BIBLIOTECA DELL'« ARCHIVUM ROMANICUM »

FONDATA DA

GIULIO BERTONI

Serie I: STORIA - LETTERATURA - PALEOGRAFIA   Vol. 71

DINO BIGONGIARI
Da Ponte Professor Emeritus of Italian,
Columbia University

With a Preface by
HENRY PAOLUCCI

Preface to 2000 Edition by Anne Paolucci

ESSAYS ON DANTE
AND MEDIEVAL CULTURE

CRITICAL STUDIES OF THE THOUGHT AND TEXTS OF
DANTE, ST. AUGUSTINE, ST. THOMAS AQUINAS, MARSILIUS OF PADUA,
AND OTHER MEDIEVAL SUBJECTS

FIRENZE · LEO S. OLSCHKI EDITORE · MCMLXIV
NEW YORK AND WILMINGTON · THE BAGEHOT COUNCIL · MM

Library of Congress Cataloging–in–Publication Data

Bigongiari, Dino.
    Essays on Dante and medieval culture : critical studies of the thought and
texts of Dante, St. Augustine, St. Thomas Aquinas, Marsilius of Padua, and
other medieval subjects / Dino Bigongiari / Preface by Anne Paolucci.
        p. cm.
    Originally published with Preface by Henry Paolucci : L.S. Olschki, 1964.
(Biblioteca dell' "Archivum Romanicum." Serie I, Storia, letteratura, paleografia ; vol. 71)
    Includes bibliographical references.
    ISBN 0-918680-86-7 (cloth).
    1. Dante Alighieri, 1265-1321--Knowledge and learning. 2. Civilization,
Medieval, in literature. 3. Middle Ages. I. Title.

    PQ4390 .B63 2000
    751'.1--dc21

                                                                    00-042175

PUBLISHED BY
THE BAGEHOT COUNCIL
GRIFFON HOUSE PUBLICATIONS
1401 PENNSYLVANIA AVE., SUITE 105, WILMINGTON, DE 19806

TABLE OF CONTENTS

PREFACE TO 2000 EDITION

A limited edition of this book was published in Florence, by Leo S. Olschki, Editore, in 1964. My husband, who edited the volume, intended to reissue the book, for he was convinced, like so many others who were fortunate enough to have been students of Bigongiari (myself included), that Bigongiari's work would never be dated, his style – scholarly rigor tempered by an ease of expression which makes even the most difficult ideas accessible to the general reader – would continue to serve for years to come as a model of academic writing. Accordingly, after my husband's death, I undertook to re-issue this invaluable collection.

Henry was Dino's last disciple and close friend. He knew, better than most, what his formidable teacher had to offer. Henry was already deep into Hegel, St. Augustine, medieval and modern philosophy, and Machiavelli, when he first entered Professor Bigongiari's graduate course on "Dante and Medieval Culture." One day, he challenged Bigongiari's explanation about St. Augustine's paradoxical insistence that man is free and God is omnipotent. "On that subject St. Augustine would urge," Bigongiari replied, placing his finger on his lips, "silence." My husband countered: "That answer may satisfy others, but not me." In the weeks that followed, contrary to what one might have expected from such an arrogant student, Henry continued to attend class but kept silent. Finally, one afternoon, Bigongiari intercepted him as the other students were leaving and asked: "Why don't you raise questions any more?" Henry answered: "Because I know everything you know . . . you've just turned it right side up for me."

I heard this story long after I myself had joined the class. Bigongiari indeed knew how to shock us into intellectual honesty. He also knew how to hold his audience. Speaking for myself, I never had a more exhilarating intellectual experience. Both Henry and I sat in Bigongiari's class for at least four more years, as we each continued research for the Ph.D. Later, I discovered that I had absorbed much more than was obvious at the time, including Bigongiari's unobtrusive Socratic approach, his "nudging" us into questions and giving us, by way of answer, a long "footnote" on the large cultural implications of what often was an obvious question . . . . There is much more, but I will let Henry say it.

ANNE PAOLUCCI
September 2000

PREFACE

As a new student at Columbia University in 1946, I heard the chairman of a large department of the Graduate School musing aloud, before an assembly of newcomers, upon the lesson of his long career, which was about to end. Protesting the futility of most teaching, as hoary academicians seem irresistibly tempted to do, he said that if the future of Columbia were entrusted to him there would be an end to classroom teaching, and the campus would be turned into one vast library. "After all," he concluded, "except for Dino Bigongiari, which of us here knows enough about anything really worth knowing that we should presume to teach?"

By 1946, after almost five decades on Morningside Heights, Dino Bigongiari had come to enjoy an extraordinary reputation among his colleagues — extraordinary, because many who paid him intellectual homage were scholars of far wider fame than he, scholars whose academic labors had borne fruit, as his had not, in weighty and numerous publications. In the course of many years, one after another of them, pursuing specialized interests, had become aware of the depth of his learning in this or that field. But only after they had matched notes, so to speak, did they come to realize that his cultural acquirements were truly immense. Literally by word of mouth, respected colleagues carried his reputation — especially the part of it that pertained to his medieval culture — far beyond the confines of Columbia. Speaking for the University in 1955, Vice-President John A. Krout could therefore say of him without exaggeration: "As a scholar, he is pre-eminent in medieval learning, especially in the depth of his understanding of St. Thomas Aquinas and his scholastic philosophy. He is known also to his colleagues of Europe and America as one of the first among them in knowledge and interpretation of Dante."[1] And we cannot

---

[1] *The New York Times*, Thursday, June 2, 1955.

neglect to mention here that William L. Westermann in the field of ancient history, Lynn Thorndike in the history of science, Richard McKeon in ancient philosophy, Paul O. Kristeller in Renaissance philosophy, Lindsay Rogers and Franz Neumann in public law, Kurt von Fritz in classical philology, Marjorie Nicolson and Harry Morgan Ayres in the modern literatures, and before them Nicholas Murray Butler, Frederick J. E. Woodbridge, and John Bassett Moore, in their fields, have all borne witness to the universal character and profundity of his learning.

Yet the witness of so many eminent scholars cannot quiet the inevitable question: what was the good of all that learning? what use did its possessor make of it? where are the fruits?

Examination of the catalog of the library of Columbia University under Dino Bigongiari's name reveals that he wrote an introduction for a translation of Dante's Monarchia, *that he edited and partially retranslated a selection of readings illustrating* The Political Ideas of St. Thomas Aquinas, *that his name is linked with those of Giovanni Gentile and Benedetto Croce as translator of Gentile's* The Reform of Education, *for which Croce had written an introduction. Add to this the translation of a political treatise by Alfredo Rocco, commissioned by The Carnegie Endowment for International Peace, and the catalog listing is complete. It isn't much; and most of it was, evidently, pried out of him. The question therefore repeats itself: what use has Dino Bigongiari made of his vast learning?*

The temptation is great to answer with Lord Acton's words, originally applied to his master and friend Döllinger and later applied to Lord Acton himself by Frederic W. Maitland: "Everybody has felt... that he knew too much to write." But that is not quite the truth. For his learning was in no sense a burden to him. It did not stifle him and could not of itself have stayed his pen. Much less can it be said that he was a fascinated hoarder. The truth is, rather, that he was, like Lord Acton, "a very spendthrift of his hard-earned treasure... ready to give away in half an hour the substance of an unwritten book."[1] *Books get to be written by shutting oneself up, by denying the claims of others on one's time. Dino Bigongiari denied no one. He was lavish*

---

[1] FREDERIC W. MAITLAND, *The Collected Papers of Frederic William Maitland*, Cambridge, 1911, Vol. III, pp. 516-518.

*beyond belief in assisting all who called on him; and the reservoir
of his learning was only too easy to tap. As his friend and colleague
Giuseppe Prezzolini expressed it:*

a hemistich, a word, a mere root sufficed to draw out of his prodigious
memory endless sequences, chains, networks of relationships, striking for
their novelty, but even more for their relevance: involving not only a
wealth of etymological fact, but aesthetic judgments and comparisons also,
and what mattered most, discursive elaborations of ideas.[1]

*Colleagues sent a stream of students to him annually, including, from
time to time, doctoral candidates badly in need of the substance of an
unwritten book. If the rush of his words was too great for an un-
retentive memory, he would not hesitate to write the whole matter
out, sheet upon sheet, to be carried away for restudy and eventual
incorporation in a dissertation. It is true that some who received his
gifts bore them away as the ass bears gold, to groan and sweat under
the business; but even they, like the pupils of Socrates who brought
forth wind, learned at least not to fancy that they knew what they
did not know.*

*In the preface to one exceptionally erudite dissertation, we read
the perhaps too candid acknowledgment: "The material of this work
was presented to me and the ideas concerning it were elaborated in
the... seminar of Professor Dino Bigongiari. To him I owe an inex-
pressible debt of gratitude." In many other dissertations, grateful
students speak of having been "guided always by his learning," or of
having received "invaluable aid" in the "identification of the numerous
quotations from Aristotle and civil and canon law," or in the "interpretation of the highly technical philosophic passages" in this or that
medieval author. Even more numerous, unfortunately, are the dissertations in modern as well as medieval or ancient subjects which owe
most of their substance to his aid, but in which no acknowledgment
appears. The point is that he gave to all who came to him unstintingly,
with an intellectual generosity nothing short of Franciscan in its indifference to their alleged worthiness or unworthiness.*

Yet many who turned to him for assistance were exceptionally

---

[1] GIUSEPPE PREZZOLINI, *L'Italiano inutile*, Milano, 1953, p. 305. All who have
known Dino Bigongiari will want to read the lively characterization of "Dino, Ultimo
Amico," pp. 303-314.

worthy. A partial record of the value placed on his learned generosity by scholars pre-eminent in their fields may be read in a series of acknowledgments extending from Professor Lynn Thorndike's expression of gratitude, several decades ago, for invaluable assistance rendered "by his mastery of the Latin language and literature, his broad familiarity with medieval learning, and his knowledge of Italian custom and speech,"[1] to Professor Herbert Deane's tribute, in 1963, to "Dino Bigongiari, whose knowledge and love of Augustine's writings are so great that it becomes almost an impertinence for his students to say or write anything on this subject."[2]

He was indeed, much loved by those who knew his intellectual generosity. But he was also much feared, for his learning and experience had never taught him to "mince or minish" when a judgment was required of him. Those who feared him most, usually for good reason, often learned to love him for the help he so willingly gave; yet I think it only fair to say that, quando si abbia a mancare dell'una de' dua, *he preferred to be feared.*

Especially feared was his faculty for detecting blunders in textual citations from Greek and Roman authors — blunders which quickly betrayed to him the linguistic incompetence of a pretentious scholar. Equally feared was the facility with which he recognized classical quotations embedded in medieval texts. Scholars often consulted him in advance of publication on this score, for they knew that failure to recognize a quotation which might have been a learned commonplace for medieval readers can lead one to mistake its significance altogether, as if it were a statement literally medieval in origin, literally mirroring the times.

Several of the reviews and essays reprinted in this volume were by-products of the exercise of such powers. The review of Allan H. Gilbert's monograph, Dante's Conception of Justice, *examines in detail the evidences of the authors's "somewhat insecure hold on the language and subject matter of the books he uses." The review of Bruno Nardi's* Saggi di filosofia dantesca, *criticizing the work for the meaninglessness of many passages cited in Latin, attracted the notice of Giuseppe Vandelli, the eminent Dantist, who remarked that such carelessness was*

---

[1] LYNN THORNDIKE, *Science and Thought in the Fifteenth Century*, New York, 1929, p. ix.

[2] HERBERT A. DEANE, *The Political and Social Ideas of St. Augustine*, New York, 1963, p. xiii.

*"a considerable nuisance indeed, and one (let me add) only too fre-
quently encountered in documented studies of this kind, either because
good editions of the work cited do not exist, or because scholars
or critics in philosophy and theology, absorbed as they are in
their thoughts, do not take sufficient pains with the language in which
their thoughts are presented."*[1] *With works of brazen incompetence,
Dino Bigongiari was much more severe. Instances are his review of a
recently published text and translation of* Girolamo Fracastoro Naugerius, Sive de Poetica Dialogus *and his long appraisal of a new translation
of Petrarch's* Life of Solitude. *The first begins with a "warning to those
who might want to use this version for scholarly research," and the
second (not reprinted here) ends with this ominously frank apology:
"The reader might now ask, why such a long review if the book is
so bad? To which I would reply... that Petrarch has been and still is
such a fertile field for fabrication that a little exemplary rigor is
demanded."*

*His masterpiece in this genre — but on an incomparably higher
level — is the last essay of this collection: "Were There Theaters in
the Twelfth and Thirteenth Centuries?", in which an earlier work
with the same title, supporting an affirmative answer, is subjected to
devastating criticism. It is a brilliant tour de force; yet mixed with the
sense of sheer delight that permeates it is a sustained insistence on the
seriousness of the scholar's calling. Dino Bigongiari was intolerant of
pretentious mediocrity and applied himself tirelessly, with "exemplary
rigor," to the task of stemming its rising tide. But he preferred irony
and raillery to preaching.*

*There is neither raillery nor preaching, however, in the three studies
of the received texts of Dante and Marsilius of Padua reprinted in
this volume. As these are the only published results of his critical
scholarship to which he attached importance, it is fitting that their
significance as contributions to medieval scholarship be stressed here.*

*Only one portion of his labors in this area — his criticism of the
text of Dante's* Monarchia *— has been thoroughly scrutinized and
assessed by competent specialists. But there is good reason to believe
that the reception already accorded that portion will prove to have
been typical of the reception awaiting the whole.*

His first study of the text of the Monarchia *appeared in 1927,*

---

[1] « Studi danteschi », XVII, 1933, p. 170-171.

*and its textual criticisms were reviewed the following year, for the
Studi danteschi, by Augusto Mancini, a well-known Vergilian scholar
and Dantist. In keeping with an old tradition of assigning little authority to* Monarchia *MSS, Mancini favored acceptance of several
proposed emendations, but rejected most emphatically Bigongiari's suggestions that emended MSS reading be restored in two important
instances. With patronizing benevolence Mancini reminded Bigongiari,
and his readers, that one of the challenged emendations had been
introduced by Marsilio Ficino himself and that both had been universally accepted by all editors from the* editio princeps *of 1559 down
to the present.*[1]

*In 1929, however, the renowned Paget Toynbee reviewed the Bi-
gongiari article with lively interest, focusing attention on the fact that
its two chief recommendations challenged the authority of the four
major critical editions of the* Monarchia, *"namely, that of Witte (Vienna,
1874), that in the Oxford Dante (1924), that of Bertalot (Friedrichs-
dorf, 1918), and that [edited by Rostagno] in the Florentine* Testo
critico *of Dante's work." Although he himself had been largely responsible for the text in the Oxford Dante, Toynbee accepted Bigongiari's
criticism of the emendation of Mon. II, 9 (originally introduced by
Ficino) which substituted* iniustitiae *for the* iustitiae *of all MSS, in
the expressions* forum sanguinis et iustitiae *(market-place of blood and
justice) and* sanguinis et iustitiae mercatores *(merchants of blood and
justice). After reminding his readers that Dante uses the expressions
to characterize the ordeal of single combat when it has been corrupted
by a desire for money, Toynbee writes:*

As Bigongiari points out, this alteration destroys the force of Dante's
thought, and replaces it with a flat and somewhat meaningless phrase. Dante
here wishes to bring out the fact that justice is not for sale, that it is not
a merchandise to be found in the market-place (*forum*). Just as Ennius, in
the passage quoted by Dante, rebukes those who, instead of waging war,
become *cauponantes bellum*, so Dante himself here rebukes the *cauponantes
iustitiam*, the *iustitiae mercatores*, 'hucksters of justice,' as he calls them.
There can be little doubt, therefore, that *iustitiae* ought to be restored to
the text in both places.

*This acknowledgment by Toynbee was important because it
marked the beginning of what, in the end, has amounted to a complete*

---

[1] *Ibid.*, XIII, 1928, pp. 101-104.

reversal in the attitude of modern Dante scholars toward the MSS tradition. In the same review, Toynbee also accepts Bigongiari's arguments rejecting the long-standing emendation of the MSS' ab illo speculo to read ab illa specula, *in Mon. II, 10. A translation of the passage as emended reads: "Let, then, the presumptuous jurists see how far they stand below that watch-tower of reason* [quantum infra sint ab illa specula rationis] *whence the mind of man regards these principles." Tacitly accepting Bigongiari's arguments that those who introduced the emendation cannot have been familiar with the medieval commonplace notion of the* speculum rationis, *the "mirror of reason," Toynbee concludes:*

The reading *ab illa specula* made its appearance for the first time in the *editio princeps,* from which it has been reproduced, notwithstanding the consensus of the MSS, in every subsequent edition down to the present day. The alteration of the text was due presumably to a misinterpretation of the word *infra,* this being taken to relate not to inferiority in the figurative sense, but to physical position, on a lower level, which would be incompatible with the reading *ab illo speculo* — the result, as Bigongiari observes, being the substitution of a pictorial metaphor for a philosophical image.[1]

Toynbee's review of the Bigongiari article was duly noticed in the Studi danteschi *of the following year, and the MSS restorations he had accepted silently earned their way with many competent students of Dante in Italy, Germany, and England. But in 1950, the reprinting of the Rostagno testo critico of 1921 in a handsome volume, with a long introduction, translation, and notes by Gustavo Vinay, precipitated an open controversy concerning the validity of that text. In his introduction Vinay wrote:*

The Latin text reproduced is — excepting only the punctuation which I have tried to simplify here and there — that of Rostagno. I have indicated in the notes my rare dissents, too few to tempt me to undertake a critical revision for which, given the manuscript tradition, I do not see the necessity.

With marvelous self-assurance Vinay proceeded, in his notes, to reject all the Bigongiari suggestions originally rejected by Mancini, and

---

[1] Paget Toynbee, "Dante Notes," *Modern Language Review,* XXIV, 1929, pp. 51-55.

several others — especially those which challenged the authority of Ficino and Witte as well as that of Rostagno. With a distinctly abusive tone, Vinay characterized one important recommendation as "poco Dantesca" and another as simply "generalmente respinta."[1]

Unfortunately for Vinay, that same year saw the publication of Bigongiari's extensive "Notes on the Text of Dante," the first section of which fulfilled in part the promise of the earlier study that the author would in a later note take up "a whole group of textual questions dealing with the more technically logical parts of the Monarchia*." The new notes caused a stir, and seem to have precipitated a decision of the Società Dantesca Italiana to authorize the preparation of a completely revised text of the* Monarchia *for the Edizione Nazionale of Dante's works. The scholar assigned that editorial task, Pier Giorgio Ricci, began by reviewing the new Bigongiari notes for the* Studi danteschi*. Taking under consideration "only those emendations with which Bigongiari proposes to correct readings generally accepted since the edition of 1921," Ricci concluded that he felt bound to accept them all. He remarked that several were of major importance and drew particular attention to one recommending restoration of the MSS reading for a passage in* Mon. III, 16.

A translation of the MSS version reads:

Now man, considered according to both his essential parts, namely, soul and body, is corruptible; considered according to only one, namely, the soul, he is incorruptible.

This reading had been rejected as meaningless by Marsilio Ficino on the grounds that the body only and not the soul and body (animam et corpus) *may be termed* corruptibilis. *Ficino (and Witte after him) had therefore emended the text so that a literal translation, with changes and additions indicated by brackets, would read as follows:*

Now man, considered according to both his essential parts, namely, soul and body [:] is corruptible, if considered according to only one, namely, [the body, if indeed according to the other, namely,] the soul, he is incorruptible.

---

[1] DANTE ALIGHIERI, *Monarchia*, ed. and trans. by Gustavo Vinay, Firenze, 1950, p. xxvi.

In challenging Ficino's drastic alteration, Bigongiari had remarked incidentally that "from the point of view of composition, too, the emendation is bad in that with its colon after corpus *it gives us, if not an anacoluthon, at least a very harsh syntactical structure." But what is really in question here is the meaning of the conception of man as the horizon between the corruptible material and incorruptible spiritual hemispheres of being — a conception no less central to medieval cosmology and theology than the sun is to Copernican astronomy. That the renowned Marsilio Ficino might have been ill-informed on so essential a part of the scholastic doctrine could hardly have occurred to a scholar less sure of himself in medieval matters than Dino Bigongiari. Ricci thus assessed the situation:*

Bigongiari holds that the addition is not necessary. He observes, in fact, that Dante speaks of man; and of man, composed as he is of matter (body) and form (soul), it is scholastically correct to say that he is corruptible. I hold that Bigongiari is right... Here are the words of St. Thomas... Ficino's correction, which is also Witte's, attributes to Dante, therefore, a theological error.[1]

In a later study, entitled "Primi Approcci per l'Edizione Nazionale della 'Monarchia'," Ricci, evidently impressed by the general tendency of Bigongiari's textual criticism, dwells on the fact that for some not easily explicable reason, each of the chief modern editors, starting with Witte, seems to have vied with his predecessors in discounting the authority of the MSS. "With Rostagno," Ricci particularizes, "the tendency to reject the readings of the codices was accentuated... even more; he saw interpolations, lacunae, emendations everywhere, and worked himself breathless to repair the damage with a flood of conjectures which of themselves surpassed in number the combined total of all that had been introduced by previous editors." But now, according to Ricci, the tide seems on the verge of being turned. "The observations of Toynbee, of Bigongiari, of Vianello," he explains, "may constitute, when gathered together and compared, the impetus for a new line of criticism [per una nuova linea critica], *disposed to place greater trust in the MSS tradition than has heretofore been accorded it." Here, Toynbee's name has somehow been given precedence, though his*

---

[1] *Studi dant.*, XXX, 1951, pp 305-307.

article, like Vianello's, took Bigongiari's study as a point of departure.
But elsewhere in the same article, Ricci writes unequivocally:

Many of the textual corrections we have been considering are due, as
we have seen, to Dino Bigongiari who, in these last thirty years, has been
the author of the most important contribution to the critical text of the
Monarchia [in questi ultimi trent'anni autore del piú notevole contributo al
testo critico della *Monarchia*].

He adds that the series of "brevi note" of Toynbee on the same
subject are marked by a "prudente sagacia"; but he dismisses most of
the labors of Vianello as the trials of a dilettante, not worthy of our
confidence because "dal punto di vista scientifico non sono sufficiente-
mente controllate."[1]
Some months later, Ricci wrote a devastating review of Vinay's
reprinting of the Rostagno text;[2] and more recently, making extensive
use of the Bigongiari notes, he has published an article entitled "L'Ar-
chetipo della 'Monarchia'," in which he examines *"the thirty-three*
emendations which the last editor of the Monarchia *deemed necessary*
for rectification of the text as given by the entire MSS tradition," and
concludes that "no less than twenty-seven of them must be discarded
as superfluous to say the least." But what is particularly striking in
this most recent article is the treatment the new editor of the testo
critico *accords the once authoritative name of Marsilio Ficino. Review-*
ing the dispute over the forum sanguinis et iustitiae *passage of* Mon.
II, 9, Ricci ascribes the substitution of the reading iniustitiae *to "mo-*
dern editors excessively impressed [suggestionati] *by a senseless trans-*
lation of Ficino [una balorda traduzione del Ficino]." *Reconsidering*
Ficino's emendation of the animam et corpus *passage in* Mon. III, 16,
Ricci does not hesitate to characterize the addition as "una zeppa abu-
siva e scorretta."[3]
It is to be hoped that Bigongiari's published notes on other texts
of Dante, especially those on the De Vulgari Eloquentia, *with their*
fascinating excursus on "The Art of the Canzone," will soon attract
the attention of scholars of the competence of Ricci, who will put them

---

[1] *Ibid.*, XXXI, No. 1, 1953, pp. 31-58.
[2] *Ibid.*, XXXII, No. 2, 1954, pp. 223-231.
[3] *Ibid.*, XXXIV, 1957, pp. 127-162.

to good use. His notes on the Divina Commedia *have not as yet been prepared for publication, and may not be for some time to come. Yet they are the most extensive of all, and, needless to say, the most important. One day they must find their place — and it will be a prominent place — in a revised edition of the text and of the Scartazzini commentary, which they rectify and supplement.*

What gives Dino Bigongiari's textual criticism a unique value is the fact that its procedure reverses the usual practice of philological study in the narrow sense. The usual practice is to start from a familiar work and then proceed to broaden the horizon by pursuing the interpretation of difficult or suggestive passages beyond the text into the less familiar and sometimes wholly unfamiliar contexts of universal culture. The result of such philological study may, on a superficial level, resemble Dino Bigongiari's work, but really it is diametrically opposed to it. Rarely in the history of modern scholarship has such universal learning as he possessed been brought to bear in textual criticism; and it should not be forgotten that he probably would not have applied his culture to such use had not his work with students and colleagues drawn him to it.

One other aspect of his scholarly activity remains to be reviewed — and it is the most important. For while it is true that he has been much honored by colleagues at home and abroad for his self-effacing intellectual generosity and for the exemplary rigor of his criticism, he "has been honored most," as Dr. Krout has correctly emphasized, "by the affection and respect of those who knew his classroom."[1] In the classroom, and not elsewhere, his vast intellectual culture bore its richest fruit. He began his teaching career at Columbia College, his Alma Mater, *in 1904, as a member of the Department of Latin. Except for three years' voluntary service as a mounted artillery officer in the armed forces of Italy during World War I, he taught at Columbia continuously for almost fifty years, passing from Latin to French to Italian, and from the College to the Graduate Faculties, offering lecture courses and seminars, in the later years, in ancient and medieval political theory, history, and philosophy, as well as in Dante, St. Augustine, Aristotle, and early Renaissance literature and cultural history.*

In the lecture hall, as in the seminar room, he often brought along

---

[1] « The New York Times », June 2, 1955.

a text of Dante, or St. Augustine, or Aristotle for explication; but he never read a prepared discourse and never used outlines or notes of any kind, except when the day's subject called for long or numerous citations of ancient and medieval writings. After his introductory talk, in which he encouraged students to interrupt him with comments at any time, he usually began each hour with an appeal for questions and if any were raised, he would take them up as points of departure for his lecture. This procedure gave his presentation an air of casualness. And yet, as those of us who have transcribed some af them are aware, each of the lectures was highly organized, held together by a vital center of thought which seemed to work like a magnet, drawing even the most extraneous particulars into a meaningful pattern. The general effect was that of a Socratic dialogue, with the dialectical discursiveness of his presentation making even those who listened to him in silence feel, when it was over, that they had had their full say in a lively discussion.

Of course, the "master of the dialogue" always interpreted questions so as to charge them with the highest possible degree of relevance and interest. "If I have understood you correctly," he might say, graciously flattering a surprised interrogator, "you have in mind the distinction Adolph von Harnack makes in his discussion of the ancient Christian Gnostics. Perhaps you have read those profound pages of Harnack on the anti-Judaist doctrice of Marcion. Do you know Harnack — the great Lutheran historian of dogma?" Week after week, usually in response to questions, he would find occasion to introduce the names and briefly characterize the works of outstanding scholars in the fields his lectures touched upon. I have heard from his lips the most impressive appraisals I have encountered anywhere of the work of Otto von Gierke and Maitland in the sphere of law, of Pierre Duhem in the history and philosophy of science, of the great Erich Caspar in papal history, of Ueberweg, Windelband, and Grabmann in the history of philosophy and theology, of Eduard Meyer in ancient near eastern and Greek history, and of Harnack and Mommsen in their fields. And when students approached him, after a lecture, for guidance in pursuing a subject further, his response was never that of dismissing them intellectually with a labyrinthine bibliography. He would listen attentively and then question them in turn very graciously, to ascertain the state of their cultural preparation and the extent of their linguistic competence. Then he would recommend the one book he thought might best serve the student's immediate purpose. "If you're really interested in that subject, and can read German," I have heard him say, "get hold of Erich Caspar's Geschichte des Papstum *and go on from there." "Read Fritz Hofmann's* Der Kirchen Begriff des Hl. Augustinus. *It's in the library. I've worn its pages thin with repeated reading." "You should start with Möhler's* Symbolik. *There is an English translation, I believe. It is a masterful exposition of the differences between the creed of the Catholic Church and the creeds of the leading Protestant sects."*

But what was most impressive in his lectures was his capacity to trace the development of a theme through the ages, from Homer or Thales down to Goethe or Hegel. When a topic that lent itself to such treatment came up, he might stress its importance by suggesting that a serious book ought to be written on the subject. And then, suddenly, the whole substance of such an unwritten book would come pouring forth in a torrent of words — one time surveying the history of allegorical interpretation, another time reviewing the controversy over Aristotle's "four causes," or the theory of knowledge from Protagoras to Hegel, or the endless polemics over the meaning of political sovereignty, or the liberum arbitrium, *fate and fortune, mixed constitutions,* virtù, *Christian cynicism, or the high object of mathematical science:* sozein ta phainomena. *Particularly brilliant, as I recall it, was an excursus on Dante's line, "Democrito, che 'l mondo a caso pone," tracing the history of the doctrine of chance, as the ultimate indeterminate cause or principle of all things, from Democritus down to Heisenberg.*

He never treated a subject in isolation: always, in some way, directly or indirectly, his entire universe of thought was brought to bear. Speaking of Dante's involvement in the political strife of Florence, for instance, he would introduce a wealth of details from the contemporary chroniclers; but these would come bathed in the light of the theory of revolution and of the devolution of power of Plato and Aristotle, enriched by examples from Thucydides, the Constitution of Athens, *and Polybius' history of Rome; attention would be called to the use Marsilius of Padua would make of the experience of the communes in his* Defensor Pacis; *and then the shockingly frank voice of Machiavelli would be heard, followed by a chorus of champions of the sovereignty of the great national states of modern times, whose histories repeat on a grand scale and in slow motion, so to speak, the hurried pattern of development through which the microcosmic Italian communes had passed in the late middle ages. In his explication of the* Paradiso, *he*

2.

could, with breath-taking ease, pursue a question of art, or religion, or philosophy, to heights where the three lines of interest converge like meridians traced up from the equator to the pole. Whatever the way of ascent, when the heights were reached, all became one — the poesia *and the so-called* non-poesia — *in that luminous point upon which heaven and all nature hang, which is the source of all being, all beauty, all goodness, all truth.*

What these lectures were like the reader may judge for himself, in part, from the selection in this volume entitled "The Political Ideas of St. Augustine." The selection is drawn from his final course of lectures, on the philosophical and political backgrounds of the Divine Comedy, *delivered at Columbia University in 1954, a full transcription of which is now being prepared for publication.*

Had he been a little less self-effacing, just a trifle appetentior famae, *much more of his vast culture would no doubt have found its way into writing. Had he lived at another time or in another place, some public-minded administrator might have found a bureaucratic way of harnassing his boundless intellectual energies for the general good. "He knows Greek," his friend and colleague William L. Westermann once said to me, "better than any classicist I have ever known. If we could only put blinkers on him for a time, what valuable work he would accomplish for all of us, instead of dissipating his powers in assisting every chance student who calls upon him."*

Dino Bigongiari needed to be harnassed if productive labor was to be got out of him. When he worked freely, his intellectual activity easily rose to the level of sophia, *in which the highest intuitive and discursive reasoning — the* nous *and* episteme *of Aristotle — are combined in consummate knowledge of the worthiest things. From those heights a man cannot willingly call himself down to the level of utility, even when it is the general community of scholarship that would profit. Particularly applicable to him, again, are Maitland's words on Lord Acton:*

He worked while the light lasted. But to "seek a little thing to do, find it and do it," to give all his thought to a century, a nation, a fragment — "no, that's the world's way."[1]

---

[1] MAITLAND, *Collected Papers*, Vol. III, p. 517.

Yet those of us whom he served so generously, enabling us to do some little thing more or less well, ought to have found a way of giving more permanent form to the rich treasures of thought and learning he lavished on us. Our master, he made himself a servant to satisfy our needs: we whom he served ought to have cherished his words with greater care, preserving them for others, as Socrates' words, and Aristotle's, and Hegel's, were preserved by grateful students.

Humbly, therefore, and painfully conscious of our inadequacies as disciples, we offer him and the academic community this collection of some of his scattered writings. It is but a token of what ought to have been and can, perhaps, still be done, in part, to repay the great debt we owe our generous friend and teacher.

HENRY PAOLUCCI
Iona College

I

THE POLITICAL DOCTRINE OF DANTE

Dante's political doctrine consists of three fundamental theses.

I. The world should be united under one sovereign rule, all the various kingdoms and republics to be politically made subordinate to it.

This is the old cosmopolitanism of the Stoics revised to suit Christian needs and fitted into an Aristotelian system. The multiplicity of states, Dante holds, vying with one another for prestige and economic aggrandizement, is the source of unending woes, all of which would disappear if these states were made subordinate to one ruler strong enough to keep them in order, and devoid by reason of his status of any possible ambition, further aggrandizement no longer being possible. The universal empire is thus the only rule which ensures justice. It also guarantees liberty. For the world-ruler alone, in the exercise of his power, is able to do away with the corrupt forms of government (tyranny, oligarchy, ochlocracy) and to replace them with the right regimes (kingly rule, aristocracy, and genuine democracy, that is, *politeia*.) In so doing he makes it possible for peoples to be free, inasmuch as it is the lack of freedom that characterizes the corrupt political forms, each one of them subordinating the welfare and freedom of its people to the interests of a ruling group.

The basic principle, however, which controls all Dante's arguments for the necessity of a supernational government is the following: Humanity has a certain task to perform. It should actualize all that the human intellect is capable of; to produce, that is, all the arts and sciences which God meant man to work out. It is obvious that this cultural task can not be carried out by a short-lived individual, nor by a city, nor even by a kingdom, all of them limited and subject to destruction. What is needed to produce *human* culture is the collective effort of *all* humanity properly co-ordinated, unimpeded by warfare and other forms of strife. To avoid such strifes a single, supernational sovereignty is needed.

Dante here revives the old Stoic argument for the political unity of mankind, deduced from the fact of man's common possession, everywhere, of a rational faculty. But this universal *intellectus possibilis* not only takes the place of the *ratio* of Cicero and of Marcus Aurelius, it suggests the cultural actualization of what is reasonably possible. Moreover, Augustine's grand conception of *peace* as the justification of *all* political regimes serves as the capstone of a theory of humanity properly organized for its universal task. The world should therefore constitute one single state. Each one of us is a *civis* of the universal *communitas*, which is fittingly called by Dante *humana civilitas*.

II. The second fundamental principle of Dante is the independence of the head of this universal state from any political control on the part of the Church or the head thereof. The universal monarchy must be a lay state, of a kind.

Dante refutes very much in the usual way the arguments adduced by ecclesiastical opponents to such a state: the argument from the donation of Constantine, from the utterings of Christ about "two swords," his command "feed my sheep," etc. His positive argument for the political autonomy of the state is the following: man aspires to two beatitudes, one on earth, the other in heaven. The former is reached through the exercise of the moral and intellectual virtues; the other by the gift of the theological virtues. The rule over man as he strives toward the first beatitude is assigned by God himself to the Emperor; his guidance as he moves toward the second is entrusted to the Pope.

The task, thus, of the Emperor is an extraordinary one. He is responsible for keeping in line all of mankind and preventing any deviations. This mankind is varied, and lives under different conditions so that the Emperor must know much of the natural order of the world in order that he may politically rule it. He must be, as Plato said, a "philosopher king." He must have the necessary *philosophica documenta*. How is he going to be so equipped? God provides: for neither God nor nature ever *deficiunt in necessariis*, and this worldwide government is a *necessarium*. So there must be in the world at all times a man divinely equipped to be a universal Emperor in that he is fully conversant with the celestial causes that produce the various conditions here below which a ruler must take in consideration if he is to do his work well. How is such a man to be found? God selects him for He is the sole Elector; the so-called electors are merely mouthpieces of his Divine Providence. These electors will receive the proper inspiration as to the choice of the Emperor if they do not let greed and covetousness cloud their minds. And as God really elects the Emperor, so does He also confirm him — He alone, not the people nor the Pope.

We thus see that Dante in supporting his conviction of the necessity of a world-rule falls back upon the fiction of divine inspiration, so often resorted to in elections whether by reliance on chance, as in antiquity, or on spiritual visitation, as among Christians.

III. The third point is more difficult. This lay universal Empire is and must remain Roman. What did Dante mean? Obviously he had in mind some such conditions as those which obtain in the Church. Just as the *ecclesia universalis is Roman Catholic*, so should the *imperium* be *Romanum*. This *imperium* must be governed with Roman law (the *Corpus Iuris* of Justinian) for that code is not man-made; it is a holy book given or rather dictated to man by God.

His fundamental argument is that the old Roman Empire was constituted and guided directly by God. Unlike other states, where developments took place by God's permission, the Roman Empire grew by God's direct operation. All the Roman conquests therefore were the result not of power but of justice. The Roman Empire grew *de jure*, by God's will. God showing his predilection even by the way he turned the fortunes of war; wars being in reality duels by which the judgment of God was being inquired into.

So the Empire began and so it was continued under Christian rulers and so it must go on till the end of time. We still have, Dante reminds us, the divinely inspired laws of the Roman *Corpus Iuris*. With these laws, if enforced by the divinely appointed ruler, the world will do its work in peace and man will reach his earthly beatitude.

This infatuation for Rome took a humanistic turn that often verges on a repudiation of Christianity. Dante tells us at the close of Book I that mankind never was nor will it ever be as perfect as it was under the reign of Augustus. When in the Divine Comedy he comes to distinguish the good from the bad, a strange *racism* appears which seems to rout all Christian belief. The Florentines, he tells us, are partly good, partly bad. The good are those who descended from the old pagan Romans; the bad are they whose progenitors were the people of Fiesole.

What could Dante mean by this surviving Romanism? Surely he would not 'favor a solution occasionally discussed by jurists as to whether the ruler of the world should be elected by the then inhabitants of Rome. For the Romans of his day Dante had nothing but contempt. What counted for him was the ancient city as it survived under Christian dispensation; he hoped for the restoration of the old Roman virtues, the return of the old Roman prestige. Thus there is much Humanism or Classicism in this political doctrine. What inflames him is the love of Ancient Rome, pagan though it had been. It must be revived, in all its glory, but as the capital of the World, not as an Italian city. Italy must abandon its nationalistic aspirations, must accept its position as part of a world empire. Its revolts against Frederick I and his grandson Frederick II show how twisted its policies had been. Italy will again be great, yes! but only as the "Garden of the Empire."

II

THE TEXT OF DANTE'S *MONARCHIA*

The accepted text of the *Monarchia* seems marred by faulty readings which a sufficient understanding of the subject matter of the book ought easily to remedy. The character of these more or less obvious errors will be indicated by the following examples.

There are, first of all, passages in which the consistent MS. reading seems to have been rejected through a misunderstanding of the text. Such, for example, the admonition (ii, 10), "Videant nunc iuriste presumptuosi quantum infra sint ab *illo speculo rationis* unde humana mens haec principia speculatur, etc..." where "*illo speculo,*" the reading of all MSS antecedent to the Editio Princeps, has been replaced by the editors with *illa specula,* and a philosophic image has been arbitrarily rejected in favor of a pictorial metaphor.

For Dante here echoes the old view which looks upon knowledge as the beholding of a reflected image of an invisible reality, and he does so by repeating the familiar connection of speculari with speculum. This derivation had been a commonplace ever since St. Augustine (*Trin.* xv, 8), commenting on St Paul's "revelata facie gloriam domini speculantes in eandem imaginem transformamur," said, "Speculantes dixit, per speculum videntes non de specula prospicientes." Coming down to the thirteenth century we find in St Thomas (*Sum.* ii, 2, 180, 3): "speculatio dicitur a speculo non a specula," and again (in 2 *Cor.* iii, 3): "Speculantes non sumitur hic a specula sed a speculo id est ipsum Deum gloriosum cognoscentes per *speculum rationis* in quo est quaedam imago Ipsius." Endless other examples might be quoted, but this one suffices in that it contains the very words of Dante *speculum rationis.*

What, then, is the meaning of *speculum rationis*, and how does it fit the passage of the *Monarchia*?

We might proceed from the analysis of the Thomistic "omnia sic uidentur in Deo sicut in quodam speculo intelligibili," but the full force of Dante's phrase can be best brought out by recalling that this *speculum* is the objective logos placed before our mind's eye, and reflecting to it that absolute reality which is beyond our mortal ken; that it is the mirror where we see that divine image into which, as St Paul says, we must transform our being if we really mean to live humanly; that image is (see St Augustine, *loc. cit.*) "quam speculamur quia eadem imago est et gloria Dei." From this *speculum*, then, is mirrored to us the rationality of the universe and the Providence of God. And as the separate souls of Paradise look to the "specchi.. onde refulge a *lor* Dio giudicante," here the "Verbum mentis in quo tamquam in speculo videmus Verbum Dei" (Aug. *Trin.* xv, 10) inspires Dante with the scornful rebuke addressed to the jurists who can only explain *secundum sensum*.

By a similarly unjustified process (ii, 9), in the passage, "unde caueant pugiles, ne pretium constituant sibi causam quia non tunc duellum sed forum sanguinis et iustitiae esset," the word *iustitiae* of all MSS is arbitrarily changed to *iniustitiae*, a change which is repeated a few lines below in the same chapter where the MSS read: "Habeant semper si duelliones esse uolunt non sanguinis et *iustitiae* mercatores, etc."

This emendation destroys the force of Dante's thought and replaces it with a flat and somewhat meaningless phrase. Dante here wants to bring out the fact that justice is not for sale, and that it is not a merchandise to be found in the market place (*forum*). Just as Ennius, in the passage quoted by Dante, rebukes those who, instead of waging war, become *cauponantes bellum*, so Dante himself flays here the *cauponantes iustitiam*, the "*iustitiae mercatores*," as he calls them. If we accept the line, "Là dove Cristo tutto dì si *merca*," we ought to have no difficulty in undestanding how objectionable hucksters of justice are and how worthy of Dante's indignation, without trying to divert his invective against the "sale of injustice" which, if it were not meaningless, would be an act infinitely less offensive than the "sale of justice."

In Book ii, Chapter 6, the MS. reading, "Cum ergo finis humani generis sit aliquod medium necessarium ad finem naturae universalem," is emended to read, "Cum ergo finis humani generis sit *et sit* aliquod medium, etc.," without, it would seem, much justification. Dante is here speaking of an *ordo*, the *ordo naturalis*, inseparably connected with *ius*. This order which unites things, this form which makes the universe like God, contains elements arranged and graded in virtue of their relation to the end of the order itself, and having each and every one of them a particular end of its own which is therefore a means, a medium, for the attainment of the ultimate end of the *ordo*. And so for humankind, for, as our author elsewhere says (*Mon.* i, 7), "humana universitas est quoddam totum ad quasdam partes, et est quaedam pars ad quoddam totum," and "pars ad totum se habet sicut ad finem." Dante therefore says with the utmost precision and clarity, "Cum ergo finis humani generis sit aliquod medium," to mean: "since the end of humankind is a necessary means for the attainment of the ultimate ends of universal nature, etc."

It seems hard to find a reason for the emendation except the fact of the roundabout translation of Ficino. We say, "The earth is a part of the universe"; we do not say, "The Earth is, and it is a part of the Universe"; likewise we should not say, "Since the end of humankind is, and it is a means, etc."; and if we did say it (as sometimes we might if that first clause had to be followed by a demonstration), in scholastic Latin we should very likely put it, "Cum ergo humani generis finis quidam sit," or "Cum ergo sit aliquis finis, etc.," and not "Cum ergo finis humani generis sit."

In Book iii, Chapter 12, the MS. reading: "Et hoc erit vel ipse deus in quo respectus omnis universaliter unitur vel aliqua substantia deo inferior in qua respectus superpositionis a simplici respectu descendens particuletur," has been emended by adding per *differentiam superpositionis* immediately before *a simplici respectu*.

Again it is difficult to see the justification of this insertion. For it is by no means necessary every time a species is deduced from its genus that the differentia be mentioned. We can say: "In qua animal rationale a simplici animali descendens particulatur," without at all mentioning the differentia that draws the species *homo* from the genus *animal*, viz., the *rationale*. In the present case the genus generalissimum is the *ad aliquid* (relativa); the genus subalternum is *respectus simplex*; the species of this genus is the *respectus superpositionis*. The insertion of Ficino, accepted by all subsequent editors, seems to be in the nature of an explanatory gloss, and one that is not completely accurate.

On the other hand, certain readings have been retained in the text of the *Monarchia* which do not seem to be tenable. Such, for example, the sentence (*Mon.* iii, 3): "His itaque sic exclusis, excludendi sunt alii qui corvorum plumis operti *oves* albas in grege Domini se iactant."

It seems strange for *black crows* to palm themselves off as *white sheep*. What Dante here perhaps wrote is: "Sunt alii qui corvorum plumis operti *aves* albas in grege domini, etc." The presence of *grege* no doubt would favor *oves*; and the familiar allegorical references to "white sheep" and "black sheep" and "sheep of the Lord" would also incline the same way. But on the other hand, the mention of the "crow's feathers" points in the direction of the famous apologue which seems to give the tone to the entire sentence. And, above all, the words of Dante are identical with a famous quotation of Horace where we have the counterpart of Dante's *corvorum*, of his *plumis*, of his *grege*, and, it would seem, of his *aves*, too (Horace, *Ep.* i, 3, 19, "Ne si forte suas repetitum venerit olim *Grex avium plumas* moveat *cornicula* risum Furtivis nudata coloribus)."

We should then have a classical echo and a pagan proverbial expression which Dante in his customary manner integrates into a Christian thought by the addition of the word *Domini*.

In *Mon.* iii, 5, in the sentence: "Et si ferrent instantiam dicentes quod *f* sequitur ad *c* hoc est auctoritas ad nativitatem et *pro* antecedente bene infertur consequens ut animal *pro* homine dico quod falsum est," the preposition *pro* seems to be amiss. Dante is arguing from the "locus a positione antecedentis: Si est homo est animal. Sed est homo, ergo est animal." (This is the invariable example used scholastically to exemplify the *positio antecedentis*. See, among others, *Totius Logicae Summa* [published with the works of St Thomas], chapter sixteen).

Valid formal inferences, as all know, and Dante tells us, are drawn either by affirming (*ponere*) the antecedent ("ad positionem antecedentis sequitur positio consequentis," Albertus, *ad II. Priora*, iii, 1) or by negating (*destruere*) the consequent (e. g., "Si non est animal non est homo"). In the case under consideration Dante uses the former as he does in *Mon.* ii, 12, and in *Mon.* ii, 5, where he says, "cum ergo iuris finis quidam sit, ut iam declaratum est, necesse est fine illo *posito* ius *poni* cum sit proprius et per se iuris effectus. Et cum in omni consequentia impossibile sit habere antecedens absque consequente ut *hominem* sine *animali* ut patet construendo (affirming the antecedent) et destruendo (negating the consequent) impossibile est iuris finem quaerere sine iure cum quaelibet res ad proprium finem se habeat velut *consequens* ad *antecedens.*"

In the passage under consideration, therefore, the logical cogency of the argument demands not *pro* but *posito* (abbreviated), so as to mean "and if they should object, saying that *f* follows from *c*, that is, authority from nativity, and that from the positing of the antecedent the consequent is correctly inferred as *animal* is inferred from the positing of *man*, I say that this false, etc." The statement then acquires rigor and is in accordance with the strictly logical language of the text, whereas it seems difficult to see how any but a vague, inappropriate, and untechnical sense could be got out of the phrase, "*pro antecedente bene infertur consequens.*"

In Book i, Chapter 3, the Oxford text (following Witte) reads: "Essentiae tales [the intelligences or angels] species quaedam sunt intellectuales et non aliud et earum esse nil est aliud quam *intelligere, quod est sine interpolatione,* aliter sempiternae non essent." Rostagno follows this. Bertalot reads: "Et earum esse nichil est aliud quam intelligere *quid est quod sunt,* quod sine interpolatione," accepting the reading of MSS BDEHLM, as he calls them, against *quod est* of AFGPT. It seems as if the confusion of the theological knot (cut by Witte, and tentatively solved by the others) arose from a phrase which, because of its technical difficulty, was misconstrued by the scribes.

The phrase would seem to be *quod quid est.*

For Dante here makes two distinctions between angels (separate intelligences) and men. The first, that angels do not have *intellectus possibilis,* following Thomas, who says: "In substantiis separatis non est intellectus agens et possibilis nisi forte aequivoce... substantiae separatae sunt substantiae viventes nec habent aliam operationem vitae nisi intelligere. Oportet igitur quod ex sua natura sint intelligentes *actu* semper... igitur operatio propria (of the *substantiae separatae*) est in eis continua et non *intercisa.*" (*Contra Gentiles,* ii, 96, 97.)[1]

The other point is that, whereas man's comprehension needs the processes of *componere, dividere,* and *discurrere,* the angels' activity is not so broken up; for "cum in angelo sit lumen intellectuale perfectum, cum sit speculum purum et clarissimum, relinquitur quod angelus sicut non intelligit *ratiocinando* ita non intelligit *componendo, et dividendo*"

---

[1] See, however, *Summa,* i, 52, 2.

(*Summa*, i, 58, 4). What, then, is angelic *intelligere* in contrast with the human processes of predication and ratiocination, and what is its object? To put it in the language common to all scholars after the translation of Aristotle's *De Anima*, the "proprium obiectum intellectus est *quod quid est*, id est substantia rei, ut dicitur in tertio de Anima" (*Contra Gent.*, iii, 56). And therefore "angeli cognoscunt simpliciter cognoscendo *quod* quid est" (*Summa* i, 58, 4) is for "angelus intelligendo *quod quid est* intelligit quidquid nos intelligere possumus, et componendo et dividendo, per unum suum simplicem intellectum" (*loc. cit.*), and "Sic enim se habent intelligendo substantiae separatae, si penitus sunt sine materia, sicut cum nos intelligimus *quod quid est*" (St Thomas, *De Anima*, iii, lectio 11).

If, then, we have an object to the *intelligere* in the passage of the *Monarchia* here discussed — and the MSS indicate that there is one — it seems as though it should be *quod quid est*. Bertalot's reading, "intelligere quid est quod sunt," would mean either that the angels have knowledge of nothing excepting their quiddity — which could hardly be accepted — or else that angels do know other things, but through their essence and not through species, which can be said of God alone.

In Book iii, Chapter 2, the sentence (Bertalot's text): "Si enim deus non vellet impedimentum finis, prout non vellet, sequeretur ad non velle, nichil de impedimento curaret sive esset sive non esset," maks no sense either in itself or in relation to the rest of the chapter. Rostagno's reading (*curare* instead of *curaret*) patches it up without reference to the logical deduction. What, however, the sense here rigorously demands is "prout non vellet sequeretur ad non *nolle*" — "in so far as not wanting was a consequence of non nolle." But what does this mean?

Dante is here building up his argument by showing the falseness of the statement, "deum *non nolle* quod naturae intentioni repugnat" (Chapter 2, 2). He proceeds to analyze the possible consequential implications of *non nolle*, and says that it may mean either *velle*, "to want," or *non velle* in the sense, however, of suspended volition, of indifference, but *not* of active opposition. And to make his meaning clear he gives an example, which is "sicut ad non odire necessario sequitur amare aut non amare" — "not hating implies either loving or not loving" where *not loving* again is neutral, and devoid of any active opposition, which Dante makes clear by adding" non enim non amare est odire, nec non velle est nolle ut de se patet" — "for obviously not loving does not mean hating nor does not wanting mean *nolle*." Dante then clearly gives to *nolle* a meaning of active negative volition, whereas to *non velle* he gives the meaning of inactive indifference.

Having thus deduced the possible meanings of *non nolle* of the sentence on which his argument rests, Dante logically goes on to say that, whether we accept the one or the other, in both cases the sentence, "Deum *non nolle* quod naturae intentioni repugnat," implies a contradiction.

Accepting the first possibility, namely, *non nolle* equals *velle*, he goes on to prove that: "si deus *vellet* impedimentum finis," i.e., "if God wanted the impediment of Nature's ends" (that is, if God wanted "quod naturae intentioni repugnat"), the inevitable conclusion would be "Deum velle *non esse* finem naturae quem dicitur velle *esse*," which must be rejected as being a self-contradictory statement.

Taking up the remaining possibility, viz., *non nolle* equals *non velle* (in the neutral sense described), he says: "Si autem deus *non vellet* impedimentum finis prout *non velle* sequeretur ad *non nolle*," to be translated: "But if God did *not want* the impediment, *not wanting* following here from *non nolle*," or more freely rendered, "If God *did not want* the impediment of natural ends, and by *not wanting* I am now considering the remaining possible meaning that could be derived from *non nolle*, etc." He then shows that this too leads to a conclusion which is contradictory, viz., "deum velle quod non vult," and rejects it.

By following out the two possible senses of *non nolle*, the statement "Deum non nolle quod naturae intentioni repugnat," has been shown in both cases to be false, therefore its opposite, *contradictorie*, is true.

That *non vellet* is the subject of *sequeretur*, and not what the editors make it, is shown even superficially by the logical deduction: "ad non nolle alterum duorum sequitur... aut velle [subject] aut non velle [subject] sicut ad non odire sequitur amare [subject] aut non amare [subject]... prout non vellet [subject] sequeretur ad non velle." In this last sentence we should expect *non velle* instead of *non vellet*, but the subjunctive might perhaps be retained as though quoted. But whether one or the other, the meaning is clear.

There is a whole group of textual questions dealing with the more technically logical parts of the *Monarchia* which will be taken up in a later note.

NOTES ON THE TEXT OF DANTE

I. *De Monarchia*

Some of Witte's emendations which, endorsed by subsequent scholars and editors, now form part of the accepted text, do not seem to be necessary nor even acceptable.

1. So the famous passage in *Monarchia*, III, 16, the MSS' reading of which is as follows:

nam homo si consideretur secundum utramque partem essentialem *scilicet animam* et corpus corruptibilis est; si consideretur tantum secundum unam scilicet animam incorruptibilis est.[1]

The sense of this passage seems to be "if we consider man as composed of his two essential parts, viz. soul and body, he is corruptible; but if we consider only his soul he is then incorruptible."

Marsilio Ficino and after him Witte thought that this did not make sense. In their opinion it is the body only that is corruptible. Hence the latter emended the text by introducing between *scilicet* and *animam* the following: (corpus si vero secundum alteram scilicet) and by putting a full stop after *corpus* so that the passage as emended reads as follows:

nam homo, si consideretur secundum utramque partem essentialem, scilicet animam et corpus (:) corruptibilis est, si consideretur tantum secundum

---

[1] The Boni MS, the Budapest, the Laurentian and the Magliabechianus omit: "si consideretur tantum... est."

unam, scilicet (corpus, si vero secundum alteram, scilicet) animam incorruptibilis est.

This emendation is not necessary nor even plausible. For in defense
of the MSS' reading we should say that it is not the body alone that
is corruptible, but man. Dante says that Aeneas went to Hades "cor-
ruttibile ancora." Does he mean that the body went there by itself
without the soul? as a corpse? or as one possessed by the devil? If
Witte were right we should not say "man is mortal" but "the *body*
of man is mortal"; but we don't. Man's corruption is the separation
of body from soul — at death. Or in more technical language the
separation of form and matter. That is what we mean by corruption.
Says St. Thomas in *Contra Gentiles*, II, 55: "Corruptio omnis est per
separationem formae a materia"; or more explicitly in his commentary
on *De Caelo*, I, 24:

Dicimus aliquid esse corruptibile quod cum prius sit aliquid posterius
vel non est vel contingit non esse... sicut *homo est corruptibilis.*

And against the emendation we must point out that Witte's text
makes Dante responsible for a scholastically untenable statement. For
in the next lines he goes on to say that man has a double beatitude
according as we consider him corruptible or incorruptible ("in duo ultima ordinetur, quorum alterum sit finis eius prout corruptibilis est,
alterum vero prout incorruptibilis".) This *finis*, this beatitude of the
corruptible part "per terrestrem paradisum figuratur" and is reached
"per philosophica documenta" (*op. cit.*).

Following Ficino, Witte and the others, we would thus have
Dante say that it is the *body* of man that receives *philosophic* teaching, and that the body thus instructed strives towards earthly Paradise!

From the point of view of composition, too, the emendation is bad
in that with its colon after *corpus* it gives us, if not an anacoluthon, at
least a very harsh syntactical structure.

2. At the close of this 3rd Book we encounter a sentence which
in my opinion has been systematically misread, misinterpreted and
mistranslated, and consequently, wrongly punctuated. It is the following:[1] "Cumque dispositio mundi huius dispositionem inherentem celo-

---

[1] I punctuate it as I think it should be read.

rum circulationi sequatur, necesse est ad hoc (no comma here) ut utilia documenta libertatis et pacis comode locis et temporibus applicentur, (comma here) de curatore isto (no comma) dispensari ab illo qui totalem celorum dispositionem presentialiter intuetur"; which I translate as follows: "Inasmuch as the disposition of this world follows the disposition inherent in the revolution of the heavens, it is necessary, in order that the requisite philosophic teachings of freedom and of peace be applied with due regard to the difference of time and place, it is necessary, I say, that the appointment of this 'curator' (the Emperor) be administered by Him who beholds directly, in front of Himself the entire disposition of the Heavens." The phrase *de curatore isto* should be connected with *dispensari* (the Imperial rule being thus a divine dispensation). That this is the sense is clearly brought out by the conclusion of the paragraph where the act of God which consists in this *very appointment* is called a *dispensatio*. For, Dante tells us, those whom we call Electors are not electors at all; they are, or should be, mere *mouthpieces* of the divine providence ("denuntiatores divine providentie"). Their function is a *dignitas denuntiandi*. The real Elector, the sole confirmer is God ("solus eligit Deus, solus ipse confirmat"). If we get a bad Emperor the reason is that these mouthpieces, blinded by wordly considerations of self-interest, are unable to receive the divine *dispensation* ("nebula cupiditatis obtenebrati divine *dispensationis* faciem non discernunt" [*ibid.*]).

Why does God in the case of the Emperor act directly in human affairs? The answer is given in the passage under consideration: the task of the Emperor is so dependent upon the knowledge of the varying effects of the secondary causes (the celestial influences) that only God who constantly has before his eyes these causes can know who here below is capable of taking them into consideration when it comes to the establishment of peace and liberty in the different parts of the world differently related to these celestial influences.

It may properly be asked if the word *dispensari* can yield such a meaning. But if we turn to Dante's *De Aqua et Terra*, 21, 64, we read the following: "Deus gloriosus qui dispensavit *de* situ polorum, *de* situ centri mundi, *de* distantia, etc.," where *dispensare de* is used in exactly the sense required for the interpretation given above. The grammatical structure might seem hard because of the impersonal use of *dispensari ab illo*, but the accepted interpretation also encounters a harsh construction, viz. the use of *de* instead of *ab* with the ablative of the agent. But the most important objection to the accepted reading, which makes *documenta* the subject of *dispensari*, is that it does not fit in the context. Dante is not trying to prove that the philosopher Emperor is *instructed* by God. That is not the point of the controversy. What he wants to prove is that he is *elected* by God, not by the Electors; confirmed by God, not by the Pope or anybody else; and that therefore no one under God can have any power over him. That is the conclusion which Dante wants to arrive at. If it was the *documenta philosophica* that constituted the divine *dispensation*, Dante would not have proceeded to tell us about the unique divine character of the Imperial election and confirmation ("solus eligit Deus solus confirmat") but rather of the unique divine character of this philosophic teaching. He would have had to tell us that such philosophic wisdom was given to no one, not even the highest dignitary of the Church.

3. In III, 10, 104, all editors read as follows: "videtur enim in patiente disposito actus activorum inesse." The best MSS have an *et* between *patiente* and *disposito*. This *et* is indispensable. It has not been observed that this line is a precise quotation from Aristotle (*De Anima*, II, 2, 414 a 11: ἐν τῷ πάσχοντι καὶ διατιθεμένῳ etc., in which the *et* appears, as it appears in the *Translatio Vetus* and in the subsequent ones.

4. In III, 10, 25, all MSS read "Hanc *ergo* minorem interimo," in which the *ergo* seems totally incongruous, for no conclusion is here produced; Dante is merely proceeding to quash the minor premise. It might appear as though he had written "Hanc *ego* minorem interimo."

5. In II, 13, 29, all editors read "Propter *convenientiam* sciendum quod etc." The word *convenientiam* does not fit here. What is needed is *consequentiam* which MSS L, M, T offer, perhaps as an emendation of a very uncertain passage.

Dante here follows the usual procedure in dealing with an hypothesis (in this case the following: if the Roman Empire was not *de iure* then the sin of Adam would not have been atoned in Christ). The procedure in this manner of arguing (that is, *a destructione consequentis*: if the consequent is proved false then the antecedent has to be rejected) consists first in showing that the consequent is untenable and must therefore be denied; and, second, in the establishment of a logical connection between the antecedent and the consequent (to show that we are not faced with a non sequitur). This second step is always called the demonstration of the *consequentia* (so in this very chapter, ii, 12, 35: "consequentiam sic ostendo" and in half a dozen more passages). In the first part of this chapter, Dante denies (destroys) the consequent by showing the impossibility of denying the divine atonement: "Et si romanum... restat agendum." After that he must demonstrate the said logical relation (the *consequentia*) that ties the antecedent with the consequent: "Propter consequentiam... gubernans."

6. In the phrase: "Christus nascendo *presumpsit* iniustum" (ii, 12, 25), *presumpsit* given by the MSS and by all editors is very hard to accept. Dante gives us here a very elaborate logical deduction in strict geometrical fashion. His point is that if the Roman Empire was not *de iure*, Christ by the act of his birth countenanced an injustice or in his own words "*persuasit iniustum.*" This "unjust persuasion" is the substance of the entire deduction; Dante leans heavily on the word itself: "edictum fore iustum opere *persuasit*" and "qui iustum edictum *persuasit* iurisdictionem etiam *persuaserit.*" Is it possible that Dante bent on proving a *persuasion* would announce it as a *presumption*? Should not the above quoted passage be read as "Christus nascendo persuasit iniustum"?

7. In ii, 7, 36, the reading of all MSS is the following: "Cum ergo finis humani generis *sit aliquod* medium necessarium ad finem nature universalem." Witte introduced (et sit) between *aliquod* and *medium*, an emendation which has been accepted by all subsequent editors. It would seem as though this insertion was not justified. Dante is here considering the ultimate end of the entire universe, and reminds us that he who wants the end must want the means (*media*) which are requisite in order that the end be reached. In this case one of the *media* by means of which the *ultimus finis* of the universe is to be attained is the *finis* of *humana civilitas* which is therefore an indispensable *medium* for the attainment of this universal end. There is no need of stressing the existence of a *finis* of humanity; the point to be made is that this *finis* is a necessary *medium*. The inserted (et sit) should be disposed of.

8. In i, 14, 40, the MSS' reading accepted by all editors is as follows: "Habent namque nationes, regna et civitates *inter se* proprietates quas legibus differentibus regulari oportet," in which *inter se* seems faulty.

Dante is here showing that the universal rule of the Empire does not exclude the use of partial legislation of a special kind to meet the particular need of a kingdom or of a city state. Each one of these

groups has *inner* conditions which are peculiar to it, and which therefore require local provisions. What we therefore need in the text is not
"*inter* se" (Dante is not dealing with *international* legislation) but
rather "*intra* se" (internal measures).

II. *De Vulgari Eloquentia*

1. In *V.E.*, I, 9, 9 ff., the MSS all read: "Et quod unum fuerit a
principio confusionis, quod prius *probandum* est, apparet quia con-
venimus in vocabulis multis." Marigo[1] changes *probandum* into *probatum*, on the ground that the proof has already been given (*V.E.*, I, 8,
22 to I, 8, 51). It seems however that this is not the case: the needed
proof is not to be found in the passages above referred to. And if it were,
other sentences of Dante would have to be emended. The general
logical connection, moreover, demands the MSS' reading, and finally the
text as emended would yield an unsatisfactory sense.

What Dante said in the passage referred to was that the three
Romance languages proceeded from one common source. He had not
proved, what he now proceeds to develop, that the common source
was one of the tongues of the Babelic confusion (a principio *Confusionis*). The proof that Marigo supposes to have been already made
should be found in the following: "Signum autem quod ab uno eodem-
que ydiomate istorum trium gentium progrediantur vulgaria in promptu
est" (*V.E.*, I, 8, 44). In this passage Dante speaks of a *signum*, not a
demonstratio, and says nothing about the *principium Confusionis*. He
mentions the mere *sign* of a monogenesis of the Romance languages.

As the argument progresses he wants to *prove* that this common
origin previously surmised is *one of the many professional jargons*
visited upon the sinners of Babel. This he does in the passage which
contains the text emended by Marigo. The development thus runs as
follows: suppose that these three Romance tongues were not one but
several at the moment of Confusion; that would mean that three of
the professional groups engaged in the building of the tower of Babel
spoke these three languages (each one its own). This in turn would
mean, in view of the numerous words common to the three languages,

---

[1] *De Vulgari Eloquentia*, ridotto a miglior lezione e commentato da ARISTIDE MARIGO,
p. 62.

that the members of one of these professional groups would understand the members of the other two. But this is contrary to the
assumption.[1] Therefore there were not several sources for the three
Romance languages at the moment of the Chastisement. Therefore
they all proceeded from one of the Confusion jargons. Quod erat
demonstrandum. In other words the seed of the differentiation was
sown by Confusion. We cannot suppose that those common elements
came to Romance speeches from a pre-Babel God-given language.

This then is the proof we needed, viz. that French, Provençal
and Italian were one language at Babel. The next step is to show how
from the one came the many. And in fact Dante goes on to say (1, 9, 31)
"we must now proceed to inquire how and why this original speech
underwent a threefold diversification (Quare autem tripharie principalius variatum sit investigemus)." The wording of this sentence indicates
that a demonstration has just been completed and another is about
to begin.

The MSS give us therefore the required sense. What meaning could
we get out of Marigo's emendation? We would have a sentence constructed like the following: "And that Columbus discovered America,
which we have already proved, is shown by the fact that he brought
natives back with him." If a thing is proved, what need have we to
show it by some of its consequences? If Dante had followed this line
of thought he would at least have added some word like "also" after
"is shown."

2. The text (1, 9) which all MSS have: "Quare autem tripharie
principalius variatum sit" has been emended by Marigo, who replaces
principalius with *principaliter* for the following reason (page 66, note
22): "*principali*[*ter*]: principalmente nei tre volgari d'*oc*, *oïl*, e *si* che
si sono elevati a dignità letteraria ma *secondariamente* in ciascuna delle
infinite varietà dialettali." He believes in other words that Dante's
text demands a *principaliter* in contrast to a *secondariamente.* But this

---

[1] To understand this proof one must recall Dante's assumption, namely, that as
a result of the punishment visited upon the craftsmen of the Babel tower, each of the
professional groups got a speech of its own, so that the members of any given craft
(carpenters, masons, mechanics, etc.) could understand each other but were unable
to comprehend the jargon of other groups of artisans: "Solis etenim in uno convenientibus actu eadem loquela remansit... quotquot autem exercitii varietates tendebant ad
opus, tot tot ydiomatibus tunc genus humanum disiungitur" (*V.E.*, 1, 7). The three
Romance languages therefore originate from one and the same professional group of the
chastised builders of Babel.

is not the sense that Dante wants to convey, and if it were Dante would not have used *principaliter* to convey it.

As I have shown above Dante having established the original Babel unity of these three major Romance tongues wants to show how this original language branched out into these three and how each one of them in turn was further ramified. He therefore says in the sentence under discussion: "Let us now investigate why this more fundamental speech (principalius ydioma) received a threefold diversification, and why each one of the resulting varieties was further diversified."

The comparative *principalius* was regularly used. The heading of Chapter 9, Book II of V.E. (Rajna's edition) reads as follows: "ponit quod stantia in cantione *principalior* pars sit." Every scholar was familiar with the maxim "unumquodque enim maxime est id quod est *principalius* in ipso," which we find frequently in St. Thomas, Albertus, etc.

The MSS therefore give us the word and the only word which fits the need of the context.

3. The reading of all three MSS in *V.E.*, I, 10: "Dextrum *quoque* latus tyrenum mare grundatorium habet" cannot be kept. The *quoque* makes Dante utter a geographical blunder which he could not have made, being in contrast with what he is saying in this very passage. Rajna corrected the *quoque* to *quidem*.[1] Bertalot followed him. Marigo reverts to the impossible reading without giving us any reasons for his departure from the accepted text.

4. The form *Aquilegiensibus* (I, 10) (with a g instead of an i) is a current one used in Italy and outside of Italy (see *Thesaurus Orbis Latinus*, s.v., and the Lexica of the *Monumenta Germaniae Historica*). Marigo thinks it is a form due to the influence of the Venetian dialect and draws from this assumed peculiarity inferences of biographical import which of course are completely devoid of foundation.

5. In the concluding line of *V.E.*, I, 11, the text which illustrates the Sardinian speech has been changed by Marigo to read as follows: "nam *dominus nova* et domus novus locuntur," *i.e.* the Sardinians. Rajna, Bertalot, etc. read instead: "nam *domus nova* et *dominus meus* locuntur." What Dante actually wrote may be a difficult matter to establish. But surely the arguments adduced by Marigo are not valid,

---

[1] *Il trattato de Vulgari Eloquentia*, p. 53.

resting as they do on a text erroneously edited and incorrectly interpreted. Says Marigo (page 95, note 30): "Appunto per esprimere questa sua impressione che il sardo sia una parlata piena di irrazionali solecismi egli ricalca gli esempi *dominus nova* et *domus novus* sopra un emistichio [*sic*] di versi mnemonici delle scuole di grammatica riportati da Antonio da Tempo:

> 'Est barbarismus si dico: dŏmina dŏmus[1]
> Est solecismus: vir mea et sponsa meus'. "

In the first place these lines are not mere mnemonic lines, etc. They are two verses from Eberhard's *Graecismus* (Chapter 2). In the second place they read as follows:

> *Est barbarismus cum dico* domína, domínus
> *Est solecismus: vir mea et sponsa meus'."*

As given by Marigo (from da Tempo) we have no barbarism at all for the *o* of *domina* is and should be short. The barbarism pointed out by Eberhard consists in wrongly accentuating *domina* and *dominus* as though they were paroxytones.[2] That Eberhard wanted us to interpret his example thus is proved by the metrical exigencies of the line. In order that we may have a rhythmical hexameter we must read *domína, domínus* (the line following is a rhythmical pentameter so that we have here an elegiac *distich* (not a *hemistich*)).

The conclusions drawn by Marigo from this arbitrary rapprochement are therefore devoid of any foundation. Dante never said that Sardinian is "a parlata piena di irrazionali solecismi." And likewise the evaluation of Dante's knowledge of Sardinian based on these hypotheses cannot be taken into consideration.

6. In I, 14, Bertalot reads "dicimus nos duo in Latio invenisse vulgaria quibusdam *convenientiis contrariis* alternata," where the phrase *contrariae convenientiae* seems an intolerable oxymoron, which, moreover, goes counter to the meaning demanded by the passage. The Grenoble MS reads: "conuenietus contrarius," the Trivultianus: "con-

---

[1] The short-mark over the *o* of *domina* and *domus* are Marigo's own.

[2] An irresistible tendency then as now. Still today our radio announcers speak of Rapído, Espósito, Pecóra, and our lecturers of orgánum, pectóris, replíca, dramátis (personae).

venientibus contrarus." Rajna has: "convenientibus contrariis." Marigo follows Bertalot.

In Dante's discussion there is no mention of any agreement ("convenientia") whether clashing or otherwise. What he discusses is the fact that there are two Italian dialects, both *bad*, but such that their *bad traits* are of *contrary* nature. One is unduly soft, the other excessively harsh. Dante, following usage, might well call each of these defects an *inconveniens* (for that is what the word meant). But they are *inconvenientia* of a contrary nature: *contraria inconvenientia*. The Rajna reading and MS T prepare the way for the emendation, which seems easy, and which does away with a meaningless and obviously corrupt text: "Invenisse vulgaria quibusdam inconvenientibus contrariis alternata."

Forli's is taken by Dante as the example of the excessively soft speech. This city, though on the edge of Romagna, appears to Dante to have a speech characteristic of the region, as though it were situated in the very center of it: "Quorum civitas licet novissima[1] sit meditullium tamen esse videtur totius provincie."

7. In *V.E.*, I, 19, all MSS and all editions read: "quos putamus ipso (*i.e.* the "Latium vulgare") dignos uti et *propter quid* et quo modo, nec non ubi, et quando, et ad quos ipsum dirigendum sit in immediatis libris tractabimus." The enumeration here before us takes up: 1. *quis*; 2. *propter quid*; 3. *quo modo*; 4. *ubi*; 5. *quando*; 6. *ad quos*. Dante obviously has in mind the constantly used Aristotelian circumstances[2] given by St. Thomas (after Cicero) as follows: 1. *quis*; 2. *quid*; 3. *ubi*; 4. *quibus auxiliis*; 5. *cur*; 6. *quo modo*; 7. *quando*.[3] But he produces only six, omitting *quibus auxiliis*. The *propter quid* represents what under the more usual name is described as *cur*. He adds *ad quos*.

In starting the second Book Dante proceeds to discuss in detail these different categories. He begins naturally with *quis*, which is fully treated in the first chapter. Immediately after (Chapter 2) he takes

---

[1] *Novissima* does not mean *most recent* in time, as Marigo interprets it (p. 116, n. 8), defending such an impossible statement on the ground that the political regime of Forli was then of recent date. (How many were not?). The meaning demanded by the text is spatial, *not* temporal. It is near the border of Romagna, far away from its center; last *geographically*: the word had this meaning regularly in Dante's time possibly as a result of the Vulgate usage: "et cunctos populos eius a *novissimis* terminis Aegypti usque ad extremos fines eius" (*Genesis*, 47:21); and "usque ad mare *novissimum*" (*Deuteronomy*, 34, 2).

[2] *Nicomachean Ethics*, III, 2, 1111 a[3].

[3] *Summa*, III[ae], 7, 3, c.

up the unannounced *quid* at the place where it was customarily treated, after *quis*. It takes the place of the *propter quid* announced but ignored. The discussion is introduced by "*que* ipso digna." Next comes in the usual order the *quomodo* (Chapter 3). This is introduced by: "nunc autem *quomodo* ea coartare debemus..." The fourth chapter starts with a resumptive enumeration of these three topics, which corresponds to the detailed treatments but not to the original enumeration of the first Book. He says: "Quando quidem aporiavimus extricantes *qui* sint aulico digni vulgari, ct *que* nec non *modum quem*," etc. He then proceeds to discuss minutely the third topic, the *modus cantionum*. But the work breaks off without resuming the discussion of the *circumstantiae*.

There is here therefore, as we see, a textual difficulty: in the introductory enumeration of Book I, 19, there is no mention of this indispensable *quid*, its place being taken by *propter quid*. In the development of these enumerated topics, the *quid* is discussed fully in its proper and customary place and no further notice is taken of the *propter quid*. When these two *circumstantiae* and the following one are reviewed (Chapter 4), they are presented as they have been treated, *not* as they had been announced. What can be done? Insert in I, 19 (quid) immediately after *ipso dignos uti*? or remove the *propter* before the *quid*?

Marigo (page 160, note 16) thinks that to *propter quid* is devoted Chapter 2 of Book 2. This cannot be allowed. Dante introduces the topic of this chapter with a clear statement: he is going to discuss *what* themes are fitting for the aulic language ("*que* ipso digna sunt") and he treats of nothing else than the determination of *what* these themes are; and when he has discussed them he concludes: now that we understand these matters we are clear as to *what* the poetical themes should be in order that they may prove worthy of our noblest speech ("Hiis proinde visis que canenda sint vulgari altissimo innotescunt").

8. There seems to be no reason why Rajna's reading of II, 1: "quapropter si non omnibus *convenit* nec omnes ipsum debent uti quia *inconvenienter*, agere nullus debet," should be emended by changing *convenit* to *competit* (the reading of the Bini codex) as Bertalot and Marigo have done. Dante has with painstaking rigor developed the argument of *convenientia*. In the space of twenty-five lines he uses *convenire, convenientia, inconvenienter* sixteen times. And when the

moment comes to conclude the quasi geometric discussion, the word that is needed to clinch the argument, *convenit*, disappears so that the whole discourse appears as a *non sequitur*.

9. A great deal of difficulty seems to have been found with the following text (*V.E.*, II, 4) which is practically the reading of MSS C and T: "*Quando* si bene recolimus summa summis esse digna iam *fuisse* probatum, et iste quem tragicum appellamus summus videtur esse stilorum illa que summe canenda distinximus isto solo sunt stilo canenda."

Leaving undiscussed the question as to the justification of Trissino's emendation of *fuisse* (of all MSS) to *fuit*, and as to the utility of inserting, with Rajna, an *et* before *quando*, there still remains the doubt about the correctness of the *et* between *stilorum* and *illa que* which Bertalot (following Bini's MS?) and Marigo after him read.

This *et* seems untenable. It comes in a syllogism between the minor premise and the conclusion. The syllogistic procedure is as follows: The noblest subjects deserve to be sung in the noblest way (which has been proven). The tragic style is stylistically the noblest way of composition. Therefore the noblest subjects must be sung in that style. The reading therefore of the other two MSS, which omit the *et*, seems preferable.

The logical connection moreover seems to demand a *quoniam* rather than a *quando* at the beginning of the sentence. The abbreviation of the MSS is such as, in Rajna's own opinion, to yield either reading. The connection of ideas is somewhat as follows: a tragic style seems to be one that attains *supremacy* in every thing ("*superbia* carminum, *elatio* constructionis, *excellentia* vocabulorum") and it is the one we should use for the *canzone* since, as it was proven, the noblest are worthy of the noblest, etc. Marigo emends the *quando* to a *quare* and gives an explanation that errs both as to the facts of the MS readings and as to logical consistency.

10. In *V.E.*, II, 6, 20, the reading "si primordium bene *discretionis* nostre recolimus" must be kept. Marigo changes it to *disgressionis* (to mean *digressionis*) and justifies his reading by both diplomatic and logical arguments. As to the former the discussion of Rajna (page 144) should have been a sufficient answer. As to the sense of the passage it seems as though *digressionis* could not be defended. There have been no digressions in Dante's development and what Marigo refers to here is not a *digressio* but a *fundamental distinction*, already made, and

here utilized, which distinction when first introduced had in fact been called a *discretio*. What Dante here says is the following: "We cannot use incongruous expressions in this style because such expressions are of inferior grade and our style, if we recall the *distinctions* we laid down at the outset, can contain superior elements only." The statement he refers to is (II, 4): "in hiis que dicenda occurrunt debemus *discretione* potiri utrum tragice, sive comice, sive elegiace sint canenda. Per tragediam *superiorem* stilum inducimus." And he goes on to say that this tragic style must be used for the *canzone*.

11. The stylistic models given by Dante in II, 6 present certain difficulties. The "sapid" construction is illustrated by the following: "Piget me cunctis pietate maiorem quicumque in exilio tabescentes patriam tantum sompniando revisunt," which is taken to mean: "I, greater in pity than all, am sorry for all those who, consuming themselves in exile, are able to see their fatherland only in dreams." The construction, as Rajna had already remarked, is harsh, being devoid of a plural genitive governed by *piget* to serve as an antecedent to *quicumque*. The difficulty could be remedied by the insertion of *mei* after *me*, in which case the meaning would be considerably improved; the sentence would then mean: "I am sorry for myself who am more deserving of pity than any one of those who only in dreams can revisit their fatherland." The dropping of *mei* after *me* could easily be explained.

12. The style which Dante calls *sapidus et venustus* is exemplified by the following: "Laudabilis discretio marchionis Estensis et sua magnificentia *preparata* cunctis illum facit esse dilectum." The phrase *magnificentia preparata* seems strange: *prepared magnificence*. The MSS' abbreviation permits us to read *properata*. This participle would suit Dante's view of *magnificentia* which, he tells us, should never lag. As to the construction, he might be modeling his phrase on Ovid's *properata gloria* (*Metamorposes*, 15, 748), *properata mors* (*Tristia*, 3, 3, 34), or on a dozen other possible exemplars. We may even suppose that *properata* modifies *discretio* (*et* connecting *laudabilis* and *properata*), *magnificentia* then being ablative.

III. *Convivio*

In IV, 24, 34, Parodi and Pellegrini read (page 299) "e quella salita e quella discesa è quasi lo *tenere* de l'arco nel quale poco di flessione si discerne."

In settling the reading of this troublesome passage, one should remember that *tenus-tenoris* was a technical if archaic expression of archery. Servius (in *Vergilii carmina commentarii*), *Aeneid*, VI, 62, says: "*tenus* est proprie extrema pars arcus" and Balbus, *Catholicon, s.v.*, says "tenus est pars summa sagitte." It seems therefore as though we should read *tenore* rather than the vague, uncertain *tenere*. Did Dante take this word, as he did many others, out of *lexica*, or was it a word currently used in his days?

Appendix: The Art of the Canzone

In the *De Vulgari Eloquentia*, II, 9, 38,[1] we read the following definition of a stanza of the *canzone*: "stantiam esse sub certo cantu et habitudine limitata carminum et sillabarum compagem." This text is given by all editors with an emendation: *limitata* is changed to *limitatam*. The emendation does not seem necessary. This definition is of considerable importance in what we might call Dante's *Ars Poetica*. For as he tells us (*ibid.*) the stanza "enfolds the entire art," "it is the structure or the enfolding of all the things that the *canzone* receives from art." We must first therefore examine the meaning which Dante gives to *art*, a term which has been variously and perhaps not accurately discussed. Reference is regularly made in this article to Marigo's work[2] not because the criticism is primarily directed against his edition of the *De Vulgari Eloquentia* but because of a certain number of interpretations below criticized which are incorporated in his text.

Dante's doctrine of art has little to do with what we might call aesthetics in the modern sense of the word. He gives us metrical schemes that are approved on the basis of the length of the lines and of their rhyming arrangements, and on their capacity to conform to a musical partition. He deals with numbers as representing sounds and with the relations existing between them, seldom if ever with significant expressions and the qualities thereof.

By "art" Dante means a set of norms and rules that tell us what

---

[1] The numbers of the lines are those of Moore's edition.
[2] Dante Alighieri, *De Vulgari Eloquentia, ridotto a miglior lezione e commentato da Aristide Marigo*, Firenze, Le Monnier, 1938. This book is referred to in this article simply by the name of the author.

to do, what not to do, and thus also indicate how much freedom is·
left to the poet within these prohibitions and these prescriptions. Any
notion of originality or of creativeness is alien to this conception of
"art." Art has to do with a routine, directed towards definite objectives; it is not genius but the proper "regulation" of genius. Something resembling our concept of inventive, creative genius Dante, in
conformity with long established usage, called "ingenium," a term
regularly distinguished from and contrasted with "ars." In Dante's
estimate, the genuine poet is he who has a natural inventive talent
("ingenium"), which he must cultivate through long practice ("usus")
in conformity with certain norms ("ars") in order that it may be able
properly to express scientific thoughts laboriously acquired ("numquam
sine strenuitate *ingenii* et *artis* assiduitate, *scientiarumque* habitu fieri
potest," *De Vulgari Eloquentia*, II, 4, 70); of this he reminds us in
Paradiso (10, 43): "Perch'io l'ingegno, l'arte, l'uso chiami." This distinction between *ingenium* and *ars* is frequent.[1] The combination of
ingenium, ars, usus is ancient.[2] "Art" as a check to an otherwise un-
controlled talent is familiar.[3]

This view had been, was in Dante's time and was destined for
centuries to remain a current one. In all spheres of human activity,
Aristotle's definition of "ars" as "recta ratio (regula) factibilium" held.
Dante tells us (*Monarchia*, I, 3, 86): "*factibilia* quae regulantur *arte*";
and again (*De Vulgari Eloquentia*, II, 4, 23): "qui magis... arte *regulari* poetati sunt." And Herennius had taught that "Ars est *praeceptio*
quae dat certam viam *rationemque faciendi* aliquid."

In the chapter of the *De Vulgari Eloquentia* under consideration,
this view of "ars" is exclusively adhered to. When Dante says (II, 9):
"stantia totam artem ingremiat," he means that all the prescriptive
norms governing the construction of the *canzone* as such are embodied
in the structure of the stanza. And when he adds (*ibid.*): "nec licet
aliquid artis sequentibus arrogare sed solam artem antecedentis induere,"
he informs us that no "artistic" innovation ("nec aliquid artis") is
permissible in the constructing of any of the stanzas after the first one,
since they must all put on ("induere") the "artistic" garment cut out
for the first stanza ("artem antecedentis"). By which words surely

---

[1] Cf. for Dante: *Purgatorio*, 27, 130; *Purgatorio*, 9, 125; *Paradiso*, 14, 117; *Canzoniere* 14, 95.
[2] Cf. Cicero, *Pro Balbo*, 20, 45. Victorinus made it familiar to Christian writers.
[3] Cf. *Purgatorio*, 33, 141: "lo fren dell'arte."

Dante does not mean that the stanzas of a *canzone* after the first have no new poetical value. This prescriptive character of "ars" appears clearly again in *De Vulgari Eloquentia*, ii, 9: "Licet enim in qualibet stantia rithimos innovare et eosdem reiterare *ad libitum*; quod, si de propria cantionis *arte* rithimus esset *minime liceret.*" That is: the fact that a poet has the liberty to repeat, or not, the rhymes at pleasure, shows that the rhymes do not fall under those prescriptions which are the peculiar constituent of the "art" of the *canzone.*

If "art" then is rule, prescription or the resultant application of such norms, the next question is: what does the "art" of the *canzone* prescribe?

The stanza of the *canzone* is, like stanzas of other poems, made up of verses of different lengths (eleven, seven, five, and three syllables). Is the poet free to choose at pleasure among these different lengths? Can he place any of them at any point? Can he arrange these longer and shorter verses in any order he wants? Can any verse begin the stanza? If he breaks up his stanza into two parts and further subdivides these parts, can the resulting subsections (strophes) be made up of any verses the poet happens to like best? and in any order he feels like giving them? Can the stanza have any number of verses ad libitum? To all these questions Dante's answer is: *no!* The art of the *canzone* prescribes definite rules of construction which indeed allow the poet a certain freedom, provided it be kept within established limits.

On what grounds, we should now ask, does Dante formulate the "artistic" rules that result in the above limitations? His answer is clear. The prescriptions contained in the "art" of the stanza arise from three sources: (a) the musical pattern to which the *canzone* is to be set imposes certain metrical restrictions, (b) the fact that the different verses above enumerated have "poetical" values that are proportionate to their length (the number of syllables they contain) imposes conditions both as to the relative number of each of the said varieties of verses and as to their collocation, (c) the subject matter determines the length of the stanza. In Dante's own words (*De Vulgari Eloquentia*, ii, 9): "Tota igitur ars cantionis circa tria videtur consistere: primo circa cantus divisionem, secundo circa partium habitudinem, tertio circa numerum carminum et sillabarum." In developing these three points Dante brings out those limitations which art demands and reaches conclusions that seem to be something quite different from what scholars have set forth.

(a) The musical pattern imposes several conditions to the metrical scheme. This dependence is explicitly stated by Dante and one may only deny it by perverting the meaning of the words and destroying the logical consistency of his arguments. "Omnis stantia," he says (*ibid.*, II, 10, 17), "ad quandam odam recipiendam armonizata est."[1] This can only mean that the writer in constructing his *poetical* "armonia" is bound to respect certain *musical* conditions. If we say "the room is built so as to receive a certain bed," it means that the room cannot be of any size and of any form whatsoever. It must be such as to admit the bed.

This dependence of the metrical structure on the musical function is brought out in several ways. First if the melody of the stanza is broken into two sections by the diesis,[2] the metrical structure of the stanza must also show this division. And that it is the musical partition that controls the metrical scheme and not the converse Dante clearly indicates by these words (*ibid.*, II, 10): "Quedam (stantie) vero sunt diesim *patientes.*" It is the stanza that undergoes the influence; its structure is conditioned. The presence of this diesis means that the musical partition either before or after the diesis, or both before and after, must be further subdivided into two or more iterative phrases. ("Diesis esse non potest, secundum quod eam appellamus nisi reiteratio unius ode fiat, vel ante diesim, vel post, vel undique": *ibid.*) In this musical iteration is the reason why the metrical scheme is constructed with strophic repetitions capable of admitting these very musical iterations.[3] This means that the subdivision of both parts of

---

[1] Dante defines *armonizare* (*ibid.*, II, 8) as a *musical* act, thus: "cantio nil aliud esse videtur quam actio completa dictantis verba *modulationi* armonizata," where *modulatio* again is given a musical meaning as follows: "numquam modulatio dicitur cantio sed sonus, vel tonus, vel nota vel melos."

[2] Diesis is a technical musical word. Dante (*ibid.*, II, 10) uses it in the uncommon sense given to it by Isidore: "diesim dicimus deductionem vergentem de una oda in aliam" ("oda" being as we have seen a musical term).

[3] There are three possible models of the stanza when it is set to a melody that is partitioned by a diesis: 1. The one in which the strophic repetitions are found only in the part that precedes the *diesis*; they are then called "pedes" (Dante himself calls our attention to this unusual meaning of the word); the other part of the stanza (the posterior half) being undivided is then called *syrma* or *cauda*. 2. The one in which the strophic repetitions are found only in the part that follows the *diesis*; they are then called *versus* (again this word is used in a special meaning which does indeed survive in English, but has been dropped in Italian because of the intolerable confusion which it engenders; to avoid confusion Dante calls the individual verses [the metrical lines] *carmina*); the other part of the stanza, the anterior half, being undivided, is then called *frons*. 3. The one in which *both* parts are subdivided, the stanza then having both *pedes* and *versus*.

the stanza into strophes (*pedes* and *versus*) is a *metrical* response to a *musical* demand. Any doubt about it is easily removed by referring to *De Vulgari Eloquentia*, ii, 12, 81: "non aliter ingeminatio cantus fieri posset *ad quam pedes fiunt*," that is, if this adherence to the musical pattern were lacking, it would not be possible to have the reduplication of the *singing*, a situation which could not develop since it is solely that we may have this iteration of the singing that the strophic reduplications of the metrical scheme have been devised.

What this dependence of the metrical form of the stanza on the musical pattern implies we may illustrate with a few quotations from Dante, and first in connection with the strophic subdivisions. These strophes in whatever part of the stanza they may be must be made of the same varieties of lines, in the same number, in the same order. Only thus can the musical iteration rest on the proper metrical duplication: "pedes ab invicem necessario carminum[1] et sillabarum equalitatem et habitudinem accipere, quia non *aliter cantus repetitio fieri posset*. Hoc idem in versibus esse servandum astruimus" (*ibid.*, ii, 11).

This dependence is further brought out in connection with the prescriptions for the use of the seven-syllable verse (*ibid.*, ii, 12, 81): a three-line strophe ("pes") made up of two hendecasyllabic lines with a heptasyllabic in between, must be followed by a strophe ("pes") likewise made up of a heptasyllabic line between two that are hendecasyllabic (because otherwise the iteration of the song could not occur, "*non aliter* ingeminatio cantus fieri posset").

This same holds for the use of the pentasyllabic line. Dante would limit the number of this "inferior" verse to one. But of course if the pentasyllabic occurs in a strophic group ("pes" or "versus") there must be two, because the singing of the strophe (with its iterative phrasing) demands this duplication of the pentasyllabic, ("propter *necessitatem* qua pedibus versibusque *cantatur*") (*ibid.*, ii, 12, 56). Further resultant constraints or compulsions are given in *ibid.*, ii, 12, 30.

These are then conditions that limit the freedom of the poet in metrically constructing his stanza. They are external ones and come from the musical pattern.

(b) But there are others, internal ones, which are due to a canon which affirms the poetical supremacy of the eleven-syllable line (the

---

[1] *Carmina*, as has been noticed, means *verses* (individual lines).

longest admissible), after which come in order of descending excellence, the heptasyllabic, the pentasyllabic, with the trisyllabic last. (This last however is devoid of metrical substantiality and identifiable solely in connection with a rhyming arrangement.) The poet, with due regard, no doubt, for the demands of variety[1] must let himself be guided by this canon, except insofar as certain metrical features are imposed again by the *musical* structure.

The application of this canon within the framework of the limitations above mentioned results in a series of prescriptions that are enumerated in *ibid.*, II, 12: the stanza must begin with a hendecasyllabic; the number of hendecasyllabics must outweigh the other verses; the seven-syllable line should be used with moderation; the pentasyllabic only once except insofar as the musical pattern demands a metrical repetition. Instructions are given for the use of the three-syllable line.

(c) There is finally a third aspect under which the stanza must be considered, viz. the use and the arrangement of rhymes. Dante (*ibid.*, II, 13) takes up this topic, shows how extensive is the freedom allowed the poet in arranging a rhyme scheme, indicates certain beautiful effects that can regularly be produced and points out the limitations to the free choice of rhyme arrangements imposed by the musical pattern, by the demands, that is, of the *pedes* and *versus*.

With the aid of the foregoing it will be easy to rectify a certain number of what seem to be misinterpretations of Dante's text and misapplications of his theory.

Marigo in the book above referred to, and others with him, are convinced that Dante affirms that the metrical structure of the stanza is in no way dependent upon the musical partition, but rather the reverse. He says (page 244, note 10): "La canzone è dunque concepita come forma letteraria indipendente nell'atto della composizione dalla musica"; that is the meaning which he gets out of Dante's words: "omnis stantia ad quandam odam recipiendam armonizata est" (*De Vulgari Eloquentia*, II, 10); and again (*ibid.*): "la stanza è composta in modo che possa ricevere una melodia che si adatti all'armonica dispo-

---

[1] It might seem as though the best stanza would be the one consisting solely of eleven-syllable lines. But we must recall that a unison sequence, even if made up of the "best" elements, is not necessarily better than an "ordered" array of varied constituents, some of which are bound to be inferior to the "best."

sizione che il poeta ha dato alle sue parti," which statement at once affirms and denies the metrical independence. For if the stanza "is composed in a manner such as to enable it to receive a melody" it is obvious that the stanza must submit to certain conditions of this melody, and yet this melody must adapt itself to the metrical exigencies of the stanza, the structure of which it was supposed to control. The above interpretation of Marigo seems to fit not the text as Dante wrote it but the reverse of it, as though he had said: "Omnis oda ad quandam stantiam recipiendam armonizata est."

To support this metrical autonomy Marigo relies on a passage from the *Convivio* which, he thinks, should clinch the case. He says (*ibid.*): "Questa indipendenza è piú chiaramente affermata nel *Convivio* (ii, 11, 2)." But if we look at the passage referred to we find the opposite of what Marigo's thesis demands. Dante tells us that usually other poets concluded their *canzone* with a *tornata* (an epodic stanza) the purpose of which was that when the *singing* of the *canzone* was over ("*cantata* la canzone") one might return to it by the aid of a certain part of the singing ("con certa parte del *canto*"). Dante tells us that he does not usually follow this custom, and in order that people might be aware of this departure, he (except for rare occasions) avoided a metrical structure for the *tornata* which would have placed it in the same musical order with the preceding stanzas. In other words he did not produce the metrical numbers which were *demanded* by the musical pattern of the stanza of the *canzone* ("acciò che altri se n'accorgesse, rade volte la puosi con l'ordine de la canzone, quanto è a lo numero che a la nota è *necessario*"). The independence therefore here considered is not that of the stanzas from the music, but the independence of the metrical structure of the *tornata* from the *musically conditioned* metrical sequences of the other stanzas.

Equally worthless is another argument that Marigo adduces to prove his contentions. He says (page cxliv, no. 1) that according to Dante's theory the ballad did indeed have to follow a musical partition, and in that lay one difference between it and the *canzone* which was not so bound ("La ballata per l'attestazione stessa di Dante (*De Vulgari Eloquentia*, ii, 3, 5) doveva comunemente essere accompagnata pure al suo tempo dalla musica anche in questo distinguendosi dalla canzone"). The invoked passage of Dante tells however a different story. Dante says that the ballad was different from the *canzone* not because it was *sung* but because it was *danced to* ("indigent enim plausoribus"). He makes no mention of music as such. The argument therefore will be valid only when it can be demonstrated that dance = music.

But what does Marigo do with all the above quoted passages which show the dependence of the metrical scheme upon the musical figure? How does he deal with unmistakably musical terms such as *diesis, modulatio, cantus, sonus*,[1] *melos*, etc.? with the *cantare* in the passage of the *Convivio* just quoted? with all the references to singing? He disposes of them all by a theory of *ideal music* totally independent from the sung music, and resulting from the harmonious arrangement of words. He tells us (page cxliii): "per essa (the Italian lyrical poetry) la melodia è solo interiore e ideale misura armonica che si realizza sviluppandosi nel verso, nelle rime e nella proporzionata struttura della strofe." And again (page 249, 5): " '*habitudo* circa cantus divisionem' cioè del rapporto fra fronte e volte [*versus* in Dante's language] piedi e sirma, piedi e volte *rispetto ad un'ideale melodia*." But this ideal melody, when we examine the text, turns out to be nothing more than the enumeration of certain numerical rapports that may exist between the constituents of a stanza which is as ideal as the enumeration of the number of feet that animals may have and of the relative size of them. There is no trace in Dante's text of this aesthetic evaluation. All he does is to provide us with a scheme and its possibilities. The poet writes verses (lines) into groups (strophes) so that these may fit into certain musical patterns or arrangements. The composer writes the score for these lines, and thus gives concrete embodiment to those general musical partitions which had determined the metrical divisions.

Dante does not tell us how to write beautiful poetry when he discusses the strophic arrangement of the stanza. He merely gives us a list of possible metrical schemes out of which we may choose if indeed the poem is to be beautiful. And he tells us that these metrical schemes have a definite relation with certain conditions of singing, of real music. This relation consists in the fact that repetitions of more or less complicated musical phrases are matched by repetitions of more or less developed metrical strophes. The question now is: is the metrical iteration there to satisfy the demands of a musical pattern or is the musical reduplication merely a response to an original metrical formation? Dante, as we have already seen, is very explicit in his answer: these metrical strophes, he says, these *pedes* are constructed to meet the

---

[1] "Dare il suono" = compose the music.

demands of the musical iteration ("ad ingeminationem cantus pedes fiunt," *ibid.*, II, 12, 82). In every single instance in which this connection with the song is mentioned Dante explicitly stresses the subordination of the metrical to the musical figure. Without enumerating them, let us merely refer here to *ibid.*, II, 12, 54, where he tells us that a certain very definite *material* verse structure is demanded, or rather necessitated by the fact that it is to be musically sung in a *certain way* "propter necessitatem qua pedibus versibusque cantatur." What could be the necessity imposed by an "ideal melody"? Of course the stanza, even without being sung, when merely read or declaimed does have a "harmony" of its own. It is a harmony which results from many factors but *also* from the musical conditions above described.

We can now proceed to examine the text of Dante's definition of the stanza, which as we have seen reads as follows: "stantiam esse sub certo cantu et habitudine limitata carminum et sillabarum compagem," and ask ourselves the question: what is the meaning of *habitudo*? That will be useful not only to determine the validity of the MS reading but also to correct certain mistaken interpretations.

The word *habitudo*, used by Dante frequently in the *De Vulgari Eloquentia* but nowhere else, has a variety of meanings carried over from various currents of technical speech. It still bears in Dante's time the old classical significance of *condition, appearance, aspect*, etc., perpetuated by the *Vulgate*[1] and the early Christian writers. St. Augustine says (*De Civitate Dei*, 22, 14): "An infantes in ea sunt resurrecturi habitudine corporis quam habituri erant aetatis accessu" (will babes be resurrected in that bodily state into which they would have developed," etc.). Again he says (*In Psalmum*, 143, 9: "Quando resuscitatum mortale hoc corpus transfertur in habitudinem angelicam" (*i.e.*, is changed to the angelic condition).[2]

This meaning coincided broadly with the medical usage of the word as a translation of εὐεξία and καχεξία. In this sense it was brought close to the meaning of *habitus* (Apuleius, *Metamorphoses* 9, page 235): *habitus* and *habitudo*; and (St. Augustine, *De Diversis Quaestionibus*, 83, qu. 73. 1): "*habitum* corporis secundum quem dicimus alium alio esse validiorem, quae magis proprie *habitudo* dici debet"; and (St.

---

[1] *Genesis*, 41, 4, and *II Machabaeorum*, 15, 13.
[2] This meaning is very frequent in St. Augustine; see *In Psalmum*, 68, 1, 4: *De Peccatorum Meritus*, I, 3, 3; *De Genesi ad Litteram*, 6, 26.

Thomas, *II Sententiarum*, 24, 1, 1 ad 1): "Bernardus (who had called free will a *habitus*) large utitur nomine habitus pro habitudine quadam. Ex hoc enim liberum arbitrium in homine dicitur quod hoc modo *se habet* eius animus ut sui actus liberam potestatem *habeat*."

Another sense of the word was developed when *habitudo* came to be used as the equivalent of ἕξις or σχέσις, *i.e.*, relation. We find this in Boethius (*In Porphyrii Isagogen*, page 30, 10): "habent duas habitudines eam quae ad superiora, et eam quae est ad posteriora." This meaning became even of more current usage with mathematical writing (Euclid v): "Ratio est duarum magnitudinum eiusdem generis aliquatenus ad invicem aliqua habitudo." It is synonymous to relation: "Est enim *habitudo* vel *relatio* quaedam moventis ad motum" (St. Thomas, *Contra Gentiles*, ii, 33). Dante uses it in this sense in *De Vulgari Eloquentia*, i, 6, 31, and in this sense it lived on until long after the Renaissance both in Italian and Latin technical writings. *Habitudo*, moreover, like *ordo* covered both the relationship on the basis of which an arrangement was made and the resulting arrangement itself.

The Schoolmen confronted with these many significances tried to unify them by bringing them all back to the common origin: *habere*, thence differentiating them with the aid of different syntactical relationships. In this way they gave the various related meanings a technical precision which could not be maintained, but which cannot be ignored. In this process *habitudo* followed the fortune of *habitus*.[1] The clearest account of this articulation we find in St. Thomas, *Summa*, i, 11ae, 49, 1, c. There St. Thomas strives to unify the three basic meanings of *habitus*, which are: (a) fixed disposition (first species of the accident *qualitas*); (b) possession, in opposition to privation (postpraedicament); (c) the praedicamental usage as something intermediate between the one that has and the thing which is had.[2]

In this way he was able to keep alive in the word the old classical sense, the mathematical significance, the medical and ethical meanings, and justify them by a naive application of the etymological fallacy.

The relation ("habitudo") of one triangle to another is the manner in which one *se habet* to the other. *Habitus* as the first species of

---

[1] St. Thomas calls *sanitas* a *habitudo*: "Est velut habitudo quaedam sicut se sanitas se habet ad corpus" (in *II Sent.*, 26, 2, 4, ad 1). "Gratia ad genus qualitatis reducitur et ad primam speciem qualitatis, nec *proprie* tamen naturam habitus habet cum *non immediate ad actum ordinet* sed est velut habitudo quaedam."

[1] "Unum speciale genus rerum quod dicitur praedicamentum habitus de quo dicit

qualitas took care of such classical meanings as we see exemplified in the Ciceronian "iustitia est habitus animi etc."[1] *Habitus* as a praedicament carried on the classical meaning of garment, attire, justified by the Aristotelian definition above given.[2] Dante uses the word in all these senses. In the *Convivio, De Monarchia, De Vulgari Eloquentia* we find "abito di scienza," "abito di arte," "habitus philosophicae veritatis," "habitus scientiarum," etc., all of which are to be interpreted by referring them to *habitus* as first species of *qualitas*.[3] In the praedicamental meaning of "attire" it is also very frequent, and we must recall this significance when we interpret *abituati* in *Purgatorio*, 29, 146; also when we encounter the phrase (*De Vulgari Eloquentia*, II, 12, 70): "qualiter tibi carminum habituando sit stantia habitudine que circa carmina consideranda videtur," For Dante had figuratively come to consider the art as the garment of the stanza: "sed solam artem antecedentis (stantiae) *induere*" (*ibid.*, II, 9, 18).

This last example shows that writers could make more than one of these various meanings converge on the word. We see this again in the *Convivio* (I, 11, 42): "dall'abito di questa luce discretiva massimamente le popolari persone sono orbate," where the privational sense of *orbate* throws upon *abito* the postpraedicamental shade of meaning (*habitus* vs. *privatio*). In *De Vulgari Eloquentia*, II, 6, 84 ("utilissimum foret ad illam [constructionem] habituandam") it is hard not to feel the pregnant or rather polysemic force of the word.[4]

Philosophus ad V Metaphysicorum [c. 20, 1022 b 6] quod inter habentem indumentum, et indumentum quod habetur est *habitus* medius."

[1] This is the meaning we still give the word when we say that usage "doth breed habit in a man."

[2] This is the meaning we give the word when we say that "habit doth the monk display."

[3] Cf. St. Thomas, *Summa*, I, 14, 1: "scientia enim habitus est"; *Summa*, I, 11ae, 53, 1, c: "habitus conclusionum qui dicitur scientia"; *Summa*, I, 11ae, 49, 2, c: "habitus ponitur prima species qualitatis."

[4] These meanings properly grasped will help us to avoid such interpretations as we find in Marigo, p. 196, n. 44, where commenting on *scientiarum habitu* he says: "Non basta un sapere frammentario e superficiale ma occorre quello divenuto *habitus* poichè la poesia non richiede esposizione analitica di dottrina ma viva sintesi animata della fantasia e del sentimento." This no doubt brings Dante up to date, in Italian literary criticism, but far away from the poet's meaning and the language of his times. The *habitus scientiarum* has absolutely nothing whatsoever to do with a synthesis of phantasy and what not. The most prosaic writer who knew his subject would be said by everybody in Dante's time to have the *habitus scientiae*. The only way not to have the *habitus scientiarum* is not to know them.

The proper grasp of the meaning of *habitudo* will help us to understand Dante's "pedes ab invicem necessario carminum et sillabarum equalitatem et habitudinem accipere" (*op. cit.*, II, 11) and correct Marigo's translation, which is as follows (p. 253):

We may now apply this general notion of the term to Dante's definition. As we have seen, it covers three topics or questions: first, an external relation (that which subordinates the metrical structure to the song ("sub certo cantu"); second, the question before us, viz. the *habitudo limitata*; third, the matter of the number of lines and syllables.

The first one he treats in II, 10. At the close of that chapter he explicitly states that he is through with the discussion bearing on the relation of the art of the *canzone* to singing, and that he is going on with the question of the *habitudo*.

The third one he treats in Chapter 14 (unfinished). This too is stated very explicitly: "Ex quo < duo > que sunt artis in cantione satis sufficienter tractavimus, nunc de tertio videtur esse tractandum, videlicet de numero carminum et sillabarum."

It is obvious therefore that in the intervening chapters (11, 12, 13) we must find the treatment of the remaining question touched upon by the definition, viz. the *habitudo limitata*, and that we are therefore authorized to draw from these chapters what we need to clarify the term under discussion.

And if we ask what this is an *habitudo* of, the answer is given by Dante (*ibid.*, II, 9) in the following passage: "tota ars cantionis circa tria videtur consistere: primo circa cantus divisionem, secundo circa *partium habitudinem*, tertio circa numerum carminum et sillabarum." The *habitudo* of the definition is then the one resulting from the arrangement of the *parts* of the stanza.

This *habitudo partium* again deals with three matters: (a) the quantitative relation of the parts of the stanza existing in virtue of the musical partition; (b) the nature of the individual lines of the

---

"i piedi ricevono l'uno dall'altro necessariamente uguaglianza e proporzionata disposizione di versi e di sillabe." Whereas Dante says that whatever number of different lines we find in one of the two *pedes*, we must find the same variety in the same number in the other *pes* ("equalitatem") and that the order in which these different lines are arranged in one of the two *pedes* must be kept in the other *pes* ("habitudo").

And again Marigo tells us (p. 245, n. 12) that the *canzoni* of Arnautz Daniel, like Dante's own *Al poco giorno*, are marked by the "assoluta mancanza di rima entro la stanza o la presenza di *rime che non costituiscono alcuna habitudo.*" But how is it possible to have a rhyming scheme without a *habitudo*? It would be like having a father and son without any relation existing between them. The very fact of a rhyme (desinential connection of several lines) sets a *habitudo*. The only way not to have a *habitudo* is to have no rhymes. And that is exactly what Dante says (*ibid.*, II, 13, 8): "Unum est stantia *sine* rithimo in qua *nulla* rithimorum habitudo actenditur."

stanza; (c) the rhyming connections; (*ibid.*, II, 11: "Hec etenim circa cantus divisionem atque contextum carminum et rithimorum relationem consistit").

The first of these is treated in Chapter 11, the second in Chapter 12, the third in Chapter 13. Marigo misses this arrangement entirely. He says (page 253 on XII): "Dopo l'*habitudo* della divisione melodica fondamento della ripartizione strofica si passa a spiegare l'*habitudo* delle singole parti divisibili (piedi e volte) in quanto è determinata dalla posizione reciproca che in esse hanno i versi secondo il numero e qualità," whereas Dante considers here the *habitudo* of the single, individual and indivisible lines, *not* that of the "divisible parts" (*pedes* and *versus*). This latter he has already discussed in the preceding chapter and it is mentioned here in this chapter only to indicate the *limits* it sets to the application of the canon of verse lengths. Dante in this chapter mentions the strophic groups ("piedi e volte") only in the following lines: 25-32, 55-56, 72-85; and these passages, all of them, deal exclusively with said limitations. So that Marigo's interpretation should be reversed to read as follows: "Dopo l'*habitudo* delle parti divisibili (piedi e volte) fondata sulla partizione musicale si passa a spiegare l'*habitudo* delle parti indivisibili (i singoli versi) in quanto è determinata dalla qualità (lunghezza) di essi versi e limitata dalle esigenze della partizione strofica." The phrase "carmina contexendo" (*ibid.*) does not mean, as Marigo thinks: to weave *carmina* (individual lines) into larger units ("pedes et versus"). It means to weave something so as to form with it these very *carmina*, these lines. And that "something" of course is the syllabic sequence. In fact Dante, immediately after the sentence we have quoted above, starts examining the various lines from the point of view of their syllabic length. This interpretation is demanded not only by the context but also by the meaning that Dante elsewhere gives to the word. Just a few lines before the above quoted sentence he had used the verb *contexere* in connection not with individual lines but with strophes ("quin liceat plures et pedes et versus similiter contexere," *ibid.*, II, 11, 50). There obviously Dante does not mean (nor has he ever been interpreted to mean) "it is permissible to build up something by means of the strophic *pedes* and *versus*" but rather: "to weave individual lines into these *pedes* and *versus*." And the passive construction bears out this usage: "frons tribus endecasillabis et uno eptasillabo contexta" (*ibid.*, II, 11, 24), where the texture refers to the constituent, not to the thing constituted. Likewise in *contextum carminum* (*ibid.*, ii, 11, 4), *carminum* is an objective, *not* a subjective genitive.[1]

This will suffice to prove that the reasons Marigo adduces (page 253, note 12) to show how carelessly this chapter has been written by Dante are unfounded ("in nessun capitolo come in questo si accumulano gli indizi di composizione trascurata e di elaborazione non ancora ben definita della materia.") The chapter appears to be carelessly composed only if it is not correctly understood. It is not true that to the development of the topic announced only the ninth and tenth sections are devoted ("al vero soggetto del capitolo, *habitudo quedam quam carmina contexendo considerare debemus* sono dedicati in realtà solo i due 9-10," *ibid.*) *All* sections of the chapter *are* devoted to the true subject, if the subject is properly understood as Dante meant it. It is sections 9-10 instead which are *not* "in realtà" devoted to it, except in so far as they point out limitations.

A proper understanding of the other phase of the *habitudo partium*, viz. the question of the quantitative superiority or inferiority of the musically constituted subsections of the stanza, will likewise help us to correct some misunderstandings.

Within this musically determined partition, many varieties of metrical structures are possible according as in the three kinds of the subdivided stanza,[2] the superiority as to (a) number of lines, (b) number of syllables, (c) number of both lines and syllables, (d) number of strophes, passes from the section which precedes to the section that follows the diesis.

Marigo has missed the point. He says (page 251, note 31), commenting the word *numero*, "sottintendi: carminum et sillabarum," which is not correct. We must supply instead "pedum et versuum." For Dante goes on to say that in a stanza there may be three *pedes* and two *versus*, or three *versus* and two *pedes*, which clearly shows that the numerical superiority here considered is that which deals with *pedes* and *versus*, not with *carmina* et *sillabae*. This last relation is

---

[1] This is also borne out (*ibid.*, ii, 12, 13) by: "hendecasillabum propter quandam excellentiam in contextu vincendi privilegium meretur," which Marigo (p. 255) mistranslates (and finds it therefore "a fiacca espressione"). Properly rendered it is a very vigorous phrase. It does not mean as Marigo has it: "l'endecasillabo merita assolutamente il privilegio di prevalere nella testura per certa sua eccellenza"; but rather; "l'endecasillabo per la superiorità della sua testura merita il privilegio della vittoria."

[2] (a) *frons* with *versus*; (b) *pedes* with *syrma*; (c) *pedes* with *versus*.

taken up later, where he says: "Et quem ad modum de victoria carminum et sillabarum diximus *inter alia*, nunc etiam inter pedes et versus dicimus," which means something quite different from what Marigo says (page 252, note 34). Dante's words have a meaning which
may be paraphrased as follows: we have discussed the possible superiority (in the matter of the number of lines and syllables) that
may shift from one section of the stanza to the other when the stanza
is subdivided 1) in *frons* and *versus*, and 2) in *cauda* (*syrma*) and
pedes. There remains that arrangement of the stanza which is made
up of *pedes* and *versus*. In this case two things must be considered:
first, the relative number of *pedes* and *versus* (and this is the statement
that, as we say above, Marigo mistranslates); second, the relation of
superiority and inferiority possible between the *versus* and the *pedes*
as to the number of lines and syllables which constitute them, which
relation exists between them in the same way that it was previously
shown to exist between the other things ("inter alia"), viz. the parts
of the strophe when the parts were the *frons* and *versus*, and the
syrma and *pedes*.

In the third phase of the *habitudo* also, Marigo (and others) seem
to have missed Dante's thought. This is the part that deals with the
rhyming scheme. Dante informs us that he will treat of rhyme *not in
itself* and *per se* but, so to speak, *per accidens*. The *per se* treatment
he promises to give in a later book of the *De Vulgari Eloquentia* which
has not come down to us. That this is the meaning of "Rithimorum
quoque *relationi* vacemus, nihil de rithimo *secundum se* modo tractan-
tes" (Chapter 13) is obvious. "Let us at this juncture treat," he says,
"of the rhymes not *in themselves*, but only as to their relationships."
Marigo, failing to see the contrast between *secundum se* and *relatio*
(*perseitas* vs. accident of relativity), discovers in these words a musical
doctrine totally foreign to the text. He tells us (page 263, note 1):
"Parlando delle rime che sono il *segno più cospicuo per cui il verso
si avvicina nella sua cadenza alla musica* si afferma che la loro disposizione consiste in una *relatio* cioè in un rapporto armonico per il quale
poesia e musica hanno un comune fondamento ed anche la poesia è
musica." Of this quite novel doctrine there is not a word in Dante.
Nowhere does he say that rhyme is the most conspicuous sign of the
similarity between poetry and music. Nor does he give evidence of an
aesthetic theory that fuses into one mold the several arts. On what does
this important affirmation then rest? On the meaning of the word

relatio, we are told, provided we bear in mind the following passage from the *Convivio* (ii, 13, 23) quoted by Marigo: "la quale [musica] è tutta relativa si come si vede ne le parole armonizzate e ne li canti dei quali tanto più dolce armonia resulta quanto la relazione è bella." True enough that music is "relativa," but how many thousand things besides are *relative*! and what would happen if we inferred some musicality about them all? Every schoolboy in Dante's days memorized: "relatio... nihil aliud est quam ordo unius ad aliud" or "relatio est secundum quam aliquae ad invicem referentur." And having memorized this, exemplified it somewhat as follows; John (who, "substantialiter," is a man) from the point of view of the accident of relativity ("ad aliquid") is the son of someone; possibly the father of somebody; the subject of a ruler or the ruler of subjects; double the weight of some person, etc. All of which exemplifies the accident of relativity in contrast to what Dante calls *perseitas*, that is when something is not considered *secundum se*. If Dante, knowing the extent of the meaning of the word *relatio*, had meant to limit it to music, could he possibly have helped to add a specifying modifier? What he means is: I will not now say what rhymes are; I will merely discuss the way in which they are arranged.

In determining the "art" of rhyming Dante stresses the great freedom that the poet enjoys. He considers the rhymeless stanza and the stanza with the same rhyme throughout. He indicates certain predilections, viz. ending a stanza with one or more rhyming couplets, and connecting the two parts of the stanza by a beautiful rhyming *concatenatio* whereby the last line of the fore part rhymes with the first line of the aft section. And he gives definite restrictions which as usual deal with the conditions to be satisfied by the strophic formations.

He also gives instructions as to the choice of rhymes from the point of view not of their arrangement, but on the basis of their quality. These remarks obviously being foreign to the declared subject of the chapter, he presents them apologetically. We give these here, he says, as an appendix to the chapter ("appendamus capitulo") because we shall not again in the course of this book touch upon the doctrine of the rhyme.[1]

---

[1] The third element (after *habitudo*), the one "circa numerum carminum et sillabarum," Dante treats in the fragmentary 14th chapter. It is very difficult to make sense out of it. Dante seems to say that the subject matter and the disposition of the poet have much to do with the length of the stanza. The writer may be in a mood which

These are then the three aspects of what constitutes the *habitudo partium*, and in every one of them the *habitudo* has been shown to be "limitata." The poet has a considerable range for the choice of the lines and the grouping of them but he must respect the *limits* set first by the musical divisions and secondly by the intrinsic value of the individual lines according as they are longer or shorter, the use of which in turn is again regulated by the exigencies of the strophic groups and therefore in the last analysis by the musical formation. It would seem therefore as though the MS reading could be upheld. Can the same be said of the emended text? By it Dante is made to say that the stanza is a structure of lines and syllables limited by a certain melody and a certain order. This seems to mean that a thing is *limited* by the elements that constitute it, as though we said: man is a material organism limited by sensuality and rationality. Such an expression would not seem to be tolerable. But, it may be objected, are the *cantus* and the *habitudo partium* constituents of the stanza *as vehicle of the art of the canzone?* Let us examine the text.

Dante tells us (*ibid.*, II, 10, 7) that if we want to know a thing satisfactorily we must extend our inquiry to the ultimate elements that constitute that thing ("cognitionis perfectio uniuscuiusque terminatur ad ultima elementa"). An inquiry about the stanza must therefore resolve itself into a study of its elements. But what are the "artistic" elements of the stanza? What is the art of a stanza made up of? The answer is given by Dante in II, 9, 23: "tota ars cantionis circa tria videtur *consistere*: prima circa cantus divisionem, secundo circa partium habitudinem, tertio circa numerum carminum et sillabarum." These are the three *constituent* elements of the stanza. And does he say that he

---

Dante calls *dextrum* and then his words will be "persuasive," "gratulatory" or "laudatory," or he may be in a mood that Dante calls *sinistrum* and then his words will be dissuasive, ironic, contemptuous. In the first case he should proceed leisurely to the end (write a long stanza), in the latter case, he should hurry (compose a short stanza).

This last sentence of the book has been interpreted in a way which seems unsatisfactory. Dante says: "quae circa sinistra sunt verba semper ad extremum festinent e alia decenti prolixitate *passim* veniant ad extremum..." Marigo translates the last clause: "le altre (parole) vi giungano *in ogni parte* con ampiezza decorosa..." He and others have given to the word *passim* the classical sense, which here obviously does not fit. What we need is a word meaning "slowly" in contrast to "festinent" of the first clause. And that meaning is furnished by *passim* in its current medieval sense, corresponding to "a passo" in contrast to "cursim." Says Rolandinus Pataviensis (*De Factis in Marchia Tarvis.*, XII, 18): "Tendebat ad partes illas cum gente sua, non equidem sicut *fugiens*, equis immo procedentibus *passim*." (Cf. Du Cange, *s.v.* In Glossaries we find *pedetentim* equated to *passim*.)

will examine as elements of the stanza these constituents? Yes, in II, 1, 14: "et primo de cantu, deinde de habitudine et postmodum de carminibus et sillabis percontemur." And are not these the three things which we find in the definition of the stanza? These three therefore should be all treated as elements and no two of them as limits. The definition in question as it reads in the MSS correctly makes of the *carmina et sillabae* something like the matter of the stanza, of the other two something like formal elements. The question is: would Dante use the preposition *sub* to indicate such a relationship? We find in *De Aqua et Terra*, 18, 33: "ut materia prima... sit *sub* omni forma materiali"; *De Monarchia*, I, 3, 74: "ut potentia tota materiae primae semper *sub* actu sit." Though the language here is not rigorously technical, the two points of view are close enough to justify such an interpretation of *sub*. It seems therefore as though the reading of the three MSS should be maintained.

IV

DANTE'S *VITA NUOVA*

I. "J. E. Shaw's *Essays on the Vita Nuova*" *

These essays treat of various subjects: the date of the *Vita Nuova*, the meaning of its title, the significance of the work, and the interpretation of certain controverted passages, such as: 'e che dirà ne lo inferno' and 'ego tamquam centrum circuli' and 'morràti morràti' and 'non è del presente proposito.'

The author shows an extraordinarily accurate and minute knowledge of the contemporary literature on these subjects. His book is a most reliable survey of all the suggestions, hypotheses, and guesses that have grown thick, in these last years, around this lovely little book. But he does more than survey; he plentifully contributes, undismayed by the unending array of contrasting arguments which he himself has masterfully reviewed.

Given the nature of the question treated, his contributions could, naturally be nothing more than guesses issuing from the failure of previous guesses; up-to-date solutions, arbitrarily arrived at, of still indeterminate problems. Solutions that betray everywhere the author's unwillingness to stop before unsurmountable obstacles, his fondness for juggling possibilities into probabilities and these again into certainties, and his endeavor to apply would-be mathematical precision to subjects

---

* Review of: J. E. SHAW, *Essays on the Vita Nuova*. Princeton: Princeton University Press, 1929. Paper. Pp. 236.

that do not admit of such rigorous treatment. I shall illustrate these
points by three examples:

1. In the essay which bears the title 'Morràti, Morràti,' Mr. Shaw
wants to prove that these two words do not mean 'you will die' but
rather: 'she will die.' Dante, as we may recall, is here describing his
sickly nightmare (*Vita Nuova*, 23). After having thought of the inevita-
bility of Beatrice's death, he sees in his dream faces of women which
he describes as 'crucciati.' These women address to him the above
words: 'morràti, morràti.' Ordinarily these words are understood to
mean: 'you will die,' and Dante himself so interprets them in his prose
commentary to the passage. Mr. Shaw, however, is not satisfied with this
explanation and naturally, in order to change it, must first dispose of
Dante's commentary. This he does by attributing to the poet a conscious
alteration of the meaning of the words. In the dream, the said ladies
had actually appeared as jealous furies clamoring for the death of their
fortunate rival, Beatrice. And Dante had so represented them in the
poem. When, however, he came to write the prose explanation he
felt ashamed of this scene of jealousy (how scrupulous!) and decided,
in the words of Mr. Shaw (page 138) 'to obliterate the one jarring
incident of the dream.' Alas! in vain. For the searching ingenuity of a
modern scholar was destined to frustrate the poet's falsification.

How did Mr. Shaw discover this hitherto unknown trick of Dante?
What enabled him to reconstruct this dramatic incident? And by what
system of oneiromancy did he succeed in extracting out of what Dante
calls the 'vain and fallacious phantoms' of the nightmare historical
personages and true events? He does it all by rectifying the meaning
of *crucciati* and rigorously deducing therefrom.

This true meaning of *crucciati* is shown by the democratic criterion
of the majority of instances to be 'angry' rather than 'distressed'
(page 136). Then the argument proceeds: Why should women be angry
either in a dream or in real life? Naturally, because they are jealous.
Why should they be jealous? Mr. Shaw has ample data on the subject.
'It is evident,' says he on page 137, 'from the story and from other
poems of the canzoniere, that there were women who had cause for
jealousy.' And he proceeds to enumerate a few of these ladies and
the reasons for their rancour. And, finally, being jealous *et avec cause*,
what else could they do but 'be glad of her death'? (page 137). They
express this vindictive joy by the words 'morràti, morràti' which must
therefore mean '*you*'ll die.'

By postulating an exegetic mystification on the part of Dante, Mr. Shaw has given us not only a new interpretation of the text but new biographical data as well, and the facts of an hitherto unknown senti· mental crisis. Perhaps some day he will find out who the other ladies of the dream are (the ones that are crying and wailing), and who the man is who announces the death of Beatrice.

2. My second example deals with the most important essay of the book, the opening one, in which the author is confident to have es· stablished more accurately the date of the *Vita Nuova*. His argument is as follows: It can be shown from Convito II, 12 that the *Vita Nuova* is anterior to the Canzone *Voi che intendendo*. This canzone in turn can be dated. It belongs to August, 1293. It follows therefore that the *Vita Nuova* was written before August, 1293. How has the date of the said canzone been determined? As follows: Dante tells us (*Convito*, II, 2) that two synodical revolutions of Venus after the death of Beatrice, the Donna Gentile, appeared accompanied by Love. The problem now is to show that this 'apparition' is simultaneous with the writing of said canzone. And that is demonstrated as follows: The Donna Gentile, though indeed she had appeared before, was seen *to be in the company of Love* only at the time of the writing of said can· zone. This chronological question therefore can be settled by proving first that before the time of the canzone the Lady had not been in the company of Love; and, second, that at the period of the canzone she was. The arguments adduced by Mr. Shaw in order to prove the two sides of this metaphorically companionate *liaison* of Love and of the Donna Gentile are not, it seems to me, very conclusive.

Dante himself declares that the two *were* keeping company actually at the time when Mr. Shaw says they were not. These are the poet's words (*Vita Nuova*, 35): 'Ben è con quella donna quello amore.' Mr. Shaw replies that these words appear in the poem; yes, but not in the prose commentary — and what counts is the latter. As a result, we have the rather perplexing situation of Dante's affirming this com· panionship when writing the poem, denying it or somehow disclaiming it in the prose commentary, and again affirming it (under changed circumstances) in the *Convito*, as though it were happening for the first time. Mr. Shaw asks us to ignore the first affirmation. We shall do so if it will help any, and also overlook Dante's retention of the assumed iteration.

But is it true that the prose commentary keeps Love and the

Lady apart? Dante, again, seems to say *no* (ch. 35): 'E non puote essere che con quella pietosa non sia amore,' a very emphatic affirmation, couched in a very unmistakable 'modal' form. But Mr. Shaw disagrees and tells us (p. 17) that 'this thought is not a certain conviction,' so that the argument of companionship is now shifted to one of 'certainty of conviction.' But what has conviction to do here? Surely something did happen between Love and the Lady. Dante tells us that it required a 'forte immaginazione' to destroy it, and it caused great repentance. What was this something? Mr. Shaw tells us (p. 21) that in the period of the *Vita Nuova* the Lady 'aroused nothing but "diletto," "piacere," "appetito," and "desiderio",' (do these ever, in Dante, fail to appear as concomitants of love?), and adds (same page) that 'she did not, at that time, obtain any hold upon the poet's *mente*, upon his rational soul.' By which we are to understand that all the sorrow and repentance at the close of the *Vita Nuova* are for an act which did not pertain to the rational soul but was limited to his 'sensitive soul.' Indeed, a novel kind of human psychology, fraught with extraordinary ethical possibilities.

And what would Dante say of this failure of the Donna Gentile to 'obtain a hold on the poet's *mente*?' If he did not think we were silly in engaging in this logico-erotical hair-splitting, he would tell us first to read Sonnet XXII of the *Vita Nuova*, in which addressing the said Donna Gentile, he writes: 'Gentil *pensiero* che parla de vui sen vene a dimorar meco sovente E ragiona d'amor si dolcemente Che face consentir lo core in lui. L'anima dice al cor: Chi è costui Che vene a consolar la nostra *mente*, etc.' He then would ask us if a 'noble thought' which discourses of 'love' and 'consoles the mind' is limited to the sensitive soul? And he would refer us to the prose commentary of said sonnet where he tells us that 'la battaglia dei pensieri vinceano coloro che per lei [the Donna Gentile] parlavano,' and ask us if it is possible that *pensieri* fail 'to obtain a hold on the *mente*,' or if their victory could possibly mean their defeat. Finally, quoting to us his words of *Convito*, II, 2: 'E si come è ragionato per me nello allegato libello [the *Vita Nuova*] più da sua gentilezza che da mia elezione venne ch'io ad esser suo consentisse,' he would ask us if *gentilezza* operates by any chance on the 'sensitive soul' or if it is possible for a human being to give assent without the consent of reason.

In all this discussion Mr. Shaw seems to lose sight of the elementary postulates of Dante's ethics. He forgets that everlasting duel between *libitum* and *licitum*, between our sense of duty and our sense of pleasure, which must continue until we reach the top of our sacred mountain and can proceed to dismiss our Virgil. In this struggle, Reason is often gagged by our *libido*, but never choked. For Dante, and for many others as well, Reason can be gagged only because she allows it, and without this assent on her part guilt, demerit, or repentance would have no meaning. In Dante's moral universe no human being can say that 'desires,' 'appetites,' etc., triumph without 'taking a hold of the human mind.' Of course Reason, after it has allowed itself to be bound, may again break its bonds and shudder at the sight of the former *voluntary* bondage. That is what happens at the close of the *Vita Nuova* when Reason, with the help of the God-sent 'forte immaginazione,' liberates itself and wins a battle which it had once lost 'vinceano coloro che per lei parlavano,' and which it had lost, because it had *wanted* to lose it.

Very little, therefore, can be said to prove the disunion of Love and the Lady in the *Vita Nuova*, which constituted the first part of the argument. Equally inconclusive are the reasons adduced to prove the second part, which should prove the said union of the two in the canzone *Voi che intendendo*. We have there the same struggle, the same victory. The two pivotal points of the argument seem therefore to be very arbitrary and far from justifying the statement (page 35) that 'the *Vita Nuova* was almost certainly composed between June, 1291, and August, 1293.' This may indeed be so, but does not follow from the arguments of the essay.

My third example of the arbitrariness of Mr. Shaw's method deals with the question of allegorical interpretation, which, owing to its importance and to our incomprehension, can often be effectively played as a joker. Dante calls the literal meaning 'a beautiful *lie*' (*Convito*, II, 1, 3). He qualifies it (*Convito*, II, 12) as a 'parola *fittizia*' and fully shows it to be such. Yet with these statements before him, Mr. Shaw can tell us (page 28) that *both* explanations (the allegorical and the literal) were *true* for him, (Dante), and proceed to build his argument in conformity, as he believes, with Dante's intention, while negating this very fundamental statement of the poet.

* * *

The competence which Mr. Shaw gives evidence of in dealing with contemporary Dantesque literature is far greater than his familiarity with what we might call the scientific side of Dante's scholarship.

I shall give one example; viz., his astronomical remarks on pp. 46 ss., and emphasize it, because it is incomprehensible that he should give so many pages to this science, build so much on its data, criticize so vehemently other people for their mistakes, and at the same time show such a complete lack of familiarity with its elements.

In discussing the question as to whether the ancient astronomers had any notion of a 225-day (sidereal) revolution of Venus, he remarks (page 41) that if the ancient astronomers 'say nothing of this period of 225 days which is so interesting to the modern mind, it is probably because it had no particular significance for them. Had the matter been quite clear to Ptolemy, and had he pondered it sufficiently, he might have been led to discard the epicycle of Venus and present her with a simple orbit *revolving about the earth* once in 225 days.'

It is disturbing to see the great scientist of antiquity so superciliously lectured by one who, not suspecting the complexity of the problems that faced him and the genius with which he solved them, candidly tells him to commit a blunder that anyone could avoid. For with the sun moving around the earth in 365 days, how could Venus, when made to revolve around the earth in 225 days, maintain itself within the 46th degree distance from the sun, as it is always observed to do?

And when, on page 41, Mr. Shaw states that 'it could be *observed* that after 225 days Venus *returned* to a previous position with regard to the fixed stars,' he is evidently trying, as philologians are wont to do, to get scientific information out of the etymology of words (sidereal, in this case), but not very successfully. For the man in the sun would indeed be able to make the said observation, but as far as we terrestrians are concerned Venus is *never* 'observed to return to a previous position in regard to the fixed stars in 225 days.'

And as to the doubt whether the 225-day revolution of Venus meant anything for the ancients, it is obvious that even a child could, from the then known data, have made the elementary calculations which give the 225 days. All that was needed was to multiply the time of the synodical revolution of Venus (584 days) by a fraction whose numerator is 365 days and whose denominator is 365 days plus said synodical revolution (584 days). But such a step could be taken only by one who was already started on a heliocentric hypothesis; in other words, Ptolemy could easily have done it if he had been Copernicus; Aristarchus or even Heraclides might have, if they had been Ptolemy.

On page 42, speaking of the moon's epicycle, Mr. Shaw again makes a serious break when he states that 'for the moon Iacopo gives 19 years.' Weak though he was in astronomy, this son of Dante yet knew enough not to make such an elementary blunder. Here are his words (chap. xv of *Il Dottrinale*):

> In anni dicennove   17,6
> la luna a puncto muove
> il suo cerchiare *oblico*
> con quel dell'*epicico*,
> per cui regola è facta
> che si chiama la Pacta.

As is obvious from the text, Iacopo speaks of *two* motions, that of the epicycle and that of the oblique deferent, which two (as he thinks) bring a lunar phenomenon back to the same point after 19 years. Iacopo speaks here not of the revolution of the epicycle but of the decennoval or metonic cycle, at the end of which the new moons return to the same degree of the Zodiac as 19 years previously. And that the epact (Pacta) is determined by this cycle, if any one did not know it, could be seen by referring to Sacrobosco's *Computus Ecclesiasticus*, chapter 'De Aetate lunae... et cyclo decennovenali;' and also chapter 'De aetate lunae aliter invenienda,' in paragraph beginning 'Primus igitur Cycli decennovenalis epactam, etc.'

Another side of scientific scholarship which Mr. Shaw should approach with greater prudence is text criticism. I have noticed among the few Latin passages of the book some phrases stamped by Mr. Shaw as erroneous by a scornful *sic*, which yet seem to me to be correct; and others which should have been questioned and were not. So, for instance on page 166 we read: '... declarando michi qualiter ipsa domina erat anima olim generose domine *Beatrice* filie condam domini [   ] quosiquidem intellecto. (sic) Respondi etc.', where the criticized words are perfectly all right. For *intellecto* is here the participle in abl. abs. construction with *quo*, which should be separated from the *siquidem*, which latter word is here used in its normal mediaeval meaning. And naturally the period should be removed before *Respondi*, which is the main verb of the sentence beginning with *quo siquidem*. And if anyone could possibly have any doubt, all he has to do is to turn to the mediaeval Italian translation of the passage quoted by Mr Shaw on the same page, which says: 'la quale cosa poi ch'ebbi, etc.' On the other hand, *Beatrice* of the above quoted text cannot stand, the genitive being required.

II. "C.S. Singleton's An Essay on the *Vita Nuova*" *

Professor Singleton has given us here really five essays: 1. "The Death of Beatrice"; 2. "The Book of Memory"; 3. "From Love to Caritas"; 4. "Vita Nuova"; 5. "Beatrice dolce memoria." These essays, however, may well be considered as so many chapters of a book for it is one and the same topic that from different points of view is treated in each of them, viz. the divinity of Beatrice.

We find here gathered and put in order the arguments that scholars for so many years have accumulated around this theme. But more than for this ordering and this arranging, the book recommends itself by its tone. It is written with a conviction that carries the reader along, often in spite of himself, and with a lyrical fervor which attests to the devotion of the author for the poet of his predilection. It creates a spiritual atmosphere which is conducive to a proper appreciation of Dante, whatsoever we may think of the success with which any of the specific arguments may be demonstrated.

The best parts of the book are those in which the outlines are not too sharp — those expositions which are characterized by a certain persuasive vagueness. When the author tries to be mathematically precise, even though Dante himself tempts him to do so, the result is not so satisfactory. Too much for instance is made of the assumed proportion of *Vita Nuova* 24: As Giovanna is to Beatrice so is St. John to Christ. A proportion in itself says nothing about the absolute value of any member of either ratio. But, what is more, we have here no definite analogical procedure. All that Dante does is to speculate on

---

* Review of: *An Essay on the Vita Nuova.* By CHARLES S. SINGLETON. Published for the Dante Society by the Harvard University Press, Cambridge, Mass., 1949. Pp. 168.

the name of Beatrice's companion called Primavera or Giovanna and to state that whether you take one or the other you have in it the sense of forerunner. If we wanted to follow Singleton in his daring path, we would reach another conclusion. Beatrice is here much more like the Holy Spirit than like the Redeemer, for after the above quoted statement Dante goes on to say: "E chi volesse sottilmente considerare quella Beatrice chiamerebbe Amore per molta somiglianza che ha meco." For surely it has always been the Third Person that is called Love.

Likewise it is difficult to accept statements like the following (page 105): "This second time the image of Beatrice had come as Grace. But Beatrice even so does not cease to be Charity." No one can possibly contrast Charity and Grace. Charity is the outcome of Grace: one may not have Grace without Charity, nor Charity without Grace.

This will be sufficient to illustrate what I mean by the danger of being too precise. Dante's *Vita Nuova*, no doubt, has a doctrinal content. But that doctrine is so suffused with emotions, so veiled with figurative language that it is beyond the possibility of recapture; and the endeavor to make room for it in a rigid philosophic and theological structure built up with modern learned treatises does nothing but bring out the difficulty.

I am not convinced by the thesis set forth in the chapter "From Love to Caritas." The author sees in chapter 24 a sort of *peripeteia* of the little drama in the *Vita Nuova*. The fact that Love no longer appears in the prose commentary seems to indicate to him that a great change has taken place: Beatrice herself has become Love, Love however of a higher nature, *i.e.* Caritas. Before the said turning point Love was that of a troubadour; that is, as Singleton puts it, "his love of *domina* was without reference to God."

It seems as though too high a structure is raised on a point of mere composition, which is otherwise and more plausibly explicable. But what is worse, the text of Dante does not seem to give evidence of such a transformation. The "subordination to God" is not more present in the second part than it is in the first. The role of a guide to God is as much and as little present in the first canzone as it is in any of the later poems. Leaving aside all the others and considering for a moment the sonnet which closes the *Vita Nuova*, what trace is there of any "reference to God"? Dante's inconsolable sorrow at this point is in striking contrast with the interpretation of Beatrice's death which he gives to us at the close of Purgatory: in order that her beauty might guide his loving heart to God, it had to be enhanced and thus be made more divine by becoming incorporeal through death. Her departure was a necessary step in the ascent to the Almighty and All Beautiful; but Dante did not see it then in the *Vita Nuova*. Beatrice is an *ultimate* end of Dante's love at the end as she had been before.

True enough, love changes in the course of the *libello*. But the great turning point, long before the said 24th chapter, is the discovery that the lover can find bliss-beatitude in singing the *praises* of his beloved. Until then he had been tortured by anxieties and contrasts; all of a sudden the solution appears; and it comes to him as a gift of Love itself: "Lo mio Signore Amore, la sua merzede ha posto tutta la mia beatitudine in quello che non mi pote venir meno" (chapter 18). And, he goes on to say, this beatitude consists "in quelle parole che *lodano* la donna mia." This is the great moment, the solemn moment, so eloquently described by St. Augustine, so intimately felt by every Catholic soul no matter how humble: *Laus Deo.* Herein is our bliss. Dante celebrates this revelation by writing his great canzone: *Donne che avete intelletto d'amore*, a new departure in his life and in his poetry, as he himself will tell us.[1]

There is of course a development in the *Vita Nuova*. Dante's love becomes more and more *amor benevolentiae* but the subordination of Beatrice to God does not accompany the ennoblement of Dante's affection. If Dante's love was "bad" (page 73) before chapter 24 because Beatrice was supreme, it remained so to the end. From this point of view the close of the *Vita Nuova* gives us a love which is equally "bad." To find the "good" love we must proceed to the *Divine Comedy*. There Beatrice, exalted though she be, finally steps aside in order that Dante may rise nearer to God with the aid of another person. As she clasps her hands in response to Bernard's prayer her task of divine guidance is completed and Dante remains alone in front of the Trinity.

In the chapter on "The Book of Memory" Professor Singleton connects Dante's words at the beginning of the *Vita Nuova* ("Libro de la mia memoria") with the old and popular image whereby the created universe is presented as a book, the careful perusal of which enables mortals to rise from the creatures to the Creator. This book in turn

---

[1] *Purgatorio*, XXIV, 51.

is coupled with another book: that of Divine Wisdom with the "magno volume du' non si muta mai bianco nè bruno," the *liber praescientiae* as St. Thomas calls it. I do not believe that Dante's mind, when he was writing the introduction of the *Vita Nuova*, was primarily taken up by this exalted image. There is a third common trope which Professor Singleton does not mention and which seems to be much more plausibly relatable to Dante's metaphor.

According to the view of those who held that "nihil in intellectu quod non fuerit antea in sensu," man comes into the world with a mind which is like a book made up of blank sheets, that will gradually be covered with writing as perception and experience progress. This image was popular at least from the moment that Aristotle called the mind an unwritten tablet (tabula rasa).[1] This figure of speech was current in Dante's times. St. Thomas explains it as follows (*I Sent.*, 40. 1. 2. ad 5): "Sicut enim in libro aliquid scribitur ex quo in eo veritas rei intelligitur ita etiam in intellectu describuntur similitudines rerum per quas res cognoscuntur unde intellectus possibilis ante intelligere comparatur *tabulae in qua nihili est scriptum.*" Dante's *Vita Nuova* then is the copy of the first written pages of the book of memory. Before that he recalled nothingh; the *tabula* was *rasa*: "dinanzi a la quale poco si potrebbe leggere" (*Vita Nuova*, I).

The interpretation of Dante's lines in *Purgatorio*, 24, 49 ff. relative to the *dolce stil nuovo* is not convincing. In the first place I do not believe that *penne* could possibly mean *feathers* (page 93). Dante is speaking of the *writing pens* which are indeed in the hands of the poets, but in reality are moved in automatic response to the dictating love. Dante here speaks not of a new love, as Singleton says, but of a new manner of writing love poetry. There is nothing to justify the statement attributed to Bonagiunta: "as long as he had written of a love which depended for its happiness on some return from without (on a beloved's greeting) he had written in the old style" (page 93). Quite different is the message of Dante. The new poetry, genuine poetry arises when inspiration sets in: the ispiration of love. We have here one of the many solemn proclamations by which Dante strives to restore poetry to the dignity it had had in antiquity. God inspires not only philosophers as Abelard had maintained, not only the prophets

---

[1] *De anima*, III, 4, 430 a 1: ὥσπερ ἐν γραμμα τείῳ ᾧ μεδὲν ὑπάρχει γεγραμμένον.

as Christians believed, but the poets as well. Guided by love we ascend to God: by Love's inspiration we sing our divine ascent.

The notes are not as well edited as the body of the work. There are many misprints particularly in the Latin quotations which no doubt Professor Singleton has already taken notice of. The references to St. Thomas are not quite acceptable as they stand. Once a doctrine is ascribed to the Angelic Doctor though it is in opposition to his own views (page 120); regularly in referring to the body of the articles of the *Summa* we find "Ad Resp." which might to advantage, it seems to me, be replaced by the usual *c*.

In spite of these minor *naevi* the book reads well, is interesting and informing. I do not think it solves the riddle of divine Beatrice, but it does throw considerable light on that spiritual milieu which enshrouds this insoluble mystery.

V

THE PHILOSOPHICAL CULTURE OF DANTE

I. "B. Nardi's *Saggi di Filosofia Dantesca*" *

The author, well known to Dante scholars and in general to students of medieval philosophy, discusses in this book some of the fundamental problems of Dante's scholarship, and with extraordinary wealth of illustrations from the writers of Islam, Greece, and Christendom strives to give us a newer, or at least a clearer, view of the basic political and scientific theories of the poet. The numerous quotations are not presented as sources — the author wisely disclaims any such intention — but rather as elements and constituents of that body of doctrines from which the poet drew his intellectual nourishment. They are, therefore, of interest and value not only for Dante specialists but for students of mediaeval science in general.

The chapters are uneven in merit. The most thorough seem to be the last ones on the political theories of Dante. Controversial though they be, we find in them a systematic and original treatment of Dante's polity and of the changes it underwent. The first chapter, which is a long discussion on Dante's view of the nature of the heavens, amplifies and extends Proto's interpretation of the second canto of the *Paradiso*. The chapter on *Albertus Magnus and Dante* is rather illuminating. The one on the *De Causis* is unnecessarily profuse and seems to contribute very little. The last chapter on 'the myth of Eden' takes up the different views that have been held on the subject of the position of Purgatory and establishes Dante's own belief.

---

* Review of: B. NARDI, *Saggi di Filosofia Dantesca*. Milan: Soc. Anom. Edit. Dante Alighieri, 1930. Paper. Pp. xii+380. Lire 16.

Some of the doctrines advanced by Mr. Nardi do not seem to me to be tenable. And since they bear on fundamental problems, and, in part, have been held at other times and by other scholars, I propose to treat a few of them in detail. Mr. Nardi seems to misunderstand and to misrepresent Aristotle's reason for the immobility of the earth. He tells us (page 190) that Aristotle, Simplicius, etc., in order to deduce the immobility of the earth from the revolution of the heavens, had erroneously ascribed the properties of an unextended mathematical point to an extended body like the earth. This criticism shows a hasty reading of the texts concerned. For Aristotle and his commentators state the very opposite, emphasizing the necessity of an extended support and clearly indicating that the problem is not a mathematical one but one of animal kinetics. (See Aristotle, *De Caelo*, 286a 10, and *De Motu Anim.*, 699a 12, where he discards the mathematical centre 'quia nullam habet essentiam.' Cf. also Simplicius in his commentary to *De Caelo*, 286a 12, where he states 'that if any one were to speak of motion around a centre he would be talking at random, for the centre, being devoid of matter, is not capable of being at rest... The centre is not a subsistent thing (οὐ γὰρ καθ' αὑτὸ ὑφέστηκε τὸ κέντρον).' St. Thomas makes the same remark and is followed by the commentators in general.

In his chapter an *l'Arco della Vita* (p. 123) Mr. Nardi indulges in a strange, though not novel practice. He affirms that Dante's image of the 'Arch of Life' and the discussion pertaining thereto were inspired by Aristotle, *De Gen. et Corr.*, 336a 17-27. Discovering, however, that the differences far outweigh the resemblances, and that the assumed similarity resolves itself into a patent contrast, he proceeds to blame Dante for not having properly understood his authority. In reality he should blame himself for not picking out the proper source of the doctrine. For if, instead of turning to Aristotle, (who figures here only because, out of the quoted passages [479a, 29], Dante was able to extract the image of the arch) he had looked to astrology and to Ptolemy, all difficulties would have disappeared. The two 'mistakes' of Dante, which consisted in taking the half circle (the arch) instead of the entire one, and of considering the diurnal motion instead of the motion of the planets in the circle of the Zodiac, would then have become two elements of the genethliacal practice. For Ptolemy had insisted upon ignoring all but the *visible half* of the circle of geniture (as Dante says: 'per parte di quello a loro si scuopra') in his often commented rule: τό τε γὰρ ὑπὸ γῆν πᾶν εἰκότως ἀθετητέον (*Tetrab.*, III, 12), And as for considering the diurnal motion instead of that of 'accession and recession,' what else did the astrologers do? How else could the circle of geniture be drawn if not in relation to the point (horoscope) that was at a given time emerging on the Eastern horizon *in virtue of the diurnal* motion and moved westward by the same revolution? This picture of the east as birth, of the west as death, and of the middle sky as maturity, must have presented itself early. We find traces of it even among those who included the *entire* circle. So in Manilius, who speaks of the west as 'Ianua Ditis,' and so in the normal 12-house circle, where the *domus* preceding the west was regularly called ἀρχὴ θανάτου (mors) even when it did not serve to indicate that final stage. The very image of Dante's semi-circle must independently have suggested itself to many authors. I shall simply give two early examples: The commentary to Ptolemy's *Tetrabiblos Syntaxis*, ascribed to Proclus, pp. 68-69 of Wolf's edition, states that we must take into account only what passes ἐν τῷ ἐμφανεῖ κόσμῳ — just what Dante says — and not what occurs below. Hence, he says, we need only consider: the horoscope (eastern point), which symbolizes early life, the *medium caelum*, which stands for maturity, and the west, which represents old age. The author of Hermippus likewise (II, 6; Kroll, p. 44) compares life to the half circle of the diurnal revolution: ὅλως᾽ τε ὁ καθ᾽ ἡμᾶς οὗτος βίος τῷ ἀπ᾽ ἀνατολῆς ἡλίου μέχρι δύσεως χρόνῳ καὶ τόπῳ ἀπείκασται.᾽

Our author's obstinate desire to find in Dante traces of Neoplatonic and Arabic doctrines independent of those incorporated by current scholastic philosophy makes him give (page 236) to *Paradiso* XIII, 52-63, a new sense which the text cannot possibly bear. Dante says:

> Ciò che non muore e ciò che può morire   20,6
> non è se non splendor di quell'idea
> che partorisce, amando, il nostro Sire:
> chè quella viva Luce che sì mea
> dal suo Lucente, che non si disuna
> da Lui nè dall'amor che a lor s'intrea
> per sua bontade il suo raggiare aduna, etc.

This passage interpreted according to the traditional view corresponds word for word to the ordinary doctrine of the church. In the first place, Dante asserts that the creation proceeds from the Idea. St. Thomas (*Sum.*, I, 9. 4. 7) says 'Filius est universalis causa creaturarum.' Dante calls Christ the 'Idea,' and so do the Fathers (see St. Bonaventura, *I Sent.* VI, 1. 3). *Lucente* to indicate the father is frequent and natural enough. Christ of course is the *luce* (*lux vera*) and the holy spirit is constantly qualified as *amor*.

Instead of this obvious and orthodox and internally consistent explanation, Mr. Nardi brings in Plotinus and Proclus, explains the Trinity as a process of emanations, misunderstands *Splendor* which he refers to the Creator, whereas it is meant to describe the creation; does not see that *amor* and not *splendor* is the third person; confuses, contrary to his own thesis, this *splendor* with *luce,* calls it *anima mundi* (at least here he has hit upon an historical heresy) and identifies them all with the empyrean.

Mr. Nardi's interpretation of Dante's Fortuna is surely faulty. While commenting *Par.* VIII, 112-141 and particularly the verses 'Sempre *natura* se fortuna trova Discorde a se... fa mala prova,' he defines *fortuna* (page 47) as the 'virtù propria delle sfere celesti' as the 'strumento celeste di quella Provvidenza divina,' with the result that, while Dante has taken pains to contrast *natura* (*circolare*) with *fortuna* (his whole argument depending on this contrast), Mr. Nardi candidly obliterates this distinction and confuses *natura* with *fortuna*. What then does fortune mean in this passage? I should say, in conformity with the Aristotelic doctrine, that it is the *causa per accidens* which governs *external conditions* in so far as they affect a human life. In the *Magna Moralia*, II, 9 we read: 'absque *externis* bonis quorum domina fortuna est...' and 'Est fortuna in his quae *in nobis non sunt.*' In *Rhet.*, II, 11: 'Fortunam autem appello nobilitatem, divitias, potentiam et horum contraria.' In *Polit.*, VII, 1: 'Bonorum enim quae *extra animam* causa casus et fortuna.' Chalcidius, in his Commentary to the *Timaeus* (Wrobel, p. 204) says the same thing. So does Cicero; so does Servius *ad Aen.*, IV, 653: 'Fortuna ad omnia pertinet quae *extrinsecus* sunt.' And the scholastic writers accept all this. Fortuna, moreover, in conformity with Aristotle's doctrine (*Physics* II. ch. 4-6) is a *causa per accidens*. For when *natura circolare* (stellar influence) as a *causa per se*, providentially diversifying the product of heredity (*natura generata*), has produced human beings endowed with the capacities necessary to fulfill the functions of the state (which is a natural aggregate), then the origination of this naturally political animal in one milieu (*ostello*) instead of another cannot be a result of nature. 'Accidit' to a naturally 'martial' man that he is born in a military milieu: it is an *accident* that the naturally 'jovial' child should belong to a kingly dynasty. This accidental cause, or, if we will, this *concursus causarum* is what we call Fortune, which is divinely ordained and providential, even though mysterious (ἄδηλος) to us (*Inf.*, VII, 84; *De Mon.*, II, 10).

Mr. Nardi's interpretation (page 48) of Dante's reference to 'Materia prima' at the beginning of the fourth tractate of the *Convito* seems totally inadequate. In his endeavor to make Dante over into a more or less heretical anti-scholastic, he states that in the sentence: 'io mirava e cercava se la materia degli elementi era da Dio intesa,' the word *intesa* means 'produced directly' and not 'comprehended,' and the whole phrase must be interpreted as expressing the doubt that perhaps not God but the celestial intelligences had produced it. All of which is impossible. For even granting the unusual meaning of *intendere*, the 'directly' on which the claims of the creating angels rest is Mr. Nardi's own contribution. If, on the other hand, we give the words their normal meaning, we get without effort a sense which brings the text in close contact with the controversies of the day.

For Aristotle has stated (*Physics*, I, 7) that 'Subiecta materia est scibilis secundum analogiam.' For us mortals, this formless matter is surely unintelligible. But how about God? Does he know it? St. Thomas (*Sum.*, I, 15. 3. 3) says no. The Franciscans (Duns Scotus, *ii. Sent.*, 12, 1; and *iii. Sent.*, 9, 1) say yes. Dante 'wonders.'

The most classical commonplaces and the most ordinary beliefs of the Middle Ages become for our author recondite bits of Neoplatonic-Arabic lore. His discussion of dreams on pp. 59-61 is a good example of this. He believes that those who speak of the truthfulness of morning dreams have directly or indirectly obtained their notion from Avicenna (p. 61): 'quel che Avicenna aveva detto dei sogni matutini.' And yet Horace (*Sat.*, I, 10, 31) refers to the truthful morning dreams, and Ovid (*Her.*, XVIII, 195) likewise, as well as Moschus (II, 5), and Homer (*Odyssey*, IV, 841). A mediaeval writer may have got the idea from Ovid or from Avicenna, or from one of a hundred writers: that is a matter of no importance. What matters is the history of this lore which goes back to pre-classical times. The second feature of Mr. Nardi's dream doctrine, namely, the necessity of a detachment from the senses, is also ancient. It suffices to quote St. Augustine (*Gen.* ad lit., XII, 13). John of Salisbury (*Pol.*, II, 14) sums up this Pythagorean doctrine in terms very similar to those of Dante: 'contingit ut animus corporis exercitio relevatus in se ipsum liberius redeat et veritatem... contempletur.' And the third and last point that we gather from his Arabic quotations, viz., the connection of dreams with stars, also goes back to classical days. Martianus Capella (II, 150) said: 'At infra solis meatum usque lunarem globum secundae beatitatis numina supparisque potentiae per quae temen vaticinia, somniaque ac prodigia componuntur.' Hephaestio (III, 24, ap. Engelbrecht, p. 26) discusses at length the influence of the moon on dreams. Ammon (Ludwich, *Maximi et Ammonis Carminum* etc., p. 53) refers to the relation of dreams with the zodiacal position of planets.

The interpretation of Averroes' celestial physics given to us in Mr. Nardi's book does not seem to be accurate. In the first place, while discussing (p. 62 et seq.) the explanation of the moon spots given by Peter of Abano, he remarks that, in spite of Abano's assertion to the contrary, 'his (Abano's) view has nothing to do with Averroes' theory.' I should rather say that a proper understanding of both will show them to be identical.

For Averroes (*De Caelo*, II, 32; II, 42; II, 49, 1860 Ed.) explains that the varying surface of the moon (which we call its spots) is due to the varying capacity of its more or less dense parts to receive the light of the sun. Which diversity, he says, is not contrary to the nature of the fifth essence, for just as one celestial body is more luminous than another, so can one part of the same heavenly body be more adapted than another to imbibe the rays of the sun. Owing, he explains, to this condition of the moon whereby it has to depend on the sun for its light, Aristotle said that it was similar to the *element* earth (not the terrestrial sphere) in that this fourth element borrowed its light from fire, whereas the other stars which have their own light may be compared to the element fire. Peter of Abano, if we try to get some sense out of the corrupt text that Mr. Nardi gives, says *exactly* the same thing. He, too, speaks of the varying capacity of the different parts of the moon to receive the light of the sun: 'secundum illam partem...' He too says that this diversity is not inadmissable in the fifth essence where varying luminosity has already been ascertained: 'quod... non est in corporibus...' And he too clinches the identical argument by quoting the authority of Aristotle in an even more definite way.

My second objection to Mr. Nardi's interpretation of Averroes' theory deals with the general nature of the celestial bodies. Mr. Nardi says (p. 8) that Averroes, while elsewhere holding that the celestial spheres are identical not only in *genus* but also in *species* (that is, that they are individuals of the same species), in the fifth chapter of his *De Substantia Orbis* says something radically different when he affirms that 'ideo invenitur in eis plus quam unum numero et sunt species et genera.'

Now Averroes may have here changed his mind; that, at least, is the view of the editors who indicate this inconsistency in their marginal notes, from which notes perhaps Mr. Nardi took his clue. But this change of view, if it exists, can never be derived from the words quoted above. For the *eis* there refers *not* to celestial bodies but to elemental ones. Averroes states that though the stars must indeed be 'bodies' in that they are endowed with motion, yet being free from alteration and corruption they are not like elemental things here below which are diversified *numero, specie et genere*. It would indeed be strange if Averroes who had refused to introduce specific distinctions in the fifth essence had ended by advocating even generic differences, which moreover would contradict the whole theory of the *De Substantia Orbis*.

The fundamental question of Dante's view of creation and of the relation of the creatures to the creator is not accurately presented by our author. In discussing (p. 47) the poet's statement that what God immediately creates cannot die, he traces this neoplatonic doctrine back to Avicenna. Yet the Greek source (available to Dante) is before our eyes in Proclus' *Institutio Theologica*, 76: 'omne quod ab immobili causa manat immutabilem habet substantiam; omne quod a mobili causa manat substantiam habet mutabilem.' Which doctrine Dante might also have gotten from Chalcidius, who in his commentary to the *Timaeus* (Wrobel, p. 89) says: 'Quod sequitur ut quidquid a Deo fit temporarium non sit... et tempus immutationem aetatis, morbos, senectutem occasum invehit. *His ergo omnibus quod a Deo instituitur immune est.*' Or perhaps he may have been inspired directly by Plato's passage (*Tim.*, 41).

And when he studies (p. 18) the fortunes of this theory among Dante's contemporaries, he quotes Tempier's condemnation of the doctrine that 'effectus immediatus debet esse unus tantum et simillimus primo,' and suggests that some Averroist in Paris must have defended this view. This mysterious Averroist will be found to be Albertus himself. For the author of the book *De Causis Universitatis* which Mr.

Nardi unquestioningly assigns to Albertus, says (i, 1, 10) 'a primo quod est necesse esse *immediate* non potest esse nisi *unum*. Et in hoc quidem iam omnes consenserunt peripatetici licet hoc quidem non intelligentes theologi negaverint.' And he proceeds to support his statement on the authority of Dionysius.

My other objection to the book has to do with the practice of the author to accept and incorporate erroneous and meaningless texts which cannot be defended by the fact that they are taken from standard editions. This point should be emphasized because it is fast becoming a serious one. It seems to be a growing habit on the part of writers to accept long Latin and Greek quotations so replete with blunders that it may be reasonably inquired whether the person quoting them has any idea what they are all about.

For instance, Mr. Nardi (pp. 86-87) cites from the not very good edition of Baur of Grosseteste's philosophical works (Beiträge etc., IX) the following: 'Luna autem de natura perspicui densissimi in caelestibus habet *motum* de natura lucis rarissimae inter cetera caelestia minimum, de natura luminosi proprii parum.' It would be interesting to know what sense Baur and Nardi got out of this passage, and how they juggled the *motum* into the context. Of course we should read *multum* instead of *motum*, and then the passage would mean something. The moon has much of the nature of 'perspicuum densum,' a minimum of 'lux rara,' little of self-illumination. Grosseteste had said in the previous page that the moon is made up of *perspicuum* and had quoted Averroes where the latter says that the moon is *densa*.

The blunders of the editions of St. Thomas (Fretté and others) are swallowed whole. So the following passage of the *De Causis*, which has been frequently quoted from St. Thomas by other authors who did not seem to surmise how senseless it is: 'Et non est factum ita nisi propter suam propinquitatem esse puri et uni et vero, in quo *vero* est multitudo aliquorum modorum.' Here, of course, instead of the *vero*, we need a very strong *non*.

Nor is Mr. Nardi disturbed (p. 100) by this other passage from St. Thomas (Commentary to Proposition II of *De Causis*): 'Unde et Proculus dicit 191 propositione: omnis anima participans substantiam quidem aeternalem, habet operationem *aliam* secundum tempus,' which is meaningless. Instead of *aliam* we should read *autem* and connect *aeternalem* with *operationem* to mean: 'every participating soul has an eternal substance but an action in time,' which statement is amplified in the sentence of St. Thomas which immediately follows. Worse still is the case with quotations from Albertus which are taken from Borgnet and Jammy. On p. 21, Mr. Nardi quotes from Albertus: *Summa de Creaturis*, III, 12, 3, and gives us a meaningless text not only because he accept a *mobili* which should be emended into a *nobili* but introduces himself an *immobili* where a *mobili* is demanded. On p. 108, in quoting from Albertus: *De Caelo*, II, 3, 14, he accepts the same erroneous reading in: 'quia per ipsam est *mobile* quidquid est,' where *nobile* is needed. And in that same passage he endorses the following: 'necesse est autem quod sphaera quae movetur ab intelligentia primi ordinis habeat operationem unam quoniam forma quam habet est simplex et *determinata*, sphaerae aliae accipiunt formam hanc minus universalem et *minus* determinatam,' where instead of *determinatam* we need *indeterminatam*, and instead of *minus* we need *magis*. And on page 224, in quoting from *Summa de Creaturis*, I, 3, 11a, 2, he again accepts the following senseless statement: 'cum inferiores caeli... sint aeque *mobiles* cum caelo empyreo,' where again *nobiles* should be read.

Of his quotations from Dante, I wish to discuss one which, though sponsored by the editors, should have appeared suspicious to a philosophic mind like that of Mr. Nardi. In quoting from the *Epistle* to Can Grande, ch. 20, he accepts the illogical reading of the critical texts which says: 'Omne quod est aut habet esse a se aut ab alio. Sed constat quod habere esse a se non convenit nisi uni, scilicet primo seu principio qui Deus est. Et quum habere esse non arguat per se necesse esse et per se necesse esse non competat nisi uni, scilicet primo seu principio quod est causa omnium, ergo omnia quae sunt praeter unum ipsum habent esse ab alio.'

Dante is here made to say that the 'possession of being from self' (*habere esse a se*) pertains to one alone because 'necessary being through self' (*per se necesse esse*) pertains to one alone (God) inasmuch as the possession of being does not imply 'necessary being through self.' All of which is senseless. For if 'necessary being through self' is posited for one alone, what is the sense of adding that being does not imply 'necessary being through self'? And how do we establish the relation (on which Dante builds his argument) between *habere esse a se* and *per se necesse esse*? One way of remedying the faulty text would be of reading: 'cum (without the preceding et) habere esse a se arguat per se necesse esse' leaving out *non* (*cod. Mediceo*). This at least presents a logical sequence and brings the passage in harmony with the accepted doctrine of the times.

The quotations from the translation of Simplicius' Commentary to *De Caelo* are also unintelligible except by emendations, and so those of Alpetragius, particularly the one on p. 173, where in the phrase 'aliquando corrigi aerem in aliquibus locis *directis*,' should read 'dirutis,' as the sense of the passage demands.

II. "A.H. Gilbert's *Dante's Conception of Justice*" *

This book is not an original investigation. The relationships commented upon have long been established; nor is the manner of presentation entirely adequate. Even after a cursory examination, one discovers that the author has a somewhat insecure hold on the language and the subject matter of the books he uses. For example, in the passage in which he tries to connect Dante's treatment of inhuman sins with Aristotle's *Politics* (I, 1) and with St. Thomas, he translates the latter's commentary on the passage as follows (p. 7): "The word *human* indicates what is useful and what is harmful. It follows from this that it signifies the just and the unjust. For justice and injustice consist in a man's receiving equable or inequable treatment in helpful or injurious things. And this *word* is applicable only to men (!!) for the reason that" etc. Of course St. Thomas never uttered such things. He says "*Human speech* is expressive of what is useful and of what is useless, hence of what is just and of what is unjust. For justice and injustice deal with equal or unequal distribution of things useful or harmful. And therefore *speech* is peculiar to man" etc. (Sed loquutio humana significat quid est utile et quid nocivum. Ex quo sequitur quod significet iustum et iniustum. Consistit enim iustitia et iniustitia ex hoc quod aliqui adaequentur vel non adaequentur in rebus utilibus et nocivis. Et ideo loquutio est propria hominibus, etc.) Nothing here about sins human or inhuman, but simply a contrast between rational speech and irrational vocal utterances of lower animals.

On page 9, while discussing the role of the things of Fortune in human events. St. Thomas is translated as follows: "Yet man desires

---

* Review of: *Dante's Conception of Justice*, by ALLAN H. GILBERT, Duke University Press, Durham, N.C., 1925, pp. ix+244.

these in prayer to God as though they were suitable for him, and thus is made avaricious and unjust; but he ought to pray that he might choose what is good *for himself*, that he may labor as he should according to *virtue*." What St. Thomas actually says is: "But men ask these things in their prayers as though they were suitable for them *at all times* and thus are made unjust and greedy; instead we should pray that those things which are good *in themselves* (quae sunt secundum se bona) be made good for man. So that each may choose what is good for him, *namely* to act rightly in accordance with virtue (scilicet operari recte secundum virtutem)."

The scholastic technicalities are often unsurmountable obstacles. On page 14, while emphasizing the predominance of avarice, the author attributes to St. Thomas the following impossible statement: "Thus other vices can be present in a man without the avarice which is *specially* called injustice." The true meaning of the passage is "Thus the other vices can exist without avarice which is a particular kind of injustice" (Sic aliae malitiae possunt esse sine avaritia quae est specialis iniustitia). On page 33 we are told that according to Aristotle, "justice in the strict sense of the word" is *different* from "political justice." Professor Gilbert's precise words are: "Aristotle says that he is dealing at once with justice in the strict sense of the word and with political justice. The latter implies an association" etc. What Aristotle says is just the opposite of this (see the passage in *Ethics* 459). The old Latin version has it correctly and St. Thomas also, who says: "quod justum de quo quaeritur est iustum simpliciter quod est iustum politicum," which does not mean (as Prof. Gilbert translates it) "the justice here dealt with is justice in the *simplest* form which is political justice," but rather the *justum* which is here inquired into is the absolute *iustum* which is the same as the political *justum* (*simpliciter* meaning "absolutely, unrestrictedly"). On the same page (33) we also read this ineptitude ascribed to Aristotle: "Yet the doing of some injustice does not imply injustice in everything," as a rendering of "in quibus autem iniustum facere non omnibus iniustitia," which means "injustice is not present in all those who commit unjust acts," or, as the Greek text has it, "injustice always implies an unjust act, but an unjust act does not always imply injustice." The presentation here is vitiated throughout by the author's failure to see the contrast between *iniustitia* and *iniustum*, between ἀδικία and τὸ ἀδικεῖν.

The meaning of the comment of St. Thomas (page 48) is hopelessly distorted because of the misconception as to the meaning of *ratio*, which is here the *ratio essendi*. At the close of the passage we read (p. 49) that "the things which follow from the reasons may be changed as belonging to a less important group," as a translation of "illa vero quae consequuntur, mutantur ut in minori parti," which means instead: "In the actualization of a principle there are deviations, but only exceptionally" (ut in minori parte).

The technical meaning of *per se and per accidens* also causes trouble as on page 57, where the presentation of the thought of Aristotle and St. Thomas is almost unrecognizable.

On pages 29-30 we find a glaring contradiction in the following translation from St. Thomas:

"That is why money is called *numisma*, for *nomos* means law, since money is *not* a measure according to nature, but according to *nomos*, or law, *for nature can remove the value from coins and render them useless*." This passage is a translation of the following text: "Et inde est quod denarius vocatur numisma: nomos enim lex est, quia scilicet denarius non est mensura per naturam, sed nomo, idest lege; est enim in potestate *natura* transmutare denarios et reddere eos inutiles." If we correct the misprint *natura*, as both sense and grammar demand, and read *nostra* (abbreviated in both cases *nr̄a*), the contradiction disappears, and the commentary of St. Thomas is brought into agreement with Aristotle's passage which (in the *antiqua translatio*) says: "et in *nobis* est transmutare et facere inutile."

The part of Prof. Gilbert's book which deals with the analysis of the principles of punishment and reward in the *Divine Comedy* is not usually very sound. On page 130, he tries to prove against Torraca that the manner of punishment of avarice in Purgatory is not imitative of the sin. According to his view, the avaricious are forced to look down with their faces to the pavement, not because in life they had sinfully kept their souls glued to the base earth, but because their punishment consists in being (p. 132) "unable to look with longing eyes upon the *good things* of the world." (!!) No one who understands the text, the very clear text, of Dante could have any doubt on the subject. The poet says:

"Quel ch'avarizia fa, qui si dichiara
In purgazion dell'anime converse:
E nulla pena il monte ha più amara.

Sì come l'occhio nostro non s'aderse
In alto, fisso alle cose terrene,
Così giustizia qui a terra il merse,
Come avarizia spense a ciascun bene
Lo nostro amore, onde operar perdési;
Così giustizia qui stretti ne tiene
Ne' piedi e nelle man legati e presi." (*Purg.*, 19. 115-124.)

"What avarice consists in (the act of avarice) is here made manifest for the purification of the converted souls." That is: after conversion the avaricious man can remove the stain of his transgression by realizing the implications and the significance of his immoral act. This profound and recurrent thought of Dante is wiped out by our author, who, ignoring all the exigencies of language and syntax and thought, can say that "the simplest meaning here (of the first quoted *terzina*) would be: Avarice is the sin for which the souls in the circle are punished" (p. 131).

The second *terzina* makes the thought clearer: even as our eye did not uplift itself on high, but remained fastened on earthly things (not the good things, but the bad things), so divine justice here immersed it into the earth. The clear evidence of these lines is explained off by Prof. Gilbert, as follows (p. 132): "The eyes which were not raised to heaven are now plunged to earth; the eyes once fixed on things of the earth now regard the earth itself. The question arises: Are earthly things and the earth substantially identical? or can we feel that there is instead a contrast in meaning? Earthly things are the good things of this earth which the eyes of those who are now groveling in the dust no longer look upon."

Which is all impossible. Prof. Gilbert takes Dante's "earthly things" and to help along his argument, inserts the adjective "good." By such device anything can be proved: vice can be made a virtue, and rain into sunshine. But contrasting "earthly things" arbitrarily called *good* with "the earth" which is bad, would be as sensible as calling gold *base* and things of gold *precious*. Fastening the eye on earthly things is, for Mr. Gilbert, man's duty; evidently then the act of uplifting it on high (sì come l'occhio nostro non s'aderse) is a sin; and avarice becomes a virtue and Dante becomes — what?

The condemnation of the evil of avarice often is expressed in the Middle Ages by symbols connected with the *earth*. And the avaricious person is regularly compared with the mole. St. Bonaventura (Peltier's edition, vol. 13, p. 95) says for example: "avarus eligens *terrenam* habitationem cum talpa et statuens *oculos* declinare in *terram.*" And if the Latin is not satisfactory, see *Le Laie Bible* (edited by J. A. Clarke, Columbia University Press, 1923), verses 669-672:

> "Li avarissieus resamble
> Trop bien le *fouant*, ce me samble,
> C'oncques ne cesse d'assambler
> La *terre* et d'amonceler."

And there are Italian examples as well as German ones.

The same disrespect for facts and their significance is shown in the treatment of envy (pp. 123-125): In order to prove again that the penalty does not imitate the crime but is opposed to it, he begins by saying that the envious of Purgatory have their eyes sealed unto blindness because "unless one sees, either literally or figuratively, the goods of others, one can hardly be envious" (p. 123) for "this recalls the original meaning of the Latin *invidia*, coming from *invidere* (in + videre, to see), which meant *to look askance at, to look maliciously or spitefully at*. By derivation, then, envy is a matter of sight" (p. 124). According to Prof. Gilbert, then, the malice of envy consists in seeing something somehow — and therefore he triumphantly concludes: "The justice of Dante's conception is clear. The envious are redressing the balance by giving up the faculty through which they had especially sinned. The loss of sight may signify retirement from the world through sickness or exile, so that the victim is less tempted to envy, and more certain, because blind to the world, 'of beholding the high light' of heaven."

Dante's conception is the opposite of all this, as it is known *lippis et tonsoribus*. The envious man sins in that he does not want to see, in that he turns away his eyes. Dante says this explicitly (*Purg.*, 13, 133-135):

> " 'Gli occhi,' diss'io, 'mi fieno ancor qui tolti,
> Ma picciol tempo; chè poca è l'offesa
> Fatta per esser con invidia *volti*,' "

The envious are righted by being made to feel, and to make explicit to themselves and others, the malice inherent in their not want-

ing to see. They would not see on earth the good of others: here they
cannot see their own good, for to them

"Luce del ciel di sè largir non vuole." (*Purg.* 13. 69.)

All this is in accord with the ordinary views of the time. For
whatever the true etymology of *invidia* (what the author quotes is the
first *definition* of Harper's dictionary and not its derivation) an etymology popularly accepted in the thirteenth century consisted in identifying "invidere" with "*non* videre." (St. Bonaventura, 8, 136, "invidia
a non videndo quia non potest videre bona aliorum.") And the Scrip-
tures were interpreted accordingly: Job's "Per diem incurrent tenebras
et quasi in nocte sic palpabunt in meridie" is explained by the *Glossa
ordinaria* "mens *invidi* cum de bono alieno affligitur *de radio solis
obscuratur...* quia livore *caeci... caeci* circumeunt, id est *invidentes* facta
dictaque scrutantur" etc. (Wal. Strabo, *Glossa Ordinaria* s. lib. Job.)

The handling of the Paradiso is also unsatisfatory. The courage
shown in dealing with the philosophical problems of that *Cantica* is
not justified by the preparation of the author, which symptomatically
reveals itself by such statements as these (p. 176): "In the *last* heaven,
the *primum mobile*, all the saints are gathered together, for here all
have their dwelling place, without respect to their grades."

The interpretative accuracy may be sampled by reading on page 174
the discussion of Paradiso xxviii, 109-14. This passage in Dante is a
clear presentation of the intellectualist's view of beatitude in opposition
to the voluntarist's. The poet here polemically takes sides in this famous
thirteenth century controversy, and says in plain language that beatitude primarily is founded on the act of the intellect and only secondarily on the act of the will (the voluntarists held the opposite) and
that the beatific capacity of the intellect depends on grace and deeds.
Prof. Gilbert comments on this important philosophical statement in
such a way that no vestige of Dante's thought remains. He says "We
may take this as Dante's statement of the cause of the satisfaction of
men in ordinary life with the divine justice. In proportion as men
are able to see clearly they can advance from 'grade to grade' of blessed-
ness. When a man is thus graded in accord with what is within himself,
he has no dissatisfaction with his own lot, but accepts it as in harmony
with the eternal verities."

VI

THE POLITICAL IDEAS OF ST. AUGUSTINE *

We want to discuss now the by-products — social and political — of the theology of St. Augustine: by-products fully as important as the theological ideas themselves.

The political implications of that theology are not hard to trace. All depends, of course, on the profound pessimism of his theory of predestination, which one cannot dismiss by saying that it is a Lutheran or Jansenist misinterpretation, for it is too clearly present in his own pages. The doctrine hinges on two facts, both very hard to scrutinize: one, the contamination of the whole species by one man; the other, the determination of the Creator to save some and not the others. Long before Adam was created, St. Augustine says, interpreting the words of St. Paul, God knew that Adam would sin, and that all mankind would be corrupted by that sin. But out of that corrupt mass of humanity to come, God picked out certain souls whom he saved by sending them grace in the form of a summons or call of irresistible force — irresistible grace, that is the phrase St. Augustine uses. The persons thus chosen have to be saved. They are not good, and therefore saved. They are good because God has sent His irresistible saving grace.

That, briefly, is the doctrine of predestination. And as a result of it you have St. Augustine's entire political structure. God has predestined very few for salvation; the rest, the great majority, are to be damned. Of course, the word predestination is rarely used for the

---

* From *The Philosophical and Political Backgrounds of the Divine Comedy*, a series of lectures by Dino Bigongiari, Da Ponte Professor Emeritus of Italian, at Columbia University.

damned. The commonest use reserves it only for salvation; but, obviously, that leaves us to conclude that those who are not to be saved will be forever damned. These latter, always the majority of human beings, act immorally because they have no grace. They are all filled with lusts, desires for wealth, power, and pleasure. St. Augustine goes through the long pageant of their desires. They are the ones whose needs have called into existence the political state. The state is necessary because these people, with all their greed, with all their desires, would otherwise soon have exterminated themselves. To prevent such extermination, God permitted — he did not create, but permitted — the constitution of states. The one advantage that the state has is that it guarantees some kind of peace. And for what purpose is peace necessary? St. Augustine says, so that these people may satisfy some of their greed. That is what polity means; that is what the state is.

If we forget the theology for a moment, and consider merely the picture of the world St. Augustine gives us, we can easily see that his political pessimism has roots that extend way back into pagan antiquity. To approach St. Augustine's position in this way, we have only to recall a famous statement of Lucian, the satirist. The gods, according to Lucian, are primarily humorists. They have built this world as a stage for their own entertainment. Man finds his way on to that stage, and he comes with an infinite capacity to create, to produce all sorts of things. This ingenuity he uses all for the purpose of making himself happy; yet he finds that his desires are always one step ahead of his capacity to produce. In other words, man is destined to be always running after something he desires that is always beyond his reach; he cannot be satisfied, because his desires go on to infinity. As a result of this constitution of his, man, according to Lucian, is incapable of acting justly.

To understand the political significance of a statement of this sort, you have to recall some of the positions we touched upon in studying the Greek authors; particularly those of the Sophists and Epicureans. We noted that some of the best Greek philosophers, as well as Cicero, and many Christian thinkers, including Dante, held a very different view. It was their boast — we may call it a boast — that the state exists by divine providence in order that there may be justice in this world; that as long as there is justice, a community will be able to maintain itself, and as soon as justice goes — I'm quoting Cicero here — the community goes, collapses, and anarchy sets in. Now this view of man's condition is very different from the Sophist or Epicurean view; and it is the very opposite of the one St. Augustine holds.

In a violent debate with Cicero across the centuries, St. Augustine says: Not only does the removal of justice not lead to the breaking up of a state, but in fact there never has been a state that was maintained by justice. Behind this is Lucian's idea that man is incapable of justice because of his infinite desires, and also the Sophistic and Epicurean position according to which justice comes into existence as a result of a contract — a social contract. Those thinkers, especially the Epicurean philosophers of pleasure, held that all men had it in their hearts to satisfy to the uttermost, to infinity, all their desires, whatever they might be. By experience, however, they have come to realize that if they were to go all out to get such satisfaction, they would probably end up in such disorder that nobody would get anything. They concluded, therefore, that in order to have at least some satisfaction, we have to give up the possibility of satisfying all our desires, and concentrate on enjoying the maximum amount of pleasure our fellow-citizens will permit us to have. Through the centuries ideas of this sort have been presented again and again by serious thinkers. We have only to recall the name of Thomas Hobbes and his doctrine of *bellum omnium contra omnes*.

Let us see how St. Augustine's political philosophy fits into this series of pessimistic views of man. For him, too, men (though not all, not those destined for salvation) are animated with unquenchable desires for goods that are such that as you increase the share of one, the quantity that remains to be shared among the others diminishes. This is true, surely, of sexual pleasure, the possession of a woman, the attainment of glory on the battlefield or in the arena. Are there any pleasures of which it is not true? Long before St. Augustine's time the ancients had pointed out some of them. Seneca, for instance, had noted that our pleasure in contemplation, in singing, in dancing, increases the more people share in it. But it is not so with material goods. As civilization advances, and men learn how to produce more and more wealth, so that all might have more material goods, instead of diminishing, strife mounts. It seems that men contend more, the more there is to be had.

Against this argument, of course, you have the Baconian idea that has dominated our popular thinking for the last few centuries — the

idea that we can remove the occasion for struggle over material goods
not by limiting our desires but by forcing nature to do our bidding.
That's the Baconian attitude: force nature to supply all needs, to supply the means of satisfying all desires, and thereby put an end to
this economic and political striving that has characterized the life of
man on earth. Look around you, and judge for yourselves whether Lucian or Bacon was right.

Well, our interest in this sort of Baconian utopianism is limited
to St. Augustine's criticism. To be sure, St. Augustine has given us
some indication as to how we may live happily in the enjoyment of
goods which give greater pleasure the more people share in them. The
moral principle is clear and rather easy to apply individually. But
how to socialize the principle is the problem. Suggestions had been
heard even before St. Augustine's time as thinking people, like Plotinus,
became alarmed at the progress of material civilization, or rather, at
the strife that accompanies it. Centuries later we will hear St. Francis
express a similar pessimism about material progress. In a Marxian vein,
though to a very opposite purpose, St. Francis reduced all the evil
desires that lead mankind away from goodness to a common denominator: the desire for wealth. Wealth, or rather, the desire for wealth
is the source of all evil. It is in poverty, therefore, that we should
seek salvation. And if we seek it there, St. Francis believed, we will
surely find it.

You know how much of his time, of his genius, St. Francis dedicated to singing, in Italy and out of Italy, the praises of Lady Poverty.
And strangely enough, occasionally he had a response. We know of
whole communities that responded, acting as if they were indeed all
to be counted among those few who — St. Augustine would say —
are predestined for salvation. Yet it was a response and a happiness
that was obviously not to be of great duration. Dante, who sings of
that response in the eleventh canto of the *Paradiso*, the canto devoted
to St. Francis, grasps why it could not last on the social level. Realizing how destructive of individuals and communities the insatiable desire for wealth is, Dante begins the canto with a terrible invective
that has shocked many of his readers. It is a very Augustinian moment
in the *Divine Comedy*. He bundles together rulers, doctors, pharmacists,
lawyers, corrupt priests, prostitutes, idlers — all who have set for
themselves as an aim the satisfaction, the beatitude, the happiness
that comes from material goods. Whether they strive for the satisfac-

tions of political rule, or sexual indulgence, or banqueting, these people, Dante says, are all alike, all equally bad.

St. Augustine does not go quite that far. These people are not all the same, he says, though they are all of one camp. When there is a struggle for the goods they desire, and a struggle is always forthcoming, all these people will do what the old Sophists said: they will transform themselves into the powers that constitute the political order. They will form a state.

By state, remember, St. Augustine does not mean any given city or kingdom. When he speaks of the *civitas terrena*, the city of the earth, which he also calls the *civitas diaboli*, the diabolical city, he means all who through all the centuries have striven for the sort of goods I have described. It began in Adam's time, with the first fratricide, Cain, and continues through the time of Remus and Romulus, the reconstituted fratricide, down to the present. All of these people who strive for self-satisfaction in this way, as they are grouped in different states, under different rulers, constitute the city of the devil. God in His mercy has given them, as we said, this utilitarian suggestion or insight: give up that boundless lust for wealth, come to terms; take a little, let others have a little; otherwise nobody will have anything — you will all be dead. And when men, following this utilitarian suggestion, agree to give up their absolute lust, to accept a share of the common good, and to punish those who exceed their shares, we call the result a state — an association dictated by utility for the purpose of enabling a group of people to enjoy, without destroying one another, whatever goods they like best. Some people will like one thing and some will like another. We will have, therefore, a hierarchy of states, some not as bad as others, yet all corrupt to some degree, for the original sin contaminates them all. Whatever it may be that they want, it is still self-seeking that moves them to form a political community, the self-seeking that St. Augustine calls *cupiditas*. The Romans, who sacrificed enjoyment of the pleasures of the flesh that they might enjoy the satisfaction of dominating as a nation, might have been less ignoble than Sardanapolis, who said he wished he had thirty stomachs and as many genital organs so that he might indulge himself as much as he wanted; but they were not more just in the eyes of God. Their motive was that same *cupiditas* on a higher level. That's one pole of the Augustinian ethics. The other pole, the sharing of spiritual goods, is *caritas*. Everybody who has read a page of St. Augustine knows these two.

Men need the state, St. Augustine emphasizes, because they need coercion, in two ways. They need it, first of all, within the bounds of this city of the devil, to keep within proper confines the desires for material goods. And they need it, also, to keep other states from invading the territory of the commonwealth to secure by violence the goods on which they have set their hearts. That is the *civitas terrena.* It provides those who are to have no peace in eternity with a certain degree of peace on earth. It restrains civil war. When one state, at peace internally, comes up against another that it cannot coerce, the war of greed continues on a higher level, until one or the other is overcome.

In the midst of this *civitas terrena* live also those few who are predestined for salvation. Should they try to separate themselves and form a state of their own, apart from the others? They cannot, says St. Augustine; and the reason is that, if all men in a state were really such as these, you wouldn't need a state. The state is like a hospital. If mankind were to become physically perfect, you would not have a perfect hospital; you would have no hospital at all. The state exists because of the immorality of human beings. If people were not immoral, if — taking the impossible — all people were noble, there would not be any state.

And so those who are predestined to be saved — who they are nobody knows, or rather, God knows — will stay in the midst of this city of the devil, as foreigners, *peregrini, viatores,* until they are called to their true home, which is not of this world. While they are here, they are to obey the laws of the state, doing all it commands them to do, provided what it commands does not go against the commandments of God. If, in the relations of individuals to the state, or of one state to another, the constituted power should order you to do something that is against the commandments of God, then refuse, then assert yourselves; but refuse, St. Augustine insists, not by doing, but by not doing. Refuse by clinging to your duty before God to the point of martyrdom and self-sacrifice. The wars for Christ are won, St. Augustine reminds his readers, not by killing, but by dying.

That is the Augustinian scheme. It is important, even for those of us who do not accept its theological basis, because of its very powerful criticism of this life of ours. All of us, more or less, share in, or admire that certain kind of virtue — civic spirit, patriotism, world-brotherhood, call it what you will — which is built up in the hearts of people who willingly associate themselves together to pursue happiness in this world. Whether it be a tiny city-state, or a large nation-state, or empire, or some dreamed-of world community, your willing association with it makes this peace-enforcing institution dear to you. You don't want to see it fail, you don't want to see it die. You would rather die yourself. And you may wonder why everyone in the world has not rushed to associate himself willingly with your group, which you think is so wonderfully suited for the task of securing peace and happiness.

It is the general tendency of all mankind to resort to such flattering self-justification, is it not? How can those Russians — you hear some people ask — be so enthusiastic in the public square, when they have before them, in our way of life, a picture of almost perfect goodness, justice, welfare, and freedom? We can say the same for the little state of Israel, or the Arab states on its borders, for England, Spain, China, India; all are disposed to flatter themselves in this way. That is how the world goes. A certain group of people invade and occupy certain lands, arm themselves, and set about protecting the lands. Today the image of some ugly imperialist power comes to our mind when we say this. But it is true of all societies that hold or occupy territory and defend it: Switzerland, Cuba, India, Israel, as well as England, Russia, or the United States. Immediately this group of people begins to say: this is our land — these beautiful frontiers, these beautiful bays, these rivers — this is God's country, God has given it to us. So the defense of these lands and these rivers comes to seem just, and the willingness to defend them comes to seem a virtue. But in reality, the only justification, St. Augustine would say, is that the people from whom you took these lands had taken them equally unjustly. Our only real excuse for what we do is that there has been an infinite series of plunders, of iniquities behind ours. But, the other line of argument is more flattering. Here is a man on his own soil; obviously he has a perfect right to protect it against attack. It is his soil; God has given it to him. Well, if there is a fight, under these circumstances, and our side wins, we call it a "just" defense, a just war. You are familiar with the term, I am sure. You hear it and read it daily, coming from people in all parts of the world. Their wars are all *just* wars.

Of course, we must not forget that St. Augustine himself has given us the Christian theory of a just war. That is certainly true. Those knights, crusaders, of the Middle Ages — when they spoke of war, endeavoring to see if there might be a way to make wars and fighting less brutal — invariably cited the arguments of the Augustinian doctrine of a just war. Those arguments were later taken up by St. Thomas, and he did not add anything to them or take anything away. We can say, therefore, that the Roman Catholic Church today has a doctrine of just war that comes entirely out of the pages of St. Augustine.

But now we ought to ask: How can a man who says there can be no just state hold that there can be a just war? We can ask the same question with regard to his doctrine of property. We can speak of justice in the administration of property rights. St. Augustine says, provided we recall that these rights are not administered according to the law of God, but according to the law of the emperor. By divine law there should not be private property. And if some great wealth were to fall into the hands of an individual, it should immediately be used as God commands, by those who want to be perfect or, if not perfect, good. For those who want to be perfect — what does Christ say? If you want to be perfect, sell all your goods and give all to the poor. And if you want to be just good, live in such a way that all people around you will love you for having permitted them to share in the goods of the world that made you happy. Property rights exist for the peace of the city of the devil; but we cannot say they are *just* in terms of the divine law.

And the same is true of wars. Wars occur, St. Augustine tells us clearly, only in this earthly city. What he says of war, therefore, applies only to his *civitas terrena*. As with the laws of property, so with the rules of war. The main point is that the situation of man would be much worse without such rules.

What are the justifications for war? The world being what it is, defensive war is obviously justified, for what happens in defensive war is better than what would happen if a nation under attack did not defend itself. What is important in this doctrine, what chivalry saw and what people no longer see, unfortunately, is that the cruel necessities of war can be mitigated in certain things by applying a few realistic rules that can serve to confine the fighting to its proper objectives. One rule is: Never pursue a war beyond the treaty of peace; when a war is ended, let it be really ended. But above all, see to it that you never fight a war with a feeling of throughgoing hatred in your heart. Of all the people I can think of, the man who, I'm sure, would have been most horrified by the trials at Nuremberg is St. Augustine. The enemy may have been as brutal as you like, may have been wholly wrong in his conduct of the war; but, however horribly he has comported himself, the only way to make your defensive war *just* in any sense is to show mercy when victory is won. St. Thomas holds this, and he says himself that he takes it out of St. Augustine.

Related to his doctrine of a just war is St. Augustine's teaching — and here we must touch upon something you are not apt to like — concerning the use of force in matters of faith. You know how the Roman Empire used its civil power to combat heresy by force, as it had used force against the Christians before the time of Constantine. St. Augustine for a long time fought against it. Then, suddenly, for reasons we cannot go into deeply here, he changes his mind. He ceases to be the advocate of adherence according to conscience, and becomes the apostle of compulsion. *Compelle intrare.* To support his position he gives the example from the gospels of the celebration to which some who were invited did not come; the feast was then opened to the maimed, the poor, the halt, and the blind, but still there was room. The Saviour then said: compel them to come in, that my house may be filled. St. Augustine interprets it to mean: force these heretics to come in. Thus he completely reverses his original position, going from day to night, from white to black. You can imagine how many people were resentful and disturbed by this change. And he did not try to conceal the fact that he had reversed himself. Whatever else you may want to say, you have to admit of St. Augustine that he was a most honest thinker.

And remember, he distinctly said: no death penalty for heretics. Many critics have forgotten that. His attitude was that coercion is to be merely a device for facilitating eventual voluntary adherence. It is like the breaking of the shell of an egg. Once these people who have been misled into heresy come out of the broken shell, they will see how magnificent is the orthodox faith, and how much they have almost lost. We must remember that St. Augustine wrote thousands of pages on the subject. Unfortunately, many critics cite only some isolated statement, without noticing all the qualifications and limitations placed upon it, or any of St. Augustine's arguments in justification of his position.

In conclusion we must say a word about St. Augustine's philosophy of history, or rather, about his idea of the relation between providence and history. For here we see the culmination of something that had been preparing itself for a long time in the course of ancient thought. We discussed the question of teleology in connection with the Greeks. Aristotle had established that there is teleology or purpose not only in the volitional acts of man but also in nature. All that we see around us, the animal, vegetable, and mineral kingdoms, is regulated by purpose. The purpose is not conscious, not felt, not regulated by these things themselves; yet what happens is purposeful, because they are activated by a higher being which is called nature. This is, of course, the great Aristotelian doctrine of the teleology of nature. It has often been criticized, repeatedly challenged, sometimes apparently completely rejected, but always it comes back. And even today great scientists have come forward to acknowledge that it cannot be totally rejected, even in their sphere. It does not suffice to explain all phenomena; yet there are obviously large areas of natural phenomena that cannot be sufficiently explained without it.

Well, St. Augustine opened the sphere of history to teleology. There is a design in history, even though individuals have not intended the result accomplished. Historians are always talking as if the sequence of historical events were meaningful, are they not? For example: here comes the philosophical enlightenment of the eighteenth century; that, of course, was the intellectual preparation for the French Revolution; and that in turn was the basis for the appearance of Napoleon, who became, with his arms, the means of spreading the revolutionary ideas throughout Europe. And that, again, was the basis for the resurgence of nationalism in Germany and Italy — and so on. But the question is, was the enlightenment aiming at the Revolution? Did Voltaire want the Revolution? Obviously not. Did the Revolution plan Napoleon? Obviously not. Read the records of the Revolutionary Conventions. And did the France of Napoleon want the rise of the various nationalities — Italian, German? You can answer that for yourselves. Yet, if there is this concatenation, not willed by the agents involved — agents who often aimed at the very opposite effect — who shall we say willed it?

For St. Augustine and his contemporaries the sequence of events under examination was the history of Rome from the legendary fall of Troy to the attacks of the Germanic barbarians. The fall of Troy, whether it be fiction or not, and the consequent development of the Mediterranean world — the rise of Rome — was willed by divine providence. Hector fought as he did for Troy so that Aeneas would have to do what he did. It was the way to realize God's purposes. The players, the agents, had to be, like puppets, unconscious of their true roles.

In other words, externally at least, this Augustinian historical teleology resembles the modern doctrine of Hegel on the cunning of reason in history, does it not? You might say that this conception of history, which has gained a certain amount of notoriety through the Marxian version of it, is full of difficulties. Some people say it is all nonsense. And yet, admitting that the individuals involved were not conscious of the results toward which their deeds tended, how are you going to be able to see any logic in the sequence of political, economic, and social events — unless there is meaning on a higher level? If you deny providence, or the cunning of reason, it is pretty hard to justify what we are all prone to do — namely, to discern some plan in the sequence of historical events in this world.

Well, whether you are prepared to accept it or not, this Augustinian doctrine we have touched upon in our study of his political thought has made its impression.

VII

THE POLITICAL IDEAS OF ST. THOMAS AQUINAS

I. The State as a Natural Order *

A state according to St. Thomas is a part of the universal empire of which God is the maker and ruler. Its laws are, or can be made to be, particular determinations of this empire's eternal code; and the authority which enforces these laws is a power whose origin is also in God. Its goal and justification is to offer to man satisfactory material conditions of life as a basis for a moral and intellectual education which, in turn, must be such as to lend itself to the spiritual edification of the Christian man. For "God... instructs us by means of His law and assists us by His grace."[1]

St. Thomas follows the Aristotelian doctrine that makes of man a "political animal," but he modifies it in accordance with the exigencies of his Christian philosophy. The fact that man operates, not by instinct, but by reason makes social organization indispensable. This inter-dependence of reason and sociability is explained by St. Thomas as follows: by endowing man with reason and at the same time depriving him of instinct and of an available ready-made supply of the necessities of life, God decreed that man should be a political animal. For to the beasts nature furnishes food, body covering, weapons of defense and offense (claws, fangs, horns, etc.), means for survival through flight (rapid wings and quick feet), etc. But all this, and much more, man must produce for himself under the direction of reason. What lower

---

* Originally the "Introduction" to *The Political Ideas of St. Thomas Aquinas*, New York, 1953. Page references to materials in that anthology are included in the notes to this study.

[1] *S.* I-II, Q. 90, pp. 3 ff.

animals perform spontaneously and instinctively (i.e., by the exercise of the "estimative" faculty) man achieves as a result of rational processes. Beasts, without instruction, devoid of experience, deprived of models, know immediately what to do and how to act: the newly born lamb at the mere sight of a wolf runs for safety; birds hatched from eggs that have been removed from the nest, when the time comes, build a nest identical to the one from which they came and which they never saw; ailing animals istinctively pick out the herbs that will cure their illnesses. Man, however, is born with a common vague notion in place of this precise and particularized instinct. To that general notion he applies reason and thus is able to take care of himself. He, too, discovers the herbs that cure his diseases, but as the result of a process of reasoning:

Man... has a natural knowledge of the things which are essential for his life only in a general fashion, inasmuch as he is able to attain knowledge of the particular things necessary for human life by reasoning from natural principles.[1]

But for this there is need of collaborative efforts, and a division of labor is unavoidable.[2] Again in the words of St. Thomas:

It is not possible for one man to arrive at a knowledge of all these things by his own individual reason. It is therefore necessary for man to live in a multitude so that each one may assist his fellows, and different men may be occupied in seeking, by their reason, to make different discoveries — one, for example, in medicine, one in this and another in that.[3]

This social process implies collaboration not merely of the members of one generation and of one nation, but of all men at all times. Each coming generation which thrives on what its predecessors bequeathed to it in turn leaves to posterity an intellectual culture perfected by its own contributions. As our author says:

It seems natural to human reason to advance gradually from the imperfect to the perfect. Hence, in speculative sciences, we see that the teaching

---

[1] R.P. (On Kingship) I, § 6, p. 176.
[2] Cf. AVICENNA, De anima, v, 1.
[3] R.P. loc. cit. The things which our mind discovers by this process St. Thomas calls "adinventiones" (S. II-II, Q. 55, A. 2).

of the early philosophers was imperfect, and that it was afterward perfected by those who succeeded them. So also in practical matters. Discursive rationality implies progress.[1]

That man was intended to collaborate rationally is proved by the fact that he alone is endowed with the capacity to speak. Speech is the specific communication of rational beings. Lower animals convey to each other only emotions or feelings — fear, desire, hunger, etc.; for such communication all that is needed is sound, e.g., braying or roaring. But man uses words, which are the outward manifestation of concepts, that is, products of a conceiving reason.[2]

The naturally ordained distribution of tasks is described thus: "One man works for many, and many work for one." A political community is made up of artisans, farmers, soldiers, statesmen, etc. These constituents must do their work with competence, which means that they must be appropriately endowed and properly trained. A state, therefore, can function only if nature produces some men who are physically strong, others who are intellectually keen, and still others who are fearless. St. Thomas, on the authority of Aristotle, assures us that such men will always be forthcoming. Being indispensable to the state, they will be furnished by nature, since the state is "by nature," and "nature is never found lacking in what is necessary." The diversification of capacities essential to social collaboration is the unfailing gift of nature.[3]

In St. Thomas, however, the stress is placed on the fact that this "naturality" is but the execution of a decree of providence. Nature is a secondary cause and only an instrument. In his own words,

One man does not suffice to perform all those acts demanded by society, and therefore it is necessary that different persons be occupied in different pursuits. The diversification of men for diverse tasks is the result, primarily, of divine providence, which details the various compartments of man's life in such a way that nothing necessary to human existence is ever lacking; secondarily, this diversification proceeds from natural causes which bring it about that different men are born with aptitudes and tendencies for the different functions and the various ways of living.[4]

---

[1] S. i-ii, Q. 97, A. 1, pp. 78 ff.
[2] Cf. Ibid., A. 3, and In Pol. i. 1.
[3] Seneca had said: "God gave man two things which transformed him from a dependent into a master: reason and sociability" (De benef. iv, 18). St. Thomas says: "reason through sociability."
[4] Quodl. vii, 17; cf. C.G., iii, 132 and C.I., v, 27.

Man cannot satisfy his instinct for social life with the resources offered by the home, nor by those available in an estate, nor even by those furnished by a village. These are not capable of providing the economic basis for "being," nor the educative one for "well-being." For man's nature, over and above mere subsistence, longs for knowledge and virtue. ("All men by nature desire to know"; and "the desire for virtue is inborn in man.")

Because of these shortcomings, the above-named communities must be integrated into a larger and fuller body. Such is the self-sufficient group which St. Thomas (after Aristotle) calls the "perfect community." It is the city-state (*polis*), the *civitas*, or better still the *provincia*, and best of all the kingdom.

The difference between the perfect community and the others is not, as Plato thought, one of mere quantity; it is qualitative, as St. Thomas, following Aristotle, teaches. The perfect community is the goal toward which the other natural associations strive and in which they find their fulfillment. And that is one of the reasons why the state is "natural." For the Christian this naturally instituted process of moral edification which controls and regulates the production of economic goods is in turn subordinate to a third and higher interest: man's spiritual welfare, or the enjoyment of God, for the attainment of which the bonds of political society are indeed necessary but in no way sufficient.

The promotion of the appropriate conditions of life in both the economic and the cultural sphere is, then, the purpose of the state. Herein lies the common good of man and his highest worldly end. As such it sets in motion our actions and should control our individual aspirations. Its demands justify the employment of all the varied means that are required for its attainment. Reason tells us what these subordinate tasks, these indispensable occupations are; nature furnishes the appropriate workers for them; authority must see to it that the right man is put in the right place. When this is done, we say that "order" has been introduced, which means that multiplicity has been reduced to unity, and that, consequently, action is possible within the sphere affected by the desire for the common end. "Society is obviously nothing else than the unification of men for the purpose of performing some one thing in common," says St. Thomas.[1]

---

[1] *C.I.*, III.

The divine intention is primarily directed to the order and then to the components unified in it and by it. As St. Thomas says, "If we remove order from created things, we remove the best they have. For though the individual beings are good in themselves; joined, they rise to the highest goodness because of the order of the universe."[1] Evil, on the authority of St. Augustine, is a condition that obtains when *order* is removed. An angel is superior to a stone. But a universe of angels and stones is better than one made solely of angels.[2] (Or, as one might say, a violin is better than a banjo. Yet an orchestra, with all sorts of instruments including the banjo, is preferable to an ensemble composed solely of violins.) The reason for this is "that the perfection of the universe is obtained essentially through a diversification of natures, which natures, so diversified, fill the various ranks of goodness; it is not obtained through the plurification of the individuals in any of these given natures."[3] The Angelic Doctor goes so far as to say:

A universe in which there was no evil would not be of so great goodness as our actual one; and this for the reason that there would not be in this assumed universe so many different good natures as there are in this present one, which contains both good natures free from evil as well as some conjoined with evil; and it is better to have the combination of both rather than to have one only.[4]

II. Public Power

1. The Ruler

Order, then, comes into existence when a multiplicity of individuals are brought together and so arranged that by their united efforts a common end may be attained. But the "ordering" toward an end implies the action of a commanding authority. "In every multitude there must be some governing power," according to St. Thomas:

For where there are many men together and each one is looking after his own interest, the multitude would be broken up and scattered unless there

---

[1] *C.G.*, III, 69.
[2] I *Sent.*, 44, 1, 2, 6.
[3] *Ibid.*, 44, 1, 2, 5.
[4] *Ibid.*, 44, 1, 2, 6.

were also an agency to take care of what appertains to the common weal...
Indeed it is reasonable that this should happen, for what is proper and
what is common are not identical. Things differ by what is proper to each;
they are united by what they have in common. But diversity of effects is
due to diversity of causes. Consequently, there must exist something which
impels toward the particular good of each individual. Wherefore also in
all things that are ordained toward one end, one thing is found to rule
the rest.[1]

This applies pre-eminently to the order on whose existence all
others depend, viz., the state, which Aristotle taught rests on the
necessary relationship of "ruler and ruled." St. Augustine, too, as
St. Thomas reminds us, had taught that men greedy for worldly goods
were about to exterminate one another in their bloody competitions
when by divine mercy it was permitted that "concord be established
by means of a regime of *commanding* and *obeying*."[2] Today we still
hear: "Obedience is the tie of human societies."[3]

That this subordination to authority is in accord with the intentions
of nature is shown by the fact that some men are born with a capacity
for ruling, while others are endowed with aptitudes for performing
tasks under the direction of a commanding power. "Among men an
order is found to exist, inasmuch as those who are superior by intellect
are by nature rulers."[4] And the authority of St. Augustine is again
adduced: "Ruling power is given by nature to the best."[5] This relationship of ruler and ruled is not the result of the Fall. It would have
existed in the state of innocence.[6] Of course, the common goal aimed
at by the ruler in the state of innocence would have been different
from the actual one; the element of coercion would have been absent.
"There would have been no need for protection, there being no hostility
either internal or foreign, and no need of correcting transgressions, all
men desiring the real good."[7] The ruler would not have been expected
to guarantee conditions for material subsistence (*esse*) nor for moral

---

[1] *R.P.*, I, §§ 8-9, pp. 176-7.
[2] *De civ. Dei*, XIX, 17.
[3] PREVOST-PARADOL, *La France Nouvelle*, Ch. 4.
[4] *C.G.*, III, 81.
[5] *Contra Iulianum*, IV, 61.
[6] *S.*, I, Q. 92, Aa. 1, 2; Q. 96, Aa. 3, 4.
[7] II *Sent.*, 44, 1, 3.

betterment (*bene esse*). The only use for a ruler would have been "to guide in active life and in the field of studies according as one was wiser and intellectually more enlightened than another."[1]

Because of the Fall this spontaneous adherence to Order could not be maintained. The regime of *concupiscentia,* the *lex fomitis,* made coercion necessary. The authority over spontaneously obedient men was replaced by a power of making laws and of compelling observance through penalties: loss of property, liberty, life. This dread power imposes itself not only because of necessity but also and above all because it is authorized by God. Political power is divinely instituted. St. Paul proclaims this: "All power comes from God."[2] His divine commission, which transforms what would otherwise be brute force into just power, creates the *public person*[3] with unique attributes; to it belongs the exercise of the *publica, suprema potestas.*[4] No one else may inflict major punishment on a human being. The words of St. Augustine admonish us: "He who, without being authorized by the governing power, kills a malefactor shall be adjudged to be a murderer and this all the more because he did not hesitate to usurp a power that God had not given him." This text was incorporated in the canon law.[5]

The doctrine of the divine origin of power must not be interpreted to mean that St. Thomas looked upon the state as existing in virtue of divine law. The state is an organization that rests on human law. "Dominium," he says, "was introduced by *ius gentium,* which is a human law."[6] Power comes from God, but the various political formations which are made possible by the exercise of this power are the result of natural law, for the state is natural. St. Thomas here says that it is by *ius gentium,* giving to this word the sense which it has elsewhere, viz., of a rational elaboration of the principles of natural law, valid for all humanity and not too far removed from the original proposition.[7]

What St. Thomas means when he speaks of this divine origin of power may be clarified by the following. There are, he says, three factors

[1] *Ibid.*
[2] Rom. XIII, 1.
[3] For public power and public person, cf. *S.* II-II, Q. 65, A. 1.
[4] For *plenaria potestas* of the sovereign, cf. *S.* II-II, Q. 67, A. 4.
[5] Can. *quicumque percusserit,* causa 23, qu. 8.
[6] Cf. *S.* II-II, Q. 12, A. 2. That dominion here has to do with political control and not with the rights of a master over his slave is made clear by the context of the passage (*subditis fidelibus,* etc.).
[7] Cf. *S* I-II, Q. 94, A. 5 *ad* A, pp. 52 f.

involved in power: first, the manner of acquisition; secondly, the use to which it is put; thirdly, the mode or *form*.[1] This last one is always blameless. *Formally*, we are told, all power is good and comes from God, for it consists of a certain order connecting someone who rules with someone who is subject to this rule.[2] Therefore, when we speak absolutely and unrestrictedly, we say that power, as such, is good, because a thing in its unrestricted absoluteness is judged on the basis of what is *formal* in it.[3] But if we proceed to examine what relationships may affect this absolute goodness, we discover that they proceed from one or the other of the remaining two factors: either the "manner of acquisition" or "the use to which power is put." This "manner" (the origin) may be bad (and therefore not divine) in two ways: either because of the unworthiness of the ruler or because of the illicit practices (violence, simony, etc.) resorted to in the acquisition of it.[4] The latter vitiates the competence of the ruler so completely that "his power under these circumstances should be disowned as soon as the opportunity for so doing presents itself."[5] The former does not justify disobedience, "for inasmuch as power *formally* is always from God and creates the obligation of obedience, subjects are held to obey rulers even though unworthy." As for the third factor, St. Thomas teaches that the abuse of power is twofold: first, if a command is given "contrary to that for which power was instituted, as when a ruler enjoins practices destructive of those very virtues for the upholding of which power was ordained."[6] Here disobedience is obligatory. Secondly, if a command transcends the sphere of a given authority, in which case neither obedience nor disobedience is required.

Power is given by God to the ruler in order that he may realize justice on earth. In fact, we find that in the Middle Ages people looked upon the king as the person entrusted with "the maintenance of order and peace through justice."[7]

---

[1] II *Sent.*, 44, 1, 2; 44, 2, 2.
[2] *Ibid.*
[3] That is: a man, absolutely speaking, because of his form (the rational soul) is a reasoning animal, which does not mean that he is exempt from irrationality.
[4] II *Sent.*, *loc. cit.*
[5] *Ibid.*
[6] *Ibid.*
[7] Cf. Luchaire's statement that monarchy rested on the belief "That God instituted Kingship so that rulers might render justice to men and establish peace, which is their first and most essential duty." *Histoire des Institutions Monarchiques de la France sans les premiers Capétiens.* I, 40, (Paris, 1883).

As custodian of justice, the ruler is or may be the legislator, the executor of the law, or the supreme judge.

a) The extent of the legislative power of the ruler depends naturally on the nature of the political regime. St. Thomas considers the case of "a free multitude which can legislate for itself" in contrast to one which is not free to do so. In the first instance the people (*multitudo*) as a whole may make laws or they may authorize the sovereign to do so, in which case the latter "has the power of legislating only in so far as he bears the person of the multitude."[1] This representative role of the legislative sovereign may be set forth thus: commands which are essential to the political order are not actions of the sovereign will on the *will* of the subjects; they are directed to their *reason* and therefore take the form of rational propositions. These propositions properly formulated are what we call laws and as such are necessary for the "ordering" to the common good. But the ordering of anything toward the common good belongs either to the whole people or to someone who is the vicegerent of the whole people (*gerentis vicem totius multitudinis*).[2] The ruler is "vicegerent." But when the definition is narrowed down to the more precise legislative terminology, we find that the representative aspect of the legislating prince is attenuated. Instead of being a *vicegerent*, we find that the ruler acts as *guardian* of the community. Says St. Thomas: "The making of a law belongs either to the whole people or to a public person who has care (*curam habet*) of the whole people."[3] The representative character of the legislator is further obscured in the article that follows (A. 4), where no mention is found of alternate possibilities, law being made to proceed solely from the one who is in charge of the community. And, finally, in the first article of the following Question (91) even the references to the *cura* are omitted, and law is defined as a "dictate of practical reason emanating from the ruler who governs a perfect community."

This definition is the one to which St. Thomas normally resorted, so that its formulation cannot be considered merely casual. It is essential to human law, he tells us, that "it be framed by that one who governs the community" (*a gubernante civitatis*).[4]

---

[1] *S.* I-II, Q. 97, A. 3 *ad* 3, p. 83.
[2] *Ibid.*, Q. 90, A. 3, pp. 7-8.
[3] *Ibid.*
[4] *S.* I-II, Q. 95, A. 4, pp. 62-64.

8.

b) The ruler is not only the lawmaker; he is also and above all the judge, the supreme judicial authority.

The person who delivers a judicial sentence interprets the wording of the law by applying this wording to a particular case. But both the interpretation of the law (which is the judicial act) and the making of it pertain to the same person. Therefore just as a law can be made only by a power which is public, so a judicial sentence must be rendered by public authority.[1]

The significance of the judicial function of the ruler was extended to other phases of jurisdiction:

Judicial orders are not only those which refer to litigations, but also all those that pertain to social relations (*ad ordinationem hominum ad invicem*), which matter is under the control of the ruler in his quality of supreme judge.[2]

It was as judge, then, that the ruler exercised that unique and sacred function which might necessitate the destruction of life, limb, and property and the deprivation of liberty whenever such action was deemed necessary to uphold *justice*. That which for a private person is murder, theft, or extortion becomes in certain circumstances a praiseworthy act when performed by one who, ruling a perfect community, is vested with a public power which, being "perfect," is "plenary."[3]

c) The ruler, who is under the obligation to protect the common good from the assaults of a foreign enemy, has the right and duty to resort to the necessary measures of war. The nature of his power authorizes the destruction of life and property, provided the war is just.[4] An offensive war is just when three conditions are complied with. First, it must be declared by the sovereign. Private persons may not wage war, and this for two reasons. In the first place, war is resorted to only when there is no higher authority to which the contestants may submit their conflicting claims. In the case of private persons this does not obtain, for there is over them a superior authority qualified to

---

[1] *S.* II-II, Q. 60, A. 6; cf. Q. 67, A. 1.
[2] *S.* I-II, Q. 104, A. 1.
[3] Cf. *S.* II-II, Q. 65; A. 2; Q. 66 A. 8, pp. 139-41; Q. 67, A. 4.
[4] Cf. *Ibid.*, Q. 66, A. 8.

judge their controversies. Secondly, war demands the levying of a multitude of men, and this can be done only by one who is in charge of the multitude, hence by no private individual.[1]

The second condition is a just *cause*. Those who are attacked must, because of some fault of their own, have deserved the aggression. St. Thomas here restates the argument endorsed by St. Augustine:

> A just war is usually defined as one by which a wrong is righted, viz., when a state or a nation is attacked because it neglected to punish some crimes committed by one of its members or when it failed to make restitution of something that had been unjustly seized.[2]

The third condition is the maintenance of righteous intentions on the part of those who have declared war, viz., that the purpose of war is to lay the foundations of a better and more lasting peace. For it may well be that a war has a just cause according to the above definition and that it has been declared and is being waged by the supreme political power, which was the other condition set, yet it is made iniquitous by the evil intentions entertained by the attacking power. What these evil intentions are St. Thomas tells us in the words of St. Augustine:

> They are a desire to harm the enemy more than the conduct of hostilities demands, a spirit of revenge, implacability, recourse to destructive practices that fit beasts better than men, and finally lust of supremacy.[3]

d) It is true, then, that the ruler of a state which is a *perfect community* has a perfect (complete) power of coercion, and therefore he may inflict irreparable penalties, such as death and mutilation. But neither the slave master nor the *pater familias*, for the protection of the estate or of the household, can avail himself of the prerogative of public power. The power over slaves and the power over family are determined on the basis of *ius dominativum* and *ius paternum*, respectively, both of which are subordinate to the *ius politicum* by which public power operates. A sentence of death and or confiscation issuing from these subordinate powers is, therefore, plain murder and theft.

---

[1] Cf. *S.* i-ii, Q. 40, A. 1.
[2] *Quaestio in Heptateuchon*, 10.
[3] *Contra Faust.*, xxii, 70.

A father or a master in charge of a family or of an estate, which are imperfect communities, has an imperfect coercive power. He may inflict lighter penalties which do not carry with them an irreparable harm, such as, for example, whipping.[1]

Also:

And just as one may by public power be lawfully deprived of life because of major crimes, so he is liable because of minor crimes to be deprived of limb. This, however, a private person may not do, not even with the consent of the possessor of the limb, because of the harm that thereby results to the community.[2]

e) The political order is, then, the rule of justice. The prince is expected to govern by laws, and these laws must be just; that is, they cannot be the arbitrary expression of a will, either individual or collective, but rather the rational deduction from principles of justice imparted by God to man; the nature of their content conditions their validity. In view of this, how does St. Thomas deal with the two formulas of Roman law so often invoked in his day which seem to contradict flatly the two conditions above referred to? These two formulas are: first, "Whatever the prince wants [whatever his pleasure may be] has the vigor of law;"[3] and, secondly, "The prince is not bound by laws." (He is above the law.)[4]

These maximus could not be ignored or waved aside. They had intrigued political writers of all generations. They seemed to lead to an impasse; for, on the one hand, no Christian could deny that in some form or other positive law must derive from natural law and conform to divine law; and, on the other hand, it seemed difficult to repudiate norms which, though pagan in origin, had received the full sanction of Christian jurisprudence. The force of the autocratic formulas was further strengthened by imperial affirmations such as those of Justinian: "God subordinated all laws to the imperial sway (*fortuna imperialis*) in that He himself sent to mankind the Emperor as a living law."[5] And this

---

[1] *S.* II-II, Q. 65, A. 2 *ad* 2.
[2] *Ibid.*, A. 1 and A. 2 *ad* 2.
[3] "Quod principi placuit legis habet vigorem" (*Digest*, 1, 4, 1).
[4] "Princeps legibus solutus" (*ibid.*, 1, 3, 31).
[5] *Novella*, 105, 4.

animate law, he tells us, was providentially given because of the insufficiency of inanimate legislation. Since human nature constantly varies, he said, rigid legislation would soon become antiquated unless a man divinely prepared were on hand to adapt it to the new circumstances.[1]

Refusal to accept the doctrine that the ruler is above the law was felt to encounter this dilemma: either the ruler binds himself or he is bound by others. The first is not possible because a man may, indeed, bind himself by a vow or by a pledge, but cannot constrain himself legally. A law, it was pointed out, is the creation or rather the effect of a governing power and, as Aristotle teaches, such a power is the *principle of ruling* another *qua other*. A legal injunction presupposes a jurisdiction, and no man can have jurisdiction over himself except in a metaphorical sense. Coercion, implicit in the enforcement of law, demands two distinct parties: one which does the coercing, and one which suffers it; the *agent*, it was said, must be a different person from the *patient*. The ruler cannot appear in the double role of sovereign and subject.

The second alternative was not tenable, given the nature of supreme power, which admits of no control.

In facing this problem St. Thomas tried to reconcile the political with the moral side of the question. The supreme power of the ruler is indeed beyond the control of the subjects. They have no way of compelling him to respect the law. But supreme power is not beyond the control of God, who brings the sovereign to a voluntary observance of this (the human) law.

The explanation which he gives[2] is the one that the Church has for a long time made its own. The law, he said, binds the sovereign by its *directive*, not by its *coercive* power. And by "coercive," he means a capacity of compelling obedience by punitive sanctions; and by "directive," a power which human law derives from eternal law and which makes it capable of creating obligations in the forum of conscience.

Coercion, he tells us, cannot be practiced at the level of sovereignty, because it would result in the last analysis in self-coercion, which, as it was said above, is not possible. From his wording, one gathers that he did not hold, as many did, that a ruler's exemption from law ob-

---

[1] *Digest*, Preface II.
[2] *S.*, I-II, Q. 96, A. 5 *ad* 3, p. 74.

servance was simply a *de facto* matter, viz., that the reason why a
ruler is not bound by law is merely the fact that there is no one to
carry out a sentence delivered against him. On the contrary, for him
the exemption is *de iure*; and the impossibility exists not in the execut-
ing of a sentence but in the making of it; for eventually the sovereign,
being the supreme judge of the land, would have to judge his own
case, and as all know, no man can be a judge in his own cause. Moreover, what could be the sense of a judgment that would forever remain
inert?

Another force is therefore needed to make the ruler respect his
laws (and those which he has inherited and accepted); a force that
comes into existence when a properly formulated proposition of practical reason acquires that majesty that transforms it into a law. God,
by whose authority this transformation is effected, has implanted in us
the invincible conviction that the *power* to coerce, which He gives,
implies an *obligation* on the part of the coercer to respect voluntarily
that which he compels others to observe. Hence the power which law
has to coerce subjects can never be dissociated from the power it has
to make the ruler abide by it.[1] This latter power is exercised in our
conscience by a voluntary submission to God, the author of this power,
which, as we said, is called "directive"; and there is no difficulty
here, for though a man cannot *coerce* himself, he is quite capable of
directing himself.

The nature of this directive power requires a few words of explanation. The fact that a rational proposition can be made into an
instrument whereby one or more individuals can dispose of the life,
liberty, and property of their fellow men proves, people thought, that
the power to do this — the public power that legislates — has its
origin in God. Human law can do all it does because it is an emanation
of eternal law. The condition which God imposes on society in bestow-
ing upon it the benefit of law is that all, without distinction, accept
the conditions that accompany it. The promulgation of a just law
postulates the tacit acceptance of its provisions on the part of everybody. This, it was said, is a basic principle that all men discover in
the depths of their conscience, and which lends to law its directive
power.

---

[1] *Ibid.*

For the greater protection of society, law is furnished with the other power, that of coercing, and this one, as was said, is applicable to all except the sovereign legislator.

It was stated above that this power of creating, in *everybody*, the directive obligation of law observance is communicated to positive law by eternal law. How is this done? The answer is: just as eternal law imprints itself on human law by the medium of natural law, so it is through natural law that the moral obligation which bids all men observe the human law comes before the tribunal of conscience. The question now is: which one of the precepts that natural reason dictates to man is at the basis of this universal validity?

Caietan, in his commentary to the text of St. Thomas above quoted, says that it is the command to *do to others what we would have others do to us*, and that therefore a ruler must not impose on others a law which he does not want applied to himself. Suarez thought this was not correct, and suggested the one which, coupled with its correlative, must be postulated for the existence of the political association. This inborn principle of the political animal says to the ruler: "Respect the law you make," and says to the subject: "The superior must be obeyed."[1] This is the natural law precept which St. Thomas adduces to show the validity of the directive power of law. He finds confirmation of it in divine law (Matthew 23) and point to its embodiment in canon law. He also hints at the universality of it by quoting the maxim of an old Sage.[2] Of course this holds only when the matter and the *ratio* of a law are the same in the ruler and the ruled. Prohibition to carry weapons, therefore, cannot obligate the king. But the law of just price does.

The significance of the natural law precept above stated was shown thus: A law establishes a medium of some virtue as a step toward the common good. So, e.g., the law that regulates the price of goods fixes a means within the sphere of justice. The transgression of this medium is a repudiation of justice and therefore a sin. And sinning is not more tolerable in a ruler than it is in a subject.

The solution we find in St. Thomas was kept alive by subsequent jurists and theologians; Bossuet restates it in this form: "Kings are

---

[1] *De legibus*, III, 35, 6. Of course, the *directive* power of law is entirely different from the *vis ostensiva*, such power as the *Laws* of both Plato and Cicero might have.
[2] Dionysius Cato.

then, like everybody else, subject to the equity of the laws... but they are not subject to the penalties of the laws, or, to speak the language of theology, their submission is not to their *coercive* but to their *directive* power."[1]

The following objection might be raised: supposing the sovereign had not made a given law; he would then have been free to act without any consideration of the principle which eventually came to be incorporated in that law. This argument was met thus: eternal law, through its participant, natural law, is constantly acting on human reason so as to improve steadily the quality of legislation (St. Thomas accepts the doctrine of progress in lawmaking).[2] Eternal law is then one element; the other is the will of the legislator. The sovereign is not obliged to improve his code, but once he decides to do so and he issues a new law, then by virtue of the conditions above described and which attend to the formation of all laws, he binds himself to accept the directive power of the law he has made.

St. Thomas adds that the sovereign shows that he is above the law by the fact that he can change it. But again in its changed form he is obliged by its directive power to observe it.

The other statement, viz., that the will of the sovereign has the force of law, is explained by St. Thomas with the proviso that the will has this force when it is regulated by reason; which means that in the last resort the legislator, through a process of valid ratiocination based on the principles of natural law, must connect his enactments with eternal law. One must, of course, always recall that for St. Thomas the worst of all laws is preferable to anarchy.

2. Law

St. Thomas has left us a detailed treatise on law, embodied in those Questions of the First Part of the Second Part of the *Summa* which are here reprinted.[3] The problem comes up again in the Second Part of the Second Part, the relevant Questions of which are also included in this edition.[4] A comparison of the two is very illuminating,

---

[1] *Politique tirée des propres paroles de l'Écriture Sainte*, Book IV, art. 1 prop. 21.
[2] *S.*, I-II, Q. 97, A. 1, pp. 78 ff.
[3] Pp. 3 ff.
[4] Pp. 92 ff.

particularly in view of the disagreements to be found in them. In the first, St. Thomas is interested in deriving morality and legality from eternal law. In the latter, his intention is more juridical. He strives hard to present a theory that will embody Aristotle's teachings and, at the same time, reconcile some of the well-known contrasts in the field ol law, especially natural law.

By demonstrating that a ruler must govern in accordance with laws and that the laws of a state must be derived from natural law, or at least must not go counter to them, St. Thomas proclaims that legality is conditioned by morality and that moral conduct is indeed action regulated by reason, but a reason that is aware that it must, if it will exist, proceed from principles which God has implanted in the soul of man — of every man — viz., the fundamental, inescapable principles of practical reasons which constitute what is called natural law.

Natural law is the source of the norms of moral virtues,[1] but has a distinct significance for a particular one of them, viz., justice, the social virtue par excellence, the precepts of which, properly formulated and promulgated, constitute the civil codes of the various states.

III. Forms of Government

Political differentiation in states is the outcome of different numerical relationships between ruler and ruled.[2] Of these only three are considered, viz., those relations or ratios of ruler to ruled in which the numerator is one, a few, or many.[3] The "many" may become "all." This classification is doubled by introducing a qualitative criterion: goodness — a government being good when it concerns itself with the *common* good and bad when it aims at *private* advantages.[4] The good government of a single man is called kingship, the bad one tyranny; the good government of the few, aristocracy, the bad, oligarchy; the good

---

[1] "Virtues perfect us as to the proper prosecution of the natura inclinations which pertain to natural law, and so for every natural inclination there is a properly ordered *special* virtue" (*S.*, ii-ii, Q. 108, A. 2).

[2] *In Pol.*, iii, 6.

[3] *Ibid.*, ii, 7; *In Eth.*, viii, 10.

[4] *In Pol.*, iii, 6.

government of the many is timocracy or *politia*,[1] the bad, democracy (in the special Aristotelian sense).[2]

But the quantitative distinctions named above turn out to be accidental and derived — the outcome of something more fundamental.[3] What essentially differentiates one state from another is the end or goal toward which a government strives. Of these ends there are three: wealth, virtue, liberty. The wealthy, given the nature of the economic urge, almost always concentrate in a small group; they *happen* to form usually a numerically insignificant minority. When this group succeeds in gaining power, they form a government which, because of their very aspirations, must be bad (self-seeking) and which, because of the paucity of numbers, is called oligarchy, even though the characteristic feature is economic egoism rather than numbers. The virtuous too are few; because of their very virtue, when they rise to power they concern themselves with the common good as justice demands. If this small minority dwindles down to unity, the regime that comes into existence is called *kingship*, provided that the ruler is a virtuous man. Otherwise we have a tyranny.

A majority rule, therefore, cannot be the outcome of triumphant zeal for virtue or greed for wealth, but comes into existence when power falls into the hands of those who strive primarily for freedom.[4] Liberty in a state means self-government, which exists when *all* subjects in turn may be rulers,[5] so that the basis of freedom is political equality, implying a control by the *poor*, who are by far the most numerous. If this popular regime aims at the public good (in which the interests

---

[1] St. Thomas, following Aristotle, uses this word in two principal senses. One, the generic, means "forms of government." Our word "regime," particularly in its broader sense, seems better suited than "constitution," which is often used as the English equivalent. The "*ordo* of the *civitas*" (*ibid.*, iv, 10) which is the relation between ruler and subjects, determines the form of government. So, therefore, *politia* is also defined as "*ordo* of the rulers" (*ibid.*, iv, 12) or again as "*ordinatio* of the *civitas* in relation to all ruling powers but especially to the principal one," i.e., the government (*ibid.*, iii, 5). The form of government determines the nature of the entire community: "it is the life of the state" (*ibid.*, iv, 3), so much so that "when the *politia* is changed, one cannot say that the *civitas* remains the same" (*ibid.*, iii, 2). The second meaning is that of a particular form of government: the good popular government in contrast with *democratia*, which is the bad. It was in this sense that, in the thirteenth century, the word "politicus" come to be used as the opposite of "despotic."

[2] *R.P.*, I, § II, p. 178.

[3] *In pol.*, iii, 6; iv, 2.

[4] The difficulty with the regime of freedom is that the citizens, having secured *political* equality, tend to claim *absolute* equality. Cf. *In Eth.*, v, 2.

[5] *In Pol.*, i, 10.

of the wealthy must play a part), then the form of government is *timocracy*; but if the regime of liberty becomes domination by the populace, then we have what has been called *democracy*.[1]

On the basis of these three fundamental aspirations, it is possible to establish a standard of value for each regime. As we saw above, the dignity or excellence of a citizen in an aristocracy and in a kingdom is measured by the practice of virtue, in an oligarchy by financial success, in a democracy by devotion to freedom.[2]

These types are in no way fixed and immovable. Whatever the qualities of each may be, we find gradations that tend to destroy the rigidity of the type. Tyranny, for example, can be more or less severe; and because of these variations it is possible to say both that it is and that it is not the worst of all regimes.[3]

1. The Best Regime

A most important task of the political writers of antiquity and of their disciples in the Middle Ages was to determine the best form of government (the *optima civitas*). And naturally the question immediately arose: best for whom? St. Thomas was well aware of something that is still often forgotten, viz., that a political regime must be suitable to the cultural or moral level of the people concerned. In *S.*, I-II, Q. 97, A. 1, he quotes approvingly this passage from St. Augustine:

If the people have a sense of moderation and responsibility and are most careful guardians of the common weal, it is right to enact a law allowing such a people to choose their own magistrates for the government of the commonwealth. But if, as time goes on, the same people become so corrupt as to sell their votes and entrust the government to scoundrels and criminals, then the right of appointing their public officials is rightly forfeit to such a people, and the choice devolves to a few good men.[4]

Circumstances, too, play an important role; a given regime which has been declared inferior to another from an *absolute* point of view

---

[1] *R.P.* I, § II, p. 178; *In Eth.*, viii, 10.
[2] *S.*, II-II, Q. 61, A. 2.
[3] *R.P.*, I, §§ 21 ff. and 36 ff., pp. 181 ff., 186 ff.
[4] P. 79 (*De lib. arb.*, i, 6).

becomes, under certain conditions, superior to it. So oligarchy, which is theoretically better than any kind of tyranny, becomes less desirable when the community is threatened by disruption, because, by its greater unity, the tyrannical rule, with all its vices, is better suited to stave off anarchy, which is the worst possible evil.[1]

Of this kind of relativism we find many evidences in St. Thomas, for he looks upon human conditions realistically and is convinced that the majority of men are not the material out of which the ideal state can be built. Not reason, but egoistic self-indulgence controls the actions of great numbers of citizens.[2]

In general, monarchy is the best form of government. The reason for this is stated repeatedly:

The best regime of a community is government by one person, which is made evident if we recall that the end for which a government exists is the maintenance of peace. Peace and unity of subjects is the goal of the ruler. But unity is more congruently the effect of one than of many.[3]

And again:

Now the welfare and safety of a multitude formed into a society lies in the preservation of its unity, which is called peace. If this is removed, the benefit of social life is lost and, moreover, the multitude in its disagreement becomes a burden to itself. The chief concern of the ruler of a multitude, therefore, is to procure the unity of peace... Now it is manifest that what is itself one can more efficaciously bring about unity than a group of several. ... Therefore the rule of one man is more useful than the rule of many.[4]

The state, too, must be one. But its unity is established by *order* which, because of social exigencies, demands diversities.[5] These diversities, of course, imply inequalities, as we saw above. In the monarchical rule an essential inequality is to be found in the very great

---

[1] Provided, of course, the tyrant does not completely crush his subjects (*ibid.*).

[2] "The majority of people follow the inclinations of sensuous nature rather than the order of reason" (*S.* i-ii, Q. 71, A. 2 *ad* 3).

"The people for the most part fail to use reason" (*In Pol.*, iv, 13).

"Now human law is framed for a number of human beings, the majority of whom are not perfect in virtue" (*S.*, i-ii, Q. 96, A. 2, p. 68).

[3] *C.G.*, iv, 76.

[4] *R.P.*, i, § 17, pp. 179-80.

[5] "Every perfect whole in natural things turns out to be constituted of specifically different parts. Since the state is a perfect whole, it must consists of parts which differ among themselves specifically" (*In Pol.*, ii, 1). Therefore, complete unity destroys the

superiority of the king: "A man cannot truly be said to be king if he is not in himself equal to the task of ruling, which means that he must be super-excellent in all good endowments of mind and body and of external belongings."[1] Monarchy is a "regime in which one person excels and the others are by nature[2] constituted to obey."[3] This immense superiority is primarily a moral one. "It is necessary that the king differ *naturally* from his subjects through the possession of a certain greatness of goodness."[4] A kingly power would be unjustly exercised if the monarch were not "morally perfect" and if, in the exercise of his virtue, he differed from his subjects only quantitatively.[5] The specific kingly virtue is prudence, "which is found both in the ruler and in the subjects. But in the ruler as though in the architect; in the subjects as though in the hand-laborers."[6]

It is obvious that conditions are not always favorable to this state of affairs. There are, moreover, inherent disadvantages in a monarchical regime:

For it frequently happens that men living under a king strive more sluggishly for the common good, inasmuch as they consider that what they devote to the common good, they do not confer upon themselves but upon another, under whose power they see the common good to be. But when they see that the common good is not under the power of one man, they do not attend to it as if it belonged to another, but each one attends to it as if it were his own.[7]

And this argument is strengthened by an example drawn from contemporary life:

Experience thus teaches that one city administered by rulers changing annually is sometimes able to do more than some kings having, perchance,

---

state: "Of the unity of a state progressed beyond a certain point, the state would become a household; and if the unity of the household proceeded too far, it would turn into one individual" (*ibid.*).

[1] *In Eth.*, viii, 10.

[2] It must be recalled that nature sees to it that the needed farmers, philosophers, soldiers, etc., be always at hand: "The distribution of these functional aptitudes is done primarily by divine providence, but secondarily by natural causes, in virtue of which one man is better suited for one thing than for another" (*C.I.*, ii, 31).

[3] *In Pol.*, iii, 9.

[4] *Ibid.*, i, 10.

[5] *Ibid.*

[6] *S.*, ii-ii, Q. 47, A. 12.

[7] *R.P.*, i, § 31, p. 185.

two or three cities; and small services exacted by kings weigh more heavily than great burdens imposed by the community of citizens.[1]

A monarchical regime, moreover, fails to satisfy the natural ambition of people: "If a man of high value is the sole ruler, the many people who are deprived of the distinction of power resent it, and this resentment is the cause of dissension."[2] And dissension was for St. Thomas the worst political evil.

Both the monarchical and the aristocratic regime are defective in that they fail to take advantage of the fact that, good though an elite may be, it is never as good as the whole community which comprises, as one of its parts, the same elite. This fundamental consideration which St. Thomas encountered in commenting on the *Politics* of Aristotle[3] was to guide him in his choice of the best *practical* form of government.

2. The Mixed Government

The theoretically superior regime of monarchy can be maintained in practice provided certain conditions are met and certain difficulties obviated: first, the aspiration of all people to liberty and equality, which manifests itself in the claim to participate in public life. This is so strong that refusal to satisfy it may bring about dissension, which evil must be avoided at all costs:

In the earthly states... the variety and the abundance of public functions and roles helps to preserve the unity, because through them a great number of people are enabled to take part in public activities.[4]

A way must be found, therefore, to make the people feel that they have a stake in the public good. Secondly, the advantages of the kingly rule must not be impaired by the ever-suspended threat of relapse into tyrannical abuses. To avoid this the monarchy must be made "temper-

---

[1] *Ibid.*, § 32, but cf. § 20, pp. 180-81: "This is also evident from experience. For provinces or cities which are not ruled by one person are torn with dissensions and tossed about without peace... On the other hand, provinces and cities which are ruled under one king enjoy peace, flourish in justice, and delight in prosperity."

[2] *In pol.*, iii, 8, *et passim.*

[3] *Ibid.*, iii, 14.

[4] *S.*, II-II, Q. 183, A. 2.

ate" (*temperetur potestas*).[1] The solution was found by instituting a form of government in which the king's power would be limited and the people's desire satisfied. That form of government is what is called the "mixed regime."

The idea of fusing the main governmental forms goes back to classical days. Aristotle speaks of it and mentions the plan of some who deemed that all three forms should be compounded into one, and cited the example of Sparta.[2] Polybius further developed the idea,[3] but it was Cicero who gave it its widest scope. In the first book of *De republica*, he makes Scipio observe that the three above-named regimes tend regularly to degenerate [4] and to follow a cyclical course,[5] and that therefore, to avoid relapses and *recourses*, a fourth kind of governmental rule, composed of the said three, should be devised.[6] He makes Laelius say that the compound form is best, in that it embodies the *caritas* of the king, the *consilium* of the aristocracy, and the *libertas* of the popular regime.[7] Rome, of course, exemplified this threefold *conflatum* regime by its consuls, its senate, and its *comitia* of the people.[8]

It is difficult to say where St. Thomas got the idea of the mixed regime. In substance it is very close to Cicero's. He claims, however, that it is a generalization of what was formerly put into practice by the Hebrews:

For Moses and his successors governed the people in such a way that each of them was ruler over all, so that there was a kind of kingdom. Moreover, seventy-two men were chosen, who were elders in virtue... so that there was an element of aristocracy. But it was a democratical government in so far as the rulers were chosen from all the people.[9]

---

[1] *R.P.*, i, Ch. vi, pp. 188 ff. The word "moderatum" is also used. Cf. *R.P.*, ii, Ch. viii, and Cicero, *De repub.*, i, 29 (45): "moderatum et permixtum." The two attributes, "moderate" and "temperate", had already been joined by classical authors.

[2] *Pol.*, ii, 6.

[3] *Hist.*, vi, 1, 3, 3, 8, 9.

[4] "iter ad finitimum quoddam malum praeceps ac lubricum" (*De repub.*, i, 29).

[5] "orbes et quasi circuitus in rebus publicis commutationum et vicissitudinum" (*ibid.*).

[6] "moderatum et permixtum tribus" (*ibid.*).

[7] *Ibid.*, i, 35 (55). How this regime was to be organized we are told in *S.*, i-ii, Q. 105, A. 1, pp. 86 ff.

[8] *Ibid.*, i, 32 (56). Venice, too, claimed that its government was a fusion of the three basic forms, with the regal power in the Doge, the aristocratic in the Senate, and the democratic in the greater Council.

[9] *S.*, i-ii, Q. 105, A. 1, p. 88.

3. Tyranny

In treating of tyranny and of the justification of tyrannicide, a question often discussed in antiquity and brought to the fore again by John of Salisbury, St. Thomas moves very cautiously and, as usual, is more concerned with the stability of the state than with the upholding of individual *political* rights.

In the *Commentary to the Sentences* he seems to countenance tyrannicide by what might be looked upon as a partial approval of a statement of Cicero. He says:

Cicero here considers the case in which power was seized by an act of violence either against the will of the subjects or with a consent which was wrested by coercion, and in conditions such that no recourse could be had to a higher authority capable of passing judgment on the usurper. In these circumstances he who kills the tyrant in order to free his country is praised and rewarded.[1]

But such extreme measures proved to be not to his liking. He could not of course accept the doctrine that rulers are always right, that the king can do no wrong. So when he came to face the problem raised by St. Paul in his *Epistle to the Romans*: "Princes are not a terror to good works but to the evil,"[2] he hesitates between two interpretations: one, aiming at a doctrine that did not acquiesce in extreme resignation, is, from the point of view of the exegesis, somewhat daring. "Princes," he says, "*are not instituted* to be a terror, etc."; and later, "to be a terror to the good is not part of a Prince's function."[3] Realizing perhaps that this interpretation, though very acceptable from one point of view, was doing violence to the text and was departing from the old tradition, he fell back on the accepted explanation. Bad rulers, for such no doubt exist, cannot terrorize the good, for,

although they at times unjustly persecute the well-doers, yet the latter have no cause to fear, because the harm they suffer, if they will but patiently bear it, will turn out to their advantage, in accordance with the First

---

[1] II *Sent.*, 2, 2, 2, 5.
[2] Rom., xiii, 3.
[3] *In Ep. ad Rom.*, xiii, 1.

Epistle of St. Peter: "But if also you suffer anything for justice's sake, blessed are ye."[1] Thus it may be seen why those who resist power bring upon themselves condemnation, whether it is that which is inflicted by rulers upon rebels or that by which God punishes men.[2]

Bad kings, he concludes, come into the world with God's consent, to punish the wicked and test the good.

When, however, St. Thomas came to discuss the situation from a more political point of view, he suggested measures which are in line with his constant practice of stressing above all the conservation of the state and of discouraging any acts that might result in a revolution. He feared that removal of a tyrant might bring about fatal dissensions among the people and possibly give rise to some worse kind of tyrannical rule. His practical suggestions as to how to deal with the matter are the following:

If tyranny is not too oppressive, the subjects should put up with it for the reasons above stated. For extreme cases some, he tells us, have suggested tyrannicide, that is, execution by private persons. The individual act of one who exposes himself to rid the state of a tyrant has often been admired and was approved by the Old Testament. However, says the Angelic Doctor, the New Testament does not countenance this practice — witness St. Peter, who says: "Be subjects to your masters, not only to the good and gentle but also to the forward."[3] And he goes on to say that the attitude of the martyrs, who died but did not rebel, confirmed this doctrine. Sound political prudence likewise condemns tyrannicide, for it would be a great hazard for the people and for the government if individuals, by private presumption, were to attempt to take the life of rulers, tyrannical though they may be; and he warns us that frequently those who are quick to have recourse to violence are inferior elements of society.[4]

Not individual violence, then, but lawful opposition should be resorted to against tyranny: "We must proceed not by private presumption, but by public authority." And defense against tyranny may take several forms. If the ruler has been elected by the people, he may justly be checked or even deposed for abuse of power. Nor do the

---

[1] I Pet., iii, 14.
[2] *In Ep. ad Rom.*, xiii, 1.
[3] I Pet., ii, 18.
[4] *R.P.*, i, § 47, p. 190.

people break their contract if they depose a sovereign whom they had elected for life, inasmuch as they are not held to abide by the terms of an agreement which the ruler himself has already voided by his actions.[1]

But if the tyrant wields power by delegation from a higher authority, it is the duty of this superior power to remove him. Finally, if no remedy can be found in human procedures, we must turn to God, the Universal Ruler. He may, if he wishes, change the heart of the tyrant; and those whom he deems unworthy of conversion he removes or degrades. We should have recourse to prayer; but before we request divine intervention against a tyrannical ruler, we must be sure that we deserve to be helped. For frequently God permits tyrants to rule, so that they may chastise the subjects for their sinful conduct.

IV. Plenitudo Potestatis

We can gather from what has already been said that no state can possess absolute power, and we can infer that there is no room in St. Thomas' theory of government for a lay world-emperor. The Angelic Doctor says explicitly that the ultimate goal of an assembled multitude is not to live in accordance with virtue, but, by means of a virtuous life, to attain divine fruition. If indeed this end could be reached by the virtue of human nature, it would of necessity be in the power of the lay ruler to direct men to this goal. However, since man rises to the possession of God not by human but by divine power, the guidance to that goal must be the task not of a human but of a divine government.[2]

In St. Thomas' own words:

In order that spiritual matters might be kept separate from temporal ones, the ministry of this kingdom was entrusted not to earthly kings, but to priests and especially to the highest of them, the successor of St. Peter, vicar of Christ, the Roman Pontiff, to whom all kings must be subject just as they are subject to Our Lord Jesus. For, those to whom the care of an intermediate end pertains should be subject to him to whom the care of the ultimate end belongs and be directed by his rule.[3]

---

[1] *Ibid.*
[2] *R.P.*, II, §§ 107-108.
[3] *Ibid.*; § 110.

More uncompromising still, even if stated in feudal parlance, is the pronouncement of *Quaestiones Quodlibetales*, xii, 19:

> In old Roman days, monarchs opposed Christ. But now kings comprehend, and because of what they have learned, they serve Our Lord Jesus Christ in fear; and, therefore, today kings are vassals of the Church.

Nor is the Pope's power that of a supreme potentate removed from the actual administration of things and therefore in need of a vicar or an associate to assume his political functions and to act as a universal emperor over all earthly kings and rulers. There can be no lay King of Kings; it is the Pope who is the sovereign of all rulers: "In the Pope the secular power is joined to the spiritual. He holds the apex of both powers, spiritual and secular, by the will of Him who is Priest and King unto eternity, King of Kings and Dominus Dominantium."[1]

An indirect power (*ratione peccati*) over the wordly rulers is exercised by the other princes of the Church:

> Secular power is subject to the spiritual power as the body is subject to the soul, and therefore it is not a usurpation of authority if the spiritual prelate interferes in temporal things concerning those matters in which the secular power is subject to him, or concerning those matters the care of which has been entrusted to him by the secular power.[2]

But the authority of the Pope is quite other. For though there is a sphere of authority reserved for political power, the Pope is not excluded from it:

> In matters pertaining to salvation of the soul we should obey spiritual rather than temporal authority, but in those which pertain to the political good we should obey the temporal rather than the spiritual, for, as Matthew says, "Give unto Caesar, etc.," unless when it happens that *the spiritual and the civil power are joined in one person as in the case of the Pope*, who holds the summit of power both spiritual and secular, because of the will of Him who is both King and Priest, Priest unto Eternity according to the order of Melchisedech.[3]

---

[1] II *Sent.*, 44 expositio textus.

[2] S., II-II, Q. 60, A. 6. This analogical argumentation is constantly resorted to: "In the Church the Pope holds the place of the head and the major prelates hold the place of the principal limbs" (*In Ep. ad Rom.*, xii, 2).

[3] II *Sent.*, 44 explicatio textus. Some apply this solely to the Pontifical State. But such an interpretation does not seem to be tenable.

The uniqueness of the Pope's authority is explained in the passage that follows:

Sometimes the inferior power emanates in its totality from the superior, in which case the entire potence of the former is founded upon the potence of the latter, so that obedience is due to the higher at all times and without exceptions. Such is the superiority of the Emperor's power over that of the Proconsul [quoted from St. Augustine]; such that of the Pope over all spiritual powers in the Church, since the ecclesiastical hierarchies are or-dained and disposed by him, and his power is in some manner the foundation of the Church as it appears from Matthew 16. Hence we are required in all these things to obey him rather than the bishop or archbishop and to him the monk owes obedience in preference to his abbot. But two powers may be such that both arise from a third and supreme authority, and their relative rank then depends upon the will of this uppermost power. When this is the case, either one of the two subordinate authorities controls the other only in those matters in which its superiority has been recognized by the uppermost power. Of such nature is the authority exercised by *rulers*, by bishops, archbishops, etc., over their subjects, for all of them have received it from the Pope and with it the conditions and limitations of its use.[1]

St. Thomas could tolerate no other adjustment: "Mankind," he says, "is considered like one body, which is called the mystic body, whose head is Christ *both as to soul and as to body*."[2] Christ has one vicar, the Pope,[3] and the Pope is the "head of the republic of Christ."[4] The *ecclesia* includes the *res publica*.

The law by which the Pope governs is the divine law, which, as we saw above, includes all that natural law teaches and something else besides. Divine law includes natural law but does not abolish it. In other words, if the state remains within the limits set to it by natural law, no interference is justified. No one is allowed to appeal to divine law against the just obligations imposed by the state. According to St. Thomas, the faith of Christ is the principle and cause of justice. Hence the order of justice is not destroyed but rather enhanced by this faith. But the order of justice demands that inferiors obey superiors,

---

[1] *Ibid.*
[2] *S.*, III, Q. 8, A. 1.
[3] *C.G.*, iv, 76.
[4] *Contra errores Graecorum*, ii, 32.

for otherwise human society could not exist. Hence men may not invoke their faith in Christ as an excuse for disobeying secular rulers.[1]

St. Thomas recognizes the autonomy of the state, and this recognition is utilized in settling important questions such as that of the right of infidel rulers to demand obedience of their Christian subjects: "Infidelity in itself does not destroy the justness of power, because power was instituted by *ius gentium*, a human law, and the distinction between believers and infidels exists by virtue of divine law, which does not destroy human law."[2] An infidel, like any other ruler, may, of course, lose his power because of sins he commits; and it may well be that such sins, in that case, have some connection with his religion. "It does not pertain to the Church," he adds, "to punish the infidelity of those who never took up the faith, according to St. Paul's I Corinthians (v. 12)."[3] However, the situation of heretics is different: The Church "can sententially punish the infidelity of those who had previously accepted the faith[4]... and, therefore, as soon as a sentence of excommunication has been delivered against a ruler on account of apostasy from the faith, *ipso facto* his subjects are released from his control and from their oath of fidelity."[5]

Existing infidel rulers are therefore authorized to continue in existence, but no new infidel formations are to be permitted:

The Church cannot allow that infidels proceed to gain control over believers or that they be in any way placed in a commanding position over them. But we can speak differently about powers or authorities already existing. For, as we have seen, power and authority have been instituted by human law, whereas the distinction between infidels and believers exists in virtue of divine law. But divine law, which comes from Grace, does not destroy human law, which comes from nature.[6]

This apparently was a strong statement, for St. Thomas immediately introduced a clause that justified exceptional procedures on the part of the Church, on the basis of its possessing the "authority of God." It is important, however, to notice that here, as everywhere else, the

---

[1] *S.*, II-II, Q. 104, A. 6, pp. 171-2.
[2] *Ibid.*, Q. 12, A. 2.
[3] *Ibid.*
[4] Here follows the reason why heresy and not infidelity is punishable.
[5] *S.*, II-II, Q. 12, A. 2.
[6] *Ibid.*, Q. 10, A. 10.

point that St. Thomas stresses is the stability of the political order. For its sake the Church refrains from going the whole length in imposing this God-given authority. It is because of this fear of political disturbances that St. Thomas decides against the manumission of Christian slaves owned by Jews.

Over the natural state so organized the Pope ordinarily exercises no immediate jurisdiction. He does not wield the two swords. One of them, that of earthly justice, he hands over to the secular ruler, who is to unsheathe it, however, at his beck (*ad nutum*).[1] It is interesting nevertheless, to see that in one sphere the Pope exercises direct political authority: The *civil* authorities, St. Thomas says, have, according to Aristotle, the power to regulate the instruction of the citizens, to decide to what pursuits individual men should dedicate themselves, and how far these should be carried. "And so it is clear that the ordaining of a university pertains to him who is at the head of the state, and especially to the authority of the Apostolic See by which the Universal Church is ruled, the intellectual interests of which are taken care of in the higher institution of learning."[2]

---

[1] IV *Sent.*, 37 expositio textus; cf. *S.*, II-II, Q. 64, A. 4. *ad* 3. Cf. St. BERNARD, *De consideratione*, iv, 3, 7, and Epist. 256.

[2] *C.I.*, i, 8.

VIII

NOTES ON THE TEXT OF THE *DEFENSOR PACIS*
OF MARSILIUS OF PADUA

The recent edition of the *Defensor* by Mr Previté-Orton with its most valuable critical apparatus has marked a considerable advance in the study of Marsilius. There are, however, in this edition, and in those which have preceded it, a great number of passages — some of them of considerable importance — which, though never questioned or queried by the editors, seem to stand in need of correction either by textual emendation or footnotes. I have examined here below a certain number of these passages which, whatever their critical support, do not seem to meet the demands of reason or the requirements of that modicum of consistency and scholarship which we must, in justice, posit for our author. I have, however, left out of the present consideration a few readings which seemed, in my judgment, to demand considerable change, and have limited my attention to such sentences and phrases as are obviously erroneous and emendable with little or no departure from the critical apparatus. For the sake of convenience, I regularly refer to the edition of Mr Previté-Orton (Cambridge: University Press, 1928), although the passages I object to are usually not differently edited there from what they are in Goldast, etc.

1. One source of difficulty seems to have been the copyists' and editors' consistent practice of compounding words that should remain separate. I will give a few examples, leaving the complete enumeration to some future time. I mean, for instance, sentences like the following, in Dictio II, chapter 5, paragraph 2 (p. 145 of Previté-Orton's text) — 'Voluit ergo Apostolus eos iudicare coactivo iudicio

qui non sunt ordinati *administrandum'*... Here obviously syntax
demands *ad* as a preposition governing *ministrandum*. Again in the
sentence (p. 95) 'Unde nec sunt unum per aliquid formaliter in-
haerens unum, nec *pertangens* unum aut ea continens velut murus,'
the participle *tangens* must, for grammatical exigencies, be separated
from *per*, which is not a prefix, but a preposition needed to govern
both *tangens* and *continens*. So on p. 54, instead of 'de quibusdam
instantiis *addicta* in capitulo praecedenti,' we should read *ad dicta*.
And on p. 37 in the sentence: 'quod erit inquirere *legislatorem* seu
causam agentem ipsius,' by writing *legislatorem* as one word, the
passage is given an erroneous meaning, in that *ipsius*, as it now
stands, can only refer to *legislatorem*, whereas the sense demands that
it refer to *legis*, whose *causa agens* is here discussed and is found
to be this very *lator*, that is: the *populus*. More important is the
following sentence (I, 5, 11) 'quod *expositione* talium legum sive sectarum sapientes illi finaliter intendebant.' Here, recalling the regular,
technical, and common meaning of *ponere leges*, considering the fact
that Marsilius is not referring to *expounders* but to *law-givers*, and
remembering also his use of *ex* (pp. 15, 28, 64, 115, etc.) we should
read *ex positione*, interpreting the word in the same sense in which
it was used at the beginning of the paragraph (p. 19): — 'at extra
causas *positionis* legum,' where we are told that these *sapientes* were:
'talium legum sive sectarum *adinventores*' (not *expositores*).

2. A certain number of passages at they appear in the present editions could be maintained only on condition that we impute to Marsilius an ignorance of elementary logic, grammar, etc., which is belied
by the rest of his work. I shall discuss a few such passages which
can be rectified by drawing from the resources of the critical apparatus.

We read for instance on p. 255 (II, 14, 18) the following:... 'com-
mittitur "figura dictionis" quoniam suscipere rei dominium aut rem
cum dominio, non est suscipere *quod*, sed quo modo... Differt tamen hic
ab illo, quoniam in praesenti mutatur quid *in aliquid*, in eo vero quem
format Aristoteles e converso,' which as it stands is meaningless. Marsilius is here striving to weaken the opponent's legal argument by
imputing to him the use of the paralogism παρὰ τὸ σχῆμα τῆς λέξεώς
(Arist., *Soph. El.*, 22); that is: A gives merely one coin, but he had ten
in his possession (and not merely one). Therefore he gives what he has
not. The sophism can be solved by noticing that *merely etc.*, indicates
not a substance (τόδε) but an accident of relativity (πρός τι), as Aris-

totle himself states in the passage quoted. The scholastics regularly translate τόδε into *quid* and πρός τι into '*ad* aliquid.' The paralogism therefore comes from a change of 'quid' *into* 'ad aliquid,' or as Albertus says in his commentary to this passage of the Elenchi (ii, 2, 6), 'quando mutatur *quid* in *ad aliquid*.' This is the only way of expressing the thought, and the only one that was ever used by the scholastics. It seems reasonable therefore to read *quid* instead of *quod* (following MSS *H* and *I*); and instead of *in aliquid* read '*in ad* aliquid,' following MSS *Q* corr. and *T* corr. (where *ad*, being correctly so deciphered, should not be expanded into *aliud* as Mr Previté-Orton suggests). Marsilius by this very technical resort would conclude that his opponent is guilty of the illogism of transmuting or converting an *ad aliquid* (or a *quo modo*) into a *quid*.

The following sentence (ii, 15, 6, p. 268) also seems to me to be incorrect: 'propter quod talis *Antiochiae* sibi soli nomen "episcopi" retinuit, ceteris sibi postmodum simplex nomen retinentibus "sacerdotis" '. Marsilius is here describing the change of meaning in the word *episcopus* from simple *priest*, overseer of the congregation, to *bishop*, overseer of other priests, a change which he says took place 'post apostolicorum tempora' (par. 6, *ad init.*). It is difficult to see what Antioch has to do here. Someone, I suppose, might think of the *Praefatio Concilii Nicaeni*: 'illic primum nomen christianorum novellae gentis exortum est'. But it does not seem to have much to do with it. The construction and the sense therefore demand that in place of *Antioch* we read a phrase meaning *antonomastically*. In fact, Marsilius is made elsewhere (ii, 28, 15) to state his idea in this proper form, as follows: 'Quod vero unicus in unico templo vel diocesi posteriori tempore instituatur episcopus *antonomasice* in iconomia templi praeferendo illum, provenit ex humana institutione.' We should therefore read here too *antonomasice* or better *antonomastice* following the manuscripts which Mr Previté-Orton names: *Q, T, H, I*.

Another similar correction seems to be demanded for the title of Chap. 9 of Dictio I, where the printed editions read: 'De modis instituendi regalem monarchiam et *perfectionis* assignatione etc,' where in place of *perfectionis* we should read *perfectioris*. This chapter treats of the different ways of instituting a royal monarchy and of the determination of the *better* one of these ways, which turns out to be the one by popular election. The text itself of the chapter makes this obvious. Besides, at the beginning of the following chapter (p. 36) we read the following resumptive statement: 'Quoniam autem electionem diximus *perfectiorem* atque *praestantiorem modorum* instituendi principatum;' and on p. 31, we have the following: 'monstrabimus ipsorum [i.e., modorum] *certiorem* atque *simpliciorem.*' Nor is there any mention in the chapter, nor could there be any, of a *de perfectionis assignatione.* The mistake originated and was perpetuated in the failure to see the syntax of *perfectioris,* viz., that it modified *modi* (understood from the preceding *modis*) and the passage was corrected without paying any attention to the pertinence of the title. It seems therefore that we should follow the reading of *Q* etc., and incorporate *perfectioris* in the text, in place of *perfectionis.* The point is essential for the development of the fundamental argument.

On that same page (29), and at the beginning of the same chapter (9), we read the following sentence: 'Ex ipsorum namque natura meliori vel deteriori, provenientibus hinc civili regimini tamquam actionibus, arguere oportet causam agentem a qua tam ipsi quam pars principans per ipsos ad politiam utilius habeant provenire.' The text seems to be here badly corrupt, nor has it been possible for me to determine from the critical notes of Mr. Previté-Orton what the different readings of the generally disagreeing MSS are. I will not venture, therefore, to make any definite suggestions. The meaning, however, is clear enough and can pragmatically be established from the context. Marsilius here wants to prove that the only body that has the authority directly to establish (or institute) the ruler (*pars principans*), and through him, indirectly, the other parts of the state, is the *universitas civium,* the community or its quantitative-qualitative majority. In his ultra-scholastic method of inquiry he proves this by demonstrating that the *universitas civium* is the only possible *causa agens* which can give full efficacy (*complementum bonitatis*) to the best system (*modus*) that can be devised to install this *pars principans* or *principatus.* He reduces these *modi* to two: elective and non elective; he shows that the elective one is preferable; and finds that the *nature* of election is such that it can only find its fullest force in *popular* suffrage.

This conclusion is eventually reached in chapter 15, where Marsilius, having shown that the community must be the *causa agens* of laws, concludes that it also has to be the *causa agens* of this better *modus* of establishing the ruler, — the 'causa factiva potioris institutionis principatus.' In the chapter under discussion, however, he limits himself to proving that this better *modus* is election: 'ipsorum simpliciter (= absolutely) praestantior est electio' (page 36), and to indicating the method he is going to follow; which, *in particular*, he describes as follows (p. 31): 'Modos institutionum principatus per humanam voluntatem immediate factos [there should be no punctuation here] narrare volumus primum, deinde vero monstrabimus ipsorum certiorem atque simpliciorem. Postmodum vero ex illius modi natura meliori arguemus causam moventem a qua provenire solummodo debet et potest.' And on p. 36 (1st par.) 'Quoniam autem electionem diximus perfectiorem atque praestantiorem modorum instituendi principatum, bene se habet inquirere illius effectivam causam, a qua scilicet secundum complementum suae bonitatis habeat provenire.'

But this method is explained in more *general* terms at the beginning of the chapter in the very sentence under discussion, where the same idea is expressed in terms of proportional generalization as follows: from the better or worse nature of these *modi* considered as *actions* we have to infer the *causa agens* from which these *modi* themselves and the *principatus* set up through them can more suitably be applied to the state.

In my ignorance of the exact readings of the various *codd.*, I cannot make any definite suggestions. A few things, however, seem to be clear, viz., that *ipsorum* refers to *modis*, as does *ipsi* and *ipsos*. The argument is developed by emphasizing the connection between *causa agens* and *actio*. Therefore, recalling that Marsilius uses *modus* and *actio* interchangeably (p. 30: *modis seu actionibus* and *modus seu actio*) we should follow the MSS which read *actionum* (instead of *actionibus*) in apposition to *ipsorum*. That the text can not stand in its present form is shown also by the translation which Mr. Previté-Orton gives of the passage: 'For from their better (or their worse) nature (considering them as activities proceeding from this nature in civil government) we must deduce a *causa agens*.' For in addition to the difficulty of imagining who is meant in 'their' and 'them' (they cannot possibly refer to the same thing, which would then proceed from its own nature), this rather obscure sentence seems to have nothing to do with the argument, which is clearly enough indicated in the text, and which I have briefly outlined above. What in reality do 'proceed' here, to use the language of Marsilius, are the effects of a cause: viz., the election and the consequent establishment of the ruler for the benefit of the state.

And again, before leaving this same page (29) it might properly be asked if ·Marsilius could have written the sentence at the close of the third paragraph of the chapter: 'Democratia vero... regit sola praeter reliquorum civium voluntatem sive consensum, nec simpliciter ad commune conferens secundum proportionem convenientem.' Everyone knows that secundum quid is regularly and invariably used in opposition to simpliciter ('absolutely'... 'relatively'). Marsilius himself employs these words in this sense (See pp. 260, 49, 82). As it stands, the sentence obliterates rather harshly that familiar distinction. Would it not be preferable to insert, with H corr., the word: nec before secundum, to re-establish the needed contrast?

3. There are some instances, however, in which outright emendation seems indispensable. So in the title of chapter 4 (p. 11) where we read: 'De causa finali civitatis, et quaesitorum scibilium, et suarum partium distinctione in generali.' There is not a word in the whole chapter about any scibile, or anything connected with it that might even remotely justify its appearance in the title. For, examining carefully the content of the second part of the chapter, to which this part of the title refers, we will see that Marsilius inquires into things which are indispensable to vivere and bene vivere, the inalienable aspirations of all human beings. These things he calls and proves to be necessaria; and being directed to the satisfaction of a natural desire, being the means for nature's ends, they cannot possibly fail to be forthcoming; for the reason that 'natura non deficit in necessariis.' The organization of the functions connected with these necessaria is nothing less than the state — the civitas, whose 'naturality' Marsilius, in apparent agreement with Aristotle and with Cicero, thus tries to establish. These necessaria then are the various demands which alone have given rise to political (civil) association (congregatio), and which nature will unfailingly satisfy by endowing men with the requisite diversity of inborn aptitudes. These peremptory political demands are nothing else than civilia quaesita. These are the words of Marsilius himself: (last paragraph): 'Fuerunt igitur homines propter sufficienter vivere congregati, potentes sibi quaerere necessaria numerata pridem, illa sibi communicantes invicem. Haec autem congregatio, sic perfecta et terminum habens per se sufficientiae, vocata est civitas, cuius siquidem finalis causa et suarum partium

pluralitatis iam dicta est.' In other words, these *necessaria quaesita* for the *congregatio*, (for the *civitas*) are the *civilia quaesita*, the necessary demands whose natural satisfaction is furnished by the manifold functions of the state. The title, therefore, in place of the meaningless *scibilium* should read *civilium*.

So again, on p. 43, the quotation from Aristotle as it stands makes no sense and contradicts Marsilius' own explanation: 'Si Timotheus non fuisset, multam melodiam non haberemus: si autem Phrynes, Timotheus non fuisset.' A *non* is needed before Phrynes; and that the absence of it is not due to a slip of Marsilius is shown by what he says immediately afterwards: '*nisi* habuisset prius inventa per Phrynem.'

Likewise, the closing sentence on p. 74 contains an impossible illogism: 'De causa quidem igitur effectiva electionis partis principantis, similiter autem et reliquarum partium *et* civitatis institutione ac ipsarum invicem ordine, determinatum sit hoc modo.' The word *et* there perverts the sense. The author has discoursed concerning the *efficient cause* of the election of the ruling part and concerning the executive appointment of the remaining parts of the state. He surely cannot claim to have treated of a *whole added to the sum of its parts*, nor of having discussed 'de omnibus rebus et quibusdam aliis;' and most assuredly he cannot say that in this chapter he has reached a conclusion concerning 'civitatis institutione' when he never said a word about it. He can only say, in summing up the contents of the chapter, what these contents are and what they had been already declared to be, viz. (p. 28) 'ex *ipsius* [i.e. partis principantis] efficientiae manifestatione priori convenienter ingrediemur ad manifestationem *institutionis* et distinctionis activae *reliquarum partium civitatis*.' The word *et* should therefore be expunged from the text.

Again on p. 321-2, the clause 'quamvis eo tempore non tanta vocaret necessitas non-sacerdotum praesentiam quanta moderno propter instantium sacerdotum et episcoporum turbam *maiorem* Divinae Legis, *quantum* oporteret, ignaram,' seems to lack sense and grammar, the meaning demanding that we read '*magis* divinae legis *quam* oporteret ignaram.' So on p. 19, line 6, *ipsum* seems intolerably harsh, standing as it does for *partem* and it seems as though we should read *ipsam*.

The question might be raised why in the clause (p. 349) 'et eius iudicio *quaeque* ad cultum Dei, vel fidei stabilitatem procurandam fuerint, disponantur,' (and in other similar instances) the MSS *queque* should be expanded into *quaeque*. It would seem that *quaequae* were required if we wish to interpret the grammatical feeling of the mediaeval writers, who were fully aware of the fact that both parts of quisquis are inflected (and here it is clearly quisquis and not quisque). The editions (Hinschius, etc.) all read as Mr. Previté-Orton does.

On p. 404-5 in the sentence 'nolentes autem imperio Romano *subiecti* iam dicto episcopo... saepe dictus episcopus persequetur,' it is clear that instead of *subiecti* (as object of *persequetur*) we should read *subiectos*; and on page 457-458 in the phrase '*nec* aliunde per Evangelium posset dictum Apostoli confirmari,' if we are to avoid a contradiction we must either read *infirmari* in place of *confirmari* or else *et* instead of *nec*.

The sentence on p. 326 (II, 20, 14): 'Quod quidem asserit se licite posse, hoc etiam et quasi consimile inconveniens de facto persaepe faciens propter potentum favorem sibi quaerendum qui (super ecclesiasticorum officiorum institutionem et beneficiorum distributionem) Romanus episcopus habere se dicit, velut Christi vicarium, plenitudinem potestatis,' presents several difficulties. In the first place, the parenthesis should be removed, for grammatical considerations demand that *plenitudinem potestatis* should not be cut off from *super ecclesiasticorum* which syntactically depends on it: 'full jurisdiction over the distribution of ecclesiastic benefices.' Second, the grammatical justification of 'Romanus episcopus' is hard to see. As the phrase now stands, we have a very harsh solecism which might be eliminated by assuming that *Romanus episcopus* is an explanatory gloss to *qui*, or else, perhaps, that it is parenthetically inserted. Third, we need some punctuation after *licite posse* indicating a fuller stop.

4. There are, on the other hand, passages whose assumed faults are ascribed by the editor to Marsilius' bad grammar and awkwardness which are in need of no correction. A particular group of these passages will be treated below in connection with the errors in punctuation. Here I will call attention to the following sentence (p. 490): 'Propter quod, ubicumque legatur et a quocumque dicatur translatum fuisse Imperium, aut alter quicumque principatus vel princeps aliquis (qui per electionem assumitur) institutus per papam, etc.,' in which the editor objects to *institutus* ('Marsilius, — he says — has here slipped into the nominative case, forgetting the construction

of his sentence'). But the sentence is correct both in accordance with mediaeval as well as with classical usage, *legatur* and *dicatur* being used personally and therefore with subject and predicate in the nominative. It is a common construction with Marsilius who, a few lines below, says 'ideoque si *translatio* Imperii Romani vel imperatoris alicuius *institutio* dicatur aut scribatur rite *facta* fuisse per papam etc.'

5. But by all odds the greatest difficulty with the text of Marsilius in all its editions is the erroneous punctuation as both an index and cause of numerous misinterpretations. There are dozens and dozens of passages in which the subject is cut off from the verb by a period (occasionally by a new paragraph); where prepositions are separated by a colon from their noun; adjectives thrust in a different sentence from the one containing the noun they modify; parentheses placed where they do not belong and omitted where they are needed, etc.

I will point out only a few of these cases, to show the seriousness of the defects. On p. 101 (1, 19, 3), 1. 17, we find a concessive clause: 'et si... varietur.' But the conclusion on which it grammatically and logically depends: 'est tamen... causa,' is not only separated from it by a period, but is transferred to a new paragraph.

Another equally unintelligible passage seems to be the following: (1, 15, 7; p. 71) 'Quoniam sicut caliditas innata ipsius cordis tamquam subiecti, per quam cor seu forma eius omnes actiones complet, dirigitur, et mensuratur in agendo per cordis formam seu virtutem, nec aliter ageret ad debitum finem. Adhuc etiam sicut calor, quem "spiritum" dicunt, tamquam instrumentum ad complendas actiones, per totum corpus ab eadem virtute regitur, nec aliter horum calorum alteruter ageret ad debitum finem, quoniam "deterius" agit "ignis quam organa," ut in II *Peri Geneseos* et *De Anima*. Sic quoque auctoritas principandi alicui hominum data caliditati cordis tamquam subiecti proportionata. Sic etiam ipsius armata seu coactiva potestas instrumentalis, calori quem "spiritum" diximus proportionalis, *debet* regulari per legem... etc.'

There are many difficulties here. In the first place, there should be no period after *finem*, for the second one of the two dependent causal clauses begins here and is connected with the first one by the correlatives *adhuc etiam sicut*, continuing the *sicut* above. There should be no period after *De Anima* for there the main sentence, on which the two causal clauses depend, begins. There should be no period after *proportionata*, for we have here two connected phrases introduced by 'sic... sic' to match the 'sicut... sicut' above, with the difference that here they both have the same verb in common, so that the period separates the subject *auctoritas* from its verb *debet*. Which verb, having a plural subject, *autoritas principandi* and *armata potestas*, should be plural, so that we had better read, *debent* instead of *debet* following MSS Q, T, H.

Another important passage demands correction p. 207 (Dictio II, chap. 11, pag. 2): 'Quia enim humilitatem et huius saeculi contemptum Christus docere venerat, tamquam viam meriti salutis aeternae, ut prius humilitatem et mundi seu rerum temporalium contemptum *tam* exemplo quam verbo doceret. In summa quidem humilitate ac temporalium contemptu hunc mundum ingressus est, sciens ipse, quod non minus, imo magis opere seu exemplo docentur homines quam sermone.' Two corrections are needed here. In the first place, the *tam* before *exemplo* falsifies the sense, and we should (with T, H, I) omit it. For the meaning here is: 'that he might teach humility and contempt of worldly things by deed *sooner than* by words,' so that *quam* is not a correlative to the erroneous *tam*, but a comparative after *prius*. That Marsilius means this is shown by what he states three lines below: '*magis* opere, seu exemplo... *quam* sermone,' the argument stressing the superiority of deeds over words and not their equivalence. The second error is the period after *doceret* (l. 19) which cuts off the subordinate clause 'Quia venerat' (l. 16) from the main verb 'ingressus est.' The sense here is: Deeds being more important than words, Christ chose to enter this world in poverty and misery, so that the lesson of humility which was to be afterwards preached in words might first be affirmed in actual deeds.

A similar misinterpretation we find on p. 337 (II, 21, 11): 'Nam *illud* non est nec esse debet auctoritatis Romani vel alterius cuiusvis episcopi aut particularis cum ipso collegii clericorum. Propter *quod* omnia regna omnesque politiae maiores sive minores haeresis et dissolutionis exponuntur periculo.' The editors here have failed to see that *illud* is the antecedent of *quod*; that the phrase means: 'for that (*illud*), on account of which (*propter quod*) all kingdoms and all states may be exposed to the danger of heresy and disintegration does not and cannot pertain to the authority of the Roman bishop, etc.' The period therefore should be removed before *propter quod*.

Likewise on p. 26 (I, 7, 1) the causal clause: 'cum enim natura...'

is incorrectly separated by a period from its conclusion 'Initiavit ipsa, etc.' And on p. 69 (I, 15, 5), an erroneously inserted period (l. 7) separates the causal sentence 'Quia enim civitas...' from its conclusion 'qualis igitur est....'

The following passage (I, 16, 11) is also defective: 'Ex determinatis autem a nobis XIV huius suppositionem accipientes, oportere futurum monarcham quemlibet prudentem et bonum esse secundum moralem virtutem, praecipue iustitiam, et quasi excellenter ad reliquos cives. Amplius et cum hiis suscipientes quae de diversitate inclinationum et dispositionum in gentibus et regionibus ad regiminum diversitates diximus IX° huius, parte 10, credendum opinor, melius esse etc.' The clause *accipientes* etc. hangs in the air. By removing the period after *cives* (l. 17, p. 79), it should be connected with *suscipientes etc.* and be made to depend on 'credendum opinor' (l. 20) recalling that *oportere* etc. is the object of *accipientes* and means: 'assuming that the future monarch must be prudent, etc.'

On page 168 (II, 6, 11), ll. 19-20, 'Haec autem ecclesiae anathematizatio hanc poenam illis, qui digne percelluntur, infligit,' makes no sense with the subject *anathematizatio* cut off from its verb by a semicolon; nor do ll. 9-13 on p. 86, where the object 'morem attendendum' is separated from its verb 'cognoscere potest' by a semicolon; and a solecism is unnecessarily introduced.

The initial sentence of paragraph 18, chapter 25, Dictio II is meaningless as it stands: 'Quod ne deinceps lateat horum episcoporum fallacia, tamquam veritatis praeco clamo valenter et vobis dico, regibus, principibus, populis, tribubus, et universis linguis! per Romanos episcopos... praeiudicium fieri.' The exclamation point after *linguis* is impossible for the reason that *regibus, principibus... linguis* are all datives governed by 'praeiudicium fieri.'

It is not possible here to enumerate all these defective passages, but for the benefit of the future editor of Marsilius, I may add the following changes: Remove period after *electum* (p. 87) and, on p. 449, between *regendus* and *Quod* (the two parts of a relative sentence); on p. 377, *cogitabilia* should not be separated from its noun *inconvenientia*, nor on p. 62 *sunt* from its predicate *circa quae*, nor on p. 500 *pars* from its limiting adjective *principans*. The semicolon after *Primae* (p. 501) is faulty, and on p. 3 *ex effectu*, depending on *sumpta*, and not on *explicanda*, should have no punctuation before it. On p. 20 the *operum* should not be cut off from the genitive it supports (we have here the 'opera misericordiae'). On p. 54, *pravi et stulti* are predicates of *videntur* and should not be cut off from it. On p. 87 no period between *electum* and *Et*. On foot of p. 414, the semicolon before *per* should be removed, for it separates the verb *persequeretur* from the object *recusantes*.

6. Conversely sentences are run together which syntactically and logically should be separated. On p. 53, a wrong meaning is given by such a slip. We read there: 'aut legum lationis auctoritas ad solam civium universitatem pertinet, ut diximus, vel ad hominem unicum aut pauciores, non ad solum unum propter ea quae dicta sunt....' As it stands this sentence has already given rise to strange interpretations. There should be a full stop after *pauciores*. For with *non ad solum* the rejection (or adoption) of the alternatives begins and is continued in *Propter eandem etc.*

The following sentence (Dictio II, ch. 14, par. 18) needs a similar straightening out: 'Quamvis enim per se rem licite trasferant aut commutent in pretium aut e converso, non propter hoc transferunt in alios aut in se suscipiunt dominium rei alicuius, nisi forte secundum accidens transferre dicantur, ut quia ipsis rem licite transferentibus domini fiunt in quos transfertur; aliunde tamen per se, ut infra patebit, dominium autem nullo modo suscipiunt nec suscipere possunt perfecti manentes.' The *autem* after *dominium*, as the sentence is now punctuated, is ungrammatical and the argumentation is meaningless. There should be no semicolon after *transfertur* and there should be a period after *patebit*. The sentence will then mean (beginning with *nisi forte*) 'unless they be said to effect an *accidental* transfer (of the *dominium*) in that while they (the perfect ones) lawfully transfer the thing itself, those who receive this transfer do become *domini* (their *essential* title, however, coming from another source, as will be seen below). But the *dominium* itself, is never vested and can never be vested in those who aspire to perfection.' So on p. 5, l. 2, the sentence ends with *iniquitas* and should be so marked with a period.

7. On p. 213, l. 3 (II, 12, 1), in order to save the syntax, we should include within parenthesis 'certum... extitisse.' Parentheses, on the other hand, should be removed from the following (p. 346): 'deliberatorum quoque (tam circa fidem quam ritum ecclesiasticum sive cultum divinum *et* reliquorum ordinatorum ad pacem atque fidelium unitatem) transgressores per ecclesiasticam aliquam arcere

censuram'... For *transgressores* governs both *deliberatorum* and *reliquorum ordinatorum*, so that one cannot be inside and the other outside the parenthesis; and the phrase 'tam circa etc.' is needed for the meaning of *deliberatorum* (*et* connecting this latter with *ordinatorum*). Likewise, on p. 467 (II, 28, 27): 'in optima (convenientium humanae conversationi) dispositione,' the requisite complementary genitive is separated from the noun it modifies. And so on p. 486, where the phrase 'vicarii (Caesaris)' gives the wrong meaning: 'the vicar Caesar' instead of 'the vicar of Caesar,' i.e. (Pontius Pilate). And finally, on p. 5, the parenthetical phrase should begin after *a quo* and end with 'capitulo,' for *a quo* refers not to *teste* but to God.

The latest edition has properly italicized all the quotations identified by Marsilius himself. There are many, however, which are introduced by him without any indication. These anonymous citations are usuall well-known phrases, and should be identified, for on their significance as quotations the proper understanding of the passage often rests. There are thus some passages where the argument depends not so much on what is actually stated, but on the authority of the quotation and on its generally accepted implications. I mean such passages as the following on p. 22 (I, 6, 3): 'qui numquam facit frustra quicquam neque deficit in necessariis' where the reader will follow the argument and accept its weight only in so far as he recognizes in the phrase a quotation from Aristotle (*De An.* III, 9: 432 b and elsewhere), and supplies mentally all that was contained in that pregnant dictum. There are eight or ten such current sentences that need to be identified and italicized.

Another group is less important. It deals with words or phrases that would appear strange did the reader not know that they were quoted. Such phrases for instance as (p. 13): 'nudus nascitur et inermis' from Aristotle, *De Part. Anim.*, IV, 10 (see Plato, *Prot.* 321 C) and 'maculativa officia' (p. 21) and, on p. 31, 'nihil contristati' (from Arist., *Pol.* III, 14).

There are quotations whose recognition seems to have some literary pertinence, as the Horatian 'tonsores aut lippi' (p. 401).

And finally, there is a considerable number of self-quotations that must be identified and marked, for they are passages in which the author discusses the meaning of his own words. So, for instance, on p. 65, ll. 7, 8: 'oportet autem simul plurium intelligere non comparative idest maiorem partem sed plurium positive,' which is devoid of sense unless we italicize or put between quotation marks 'simul plurium' and 'plurium' to mean: 'the phrase *simul plurium* above used, etc.'

The same holds for *lex* and *principantis* (p. 67, ll. 24-25) and *legis* and *principantis* on p. 296, l. 27.

IX

"GIROLAMO FRACASTORO" *

A recent review of this work by Benedetto Croce and an attempted utilization of it for a doctoral dissertation have made it seem advisable to write a few words of warning to those who might want to use this version for scholarly research.

Translations are being more and more frequently resorted to, so that greater care, it seems, should be devoted to their preparation than was done in this case. The information that we gather in this version is very often erroneous, and an attempt to derive from it Fracastoro's poetical theories would lead to some strange conclusions. Some of this misinformation was used by the author of the preface who incorporates in his revision of Fracastoro's doctrines blunders of rather fundamental importance. He quotes for instance (p. 20): "He — the poet — indeed wishes also to teach and persuade and speak of other things, but, *restricted as it were by his aim, he does not develop his subject enough to explain it* (*i.e.*, he does not realize the aim of demonstrative oratory) but making a different idea for himself, of untrammeled and universal beauty," etc. Fracastoro, however, says exactly the opposite. "The poet — he writes — no doubt wants to teach, convince and speak of other things, but he is not restricted (like the philosopher or the orator, etc.) to what is useful and sufficient for the presentation of his subject *as though limited* to the attainment of *that end* (the knowledge of nature, the proof of a law-suit, etc.) but," etc. ("Vult quidem et ipse

---

* Review of: *Girolamo Fracastoro Naugerius, Sive de Poetica Dialogus.* With an English Translation by Ruth Kelso and an Introduction by Murray W. Bundy. The University of Illinois, Urbana, Ill., 1924, 88 pp.

et docere et persuadere et de aliis loqui, sed non quantum expedit, et satis est ad explicandam rem tamquam astrictus eo fine verum," etc., p. 158C). In other words, using Fracastoro's language, the philosopher, the orator, etc., achieve a relative excellence of expression, but the poet an absolute one — one that is not subordinated to the attainment of any of these particular ends. On page 15 the following blunder is made use of: "God is not the cause, but music itself, full of a sort of great, exalting wonder which makes the *pulse* beat with the rhythm as if stirred by some violent frenzy" (p. 65). Though a doctor, Fracastoro is not speaking here about *pulses*. The word *pulsum* in his text is the participle "struck," and he says something quite different: "The cause of this frenzy is not a god but music itself which strikes the soul with harmony, arousing it as though with an overpowering sting, excites it and forces it out of its own self."[1]

Graver misunderstandings are caused by the failure on the part of the translator to grasp the philosophical meaning of *simpliciter, simplex*, etc., which is not *simple*, but *absolute*, and in Fracastoro's treatise is avowedly used to mean now *universally unsubordinated*, and now *superlative* in its own given genus (p. 106C). So when we find the following rather important passage quoted in the preface (p. 13): "A poet is inspired by no other aim than *simply* to express himself delightfully about anything that proposes itself to him" (p. 158C), we must not suppose that we have Fracastoro's thought, who quite differently states that: "The poet aims at an expression which shall be beautiful absolutely" (that is, the excellence of his speech is not like the excellence of the philosophers' language subordinated to the needs of a particular subject matter). And again (p. 19) the quotation: "The poet as a poet is inspired by no other aim than *simply* to express himself well about anything that proposes itself to him" (pp. 158C; 60), retains nothing of the original which is: "But the poet as such has no end in view other than absolute excellence of expression," etc. And on the following page, instead of "a style which is appropriate and simply beautiful" (pp. 165D; 74), Fracastoro speaks of "an appropriate style of absolute beauty." On p. 60, the rendering "how and for what reason he — the poet — alone concerns himself *simply* with beautiful expression" is

---

[1] "Non est autem Deus ullus causa furoris huius, sed ipsa musica ingentis cuiusdam atque exultantis admirationis plena, quæ *pulsum* numeris, velut œstro impotente concitum, nec sese capientem animum quatit." (p. 160D).

a long ways off from the original which is "how and for what reason the poet alone aims at absolute beauty of diction" (p. 158D). And finally the misunderstanding yields its ultimate absurdity when Fracastoro is made to say (p. 60) that "except for the poet, no one expresses himself *merely* (*simpliciter*) well and appropriately," when in reality he says much more sensibly that "except for the poet no one possesses absolute beauty and propriety of expression" (p. 158B). Fracastoro himself gives us the meaning of this word when, caught in an ambiguity (which is not the ambiguity assumed in footnote 5 of p. 64), he describes the gods (p. 160C) as being beautiful *simpliciter*, he goes on to explain the sense by the addition of the phrase *et in omnibus*, and makes it equivalent to *superlative*, concluding "quare æquivocatio illius verbi simpliciter te decipiebat: interdum enim significat, quod universaliter absolute tale est, interdum quod tale in suo genere."[1·]

This meaning of *simpliciter* is also made clear by its being contrasted with the word *relatively*, which is *secundum aliquid*. And keeping this in mind we should correct (on p. 69) the meaningless: "Others strive for language that is *somewhat inferior* and beautiful only in part, but the poet seeks for what is simply beautiful," so as to make it read instead: "Others strive for expression which is beautiful *relatively* (*secundum aliquid*) whereas the poet aims at *absolute* beauty of expression" (p. 162D).

In this English version Fracastoro is made to produce elements of a new *ars poetica*. On p. 73, for instance, we read this startling sentence: "Moreover, no one in so far as he is skilled in writing tells or knows anything," but in the original we find: "It does not matter if, *qua* stylist, he is ignorant of these matters;"[2] and lower down: "It is not necessary to know a great deal, but to know exactly," where the text has "It is not only necessary to know, but also to know most accurately."[3]

After reading the following passage (p. 72) one might be tempted to write a new chapter on Plato and the poets in Renaissance criticism:

---

[1] Croce discussing this passage (*Estetica*, 208) makes a curious slip. According to him Fracastoro says that "bisogna evitare l'equivoco e il doppio senso che è nel vocabolo 'bello' (æquivocatio illius verbi)." The ambiguity (æquivocatio) is not in the word *bello* but in the word *simpliciter* (now universally superlative and now superlative within its genus), and Fracastoro does not ask us to avoid it, but calls our attention to the presence of it in his language.

[2] "Nihil autem refert an nesciat quatenus dicendi peritus" (p. 164B).

[3] "Nec scire tantum necesse est, sed exactissime scire" (*Ibid.*).

"And from that comes the third objection (of Plato): that poets very often write indecently, and belittle gods and heroes. *And he is right.* It seems just therefore, my friends, that we should carefully consider these objections, since Plato himself, *the friend of poets*, demands that they defend themselves. We are not poets, to be sure, but we are the friends of poets, and consequently consider it our duty to *play the part* of friends." There seem to be promising novelties here, but they all disappear when we turn to the original which says: "And from this comes the third objection, viz., that poets very often write indecently and represent gods and heroes *as they should not* (*secus... ac par est*). It seems therefore reasonable, my friends, that we look carefully into this matter since Plato himself asks *the friends of the poets* to defend *them* (*the poets*). We are not poets but we are the poets' friends, therefore we consider it our task to *take their side.*"[1]

In this same passage we are startled to find that "*Juppiter præ impatientia expectandi sibi tractans virilia*" (p. 164C), is rendered "Jupiter, impatient of waiting, behaving like an ordinary man," against which we should strongly protest in the name of us all "ordinary men."

The commonplace statement of Fracastoro: "poets produce (*edere*) a divine and tuneful song" (p. 163C), becomes "music and divine song *elevate*" (p. 71). The strange remark on p. 66 that "the poet does not teach from knowledge of his own" surely gives a wrong idea of the text, which says: "The primary purpose of the poet is not to teach" (p. 161B).

After reading the following on p. 58: "We must likewise inquire whether the poet's style may be determined *from himself* alone, or whether a certain kind of subject matter also is required. It seems to me beyond doubt that the style peculiar to the poet ought to be found in *him alone*," etc. — we wonder whether Fracastoro is profound or silly, but he is neither. He merely says: "We must likewise inquire whether the essential quality of a poet consists *in his style alone* (*ab ipso solo*, that is, *dicendi modo*) or whether a definite subject matter is required. And to me it surely seems that such quality must be found

---

[1] "Unde et tertium enascitur, quod poetæ sæpissime indecentia scribant, et secus Diis et heroibus tribuant, ac par est. Justum igitur o amici videtur, ut de his rationem diligenter habeamus, quoniam et ipse Plato poetarum amicos rogat, ut ipsos defendant. Nos quidem poetæ non sumus, sed poetarum amici: quare nostrum esse ducimus amicorum partes tueri" (p. 164B).

solely in his style."[1] And on that same page the same error occurs before when we are told that: "And, even more, we must show *whether* any subject matter is unfit for the poet, or whether everything which can be taught at all can be called imitation," while Fracastoro says, "We must discover this (the differentiation between the poet and the historian) especially if there is no subject matter which is the poet's own."[2] And further down the discussion of Pontano's doctrine becomes meaningless through the confusion of *admiratio, mirandi.*

The followers of Lessing need not be disturbed when they read (p. 57); "We could give the name of poet to the sculptor who had carved some marble," for the Italian critic merely says: "then we would be justified in calling *sculptor* any man who happens to carve marble" (*et eum appellare sculptorem, qui marmor aliquod incidisset.* P. 157A). The following statement (p. 54) might arouse historical curiosity: "the poet... whom even emperors have thought worthy to be crowned," but again the original states nothing more than the well-known fact of: "the poet whom the Romans deemed worthy to be crowned with the same crown used for the emperors" (*quem... Romani eadem, qua et imperatores corona ornari dignum arbitrati sunt.* P. 155D). There is something very modern and suggestive in the following (p. 53): "To give pleasure is the aim of the poet which perhaps we can accept. For what else would produce these elaborate harmonies of poetry, all these intricacies of plot, all these marvels so carefully worked out?..." The original merely says: "To give pleasure is the aim of the poet which we too perhaps think. For what other conclusion could you draw from the fact that the music of songs is so much sought after; that all compositions, complicated by fabulous inventions, and all things startling are so much in demand" (p. 155B).

There was an opportunity for an easy text emendation, or rather for the correction of a misprint in the passage which is translated (p. 61) as: "Then whose business is it to examine the common elements, the business of him who considers the particular, or rather of him who

---

[1] "Nunc venio ad dicendi modum, qui in poeta longe diversus ab aliis est: de quo similiter est inquirendum, utrum ratio poetæ ab ipso solo sumatur, an et materia certa requiratur; et certe ab eo solo mihi videtur rationem propriam poetæ sumi debere" (p. 157C).
[2] "Id assignare oportet, quo differt poeta ab historico: et siqui alii idem faciunt magis autem oportebit hoc assignare si nulla materia propria poetæ sit, et omne, quod quocumque docetur modo, imitatio dicatur" (*Ibid.*).

considers the common? (*sic*). Is it the business of whoever examines the particular, or are they different, the one who contemplates the common, and the one who contemplates the particular?" which is meaningless. The Latin text is: "Cuius igitur interest speculari communia? num ejus, qui propria, an magis ejus, qui communia considerat? interest etiam propria cujusque speculari, an diversus est, qui communia et qui propria contemplatur?" (p. 159A) which, for the sake of sense and grammar, must be corrected by removing the interrogation mark after *considerat*, placing it after *propria*, so as to read: "Then whose business is it to inquire into the common attributes? The business of him who inquires into the peculiar attributes? Or rather is it the duty of the one who considers the common attributes to investigate also the peculiarities of each? Or perhaps are those who inquire into the common qualities and those who inquire into peculiar attributes entirely separate?"

The difficulty of Latin syntax is the cause of much of the trouble. The use of *alii* is responsible for a dozen and more misrepresentations of Fracastoro's thought. On p. 63: "But if there should be some one else who should come to this orator of ours... and say that he wishes to speak of *these same matters and others*," etc., where we should read "to speak about those matters concerning which others also speak" (*de quibus et alii*. P. 160A). And on the previous page (62): "In the same way the master and guide, if he wishes to write of his own subject, imposes on himself the same law and becomes a servant to himself and uses a form of eloquence not inferior but different," where Fracastoro says: "He becomes a servant to himself and a part of eloquence just like the others" (*non secus ac alii*. P. 159C). On p. 154C, *pro viribus* means "in proportion to my strength" (p. 52); in *cum enim natura insitum sit* (pp. 155B; 53), *cum* is "since," not "although." *Verum enim vero* (same page) is not "perhaps it is right": it means "but." *Mutuo* (p. 156B) is not "mutual" (p. 55), but "borrowed"; and on the next page *conductitium* (p. 156C) means "hired," not "in a measure the concern" (p. 56). The little poem on p. 158A is full of mistakes (p. 59). *Phrix* on p. 160D means "Phrygian" (p. 65) in connection with *Magna Mater*; in the margin of p. 161 *etsi* means "although," not "whether"; etc.

Similar criticism might be carried on about the translation of Pontano's *Actius*, but enough. *Sat prata biberunt.*

X

WERE THERE THEATERS IN THE TWELFTH AND THIRTEENTH CENTURIES?

Under this title Professors R. Loomis and G. Cohen have published an article in *Speculum* (January 1945) the purpose of which is to demonstrate that contrary to a view often adhered to there were in the 12th and 13th centuries permanent buildings used for theatrical performances.

Those who are interested in the history of the theater should be grateful for this noteworthy contribution. Yet the case is far from settled and in what follows the opposite view will again be supported and the validity of the arguments so far presented will once more be tested.

Professor Loomis's conclusions are based, first, on the use of such words as *theatrum*, *scena* and their derivatives in the period under consideration; and, second, on a piece of fiction describing a devil's trial held in what seems to be the ruins of an ancient theater.

The first argument, like those of Gregorovius, De Bartholomaeis and others, seems faulty in that it assumes that the persistence of words implies the survival of the things originally signified by these words; also, that literary texts faithfully reflect contemporary conditions. An historical analysis of the quotations adduced by Professor Loomis, and of hundreds more that could be added, will show that such words as *theatrum*, *scena*, *thymele*, *theatrales*, *scenici*, *thymelici*, carried over from classical antiquity, came to be used to describe men, places, and spectacles quite different from those to which they were originally applied: namely to *jongleurs*, buffoons and jesters who performed in palaces and public squares, on street corners, in open meadows and in tents, upon platforms, on bridges — everywhere except in places which in the ancient or modern sense of the word we might reasonably call a theater.

The unhistorical approach of these investigators consists therefore, as I see it, in the failure to distinguish between what is obviously rhetorical, moralizing or encyclopedic antiquarianism and what is genuinely representative of contemporary conditions. They either fail to recognize the fact that a certain passage in a medieval writer is a more or less concealed quotation from a classical author, or else they assume that words of a remote past kept their meaning unchanged. This failure to distinguish literary fossils from living social organisms is the sole ground, it seems to me, on which scholars have systematically supported their medieval theaters.

I. The method above criticized may be illustrated by the following examples taken from Professor Loomis's quotations. He gives us (page 95) Uguccione's definition of *theatrum* which is, not in part, but in its entirety, reproduced from Isidore. What does this quotation prove? We find it repeated in exactly the same words in all centuries. Papias (eleventh century) has it. Rhabanus Maurus (ninth century) has it (*De Universo*, xx, 36; Migne *P.L.*, 111, 553). The *Graphia* (eleventh-twelfth century) contains a full account copied verbatim from Isidore under the titles *De Scena et Orcistra* and *De offitiis scene*. All this material moreover appears, broken up, in numerous glossaries. And all it proves is that these men had before their eyes not theaters but the text of Isidore.

We can also illustrate moralizing as well as erudite antiquarianism from Professor Loomis's quotations. He gives us (page 44) a passage from the *Chronicle* of Richard of Devizes which reads as follows:

Vita talum et tesseram theatrum et tabernam; plures ibi quam in tota Gallia thrasones offendes; gnathorum autem infinitus est numerus: Histriones, scurrae, glabriones, garamantes, palpones, pusiones, molles mascularii, ambubaiae, pharmacopolae crissoniae, phitonissae, vultuariae noctivagae, magi, mimi mendici balatrones hoc genus omne totas replevere domos.

These are not living words in current usage during the twelfth century. The reality described is a milieu of debauchery and sodomy, enlivened by dancers and buffoons and exploited by fakers and fawners. But the contemporary features are concealed under cant phrases, in a *cento* of moralizing contumelies patched up with pieces from all centuries and many nations. We have the *pythonissa* of Old Testament days; the burning words of St. Paul, *neque molles neque masculorum concubitores*. The early Christian revilements drawn from the characters of Terence reappear: the *gnathones*,[1] the *thrasones*. Echoes from the Roman satirists: *palpo* of Persius (v, 176), caught up by John of Salisbury (Policr. III, 4) and frequently recorded in the glossaries; an obscene usage of *pusio* from Juvenal (VI, 34), that again reappears in the 12th century. *Glabrio* is neither a medieval word nor one frequently used in classical antiquity; it is occasionally found in the glossaries (see Loewe, *C.G.L.*, v, 502, 569) *as faciei disceptor*.[2] Finally the favorite jingle from Horace, *Sat.* I, 2, 1, that was so often quoted from Flavius Vopiscus to Petrus Blesensis. All these pursuits are carried on, we are told, in a place which is called *theatrum*; naturally enough, since Isidore had said (and every century had repeated his words) that the *theatrum* is *postribulum*, or, as others called it, *a lupanar*.[3] If we consider the various pursuits enumerated above by our chronicler we should have reached the same conclusions even without the aid of Isidore.

These words are then technical terms; not, however, of dramatists or historians, but of the moralists. The latter in the period we are considering were bent on enriching their vocabulary, mainly with the aid of ancient authors and the glosses thereon. Any antiquated word that was in any way reminiscent of the foul practices connected with the more or less histrionic amusements of the ancients was eagerly picked up. This explains the wealth of abuse in the above passage and in others similar to it.

The insertion of the familiar tirade from Horace deserves notice. Surely no one should claim that the *ambubaiae* and the *balatrones* were professional terms in the twelfth century. *Pharmacolopa*, too, had lost its original sting and new meanings were being applied. How badly the details of this Horatian invective fit into the conditions of

---

[1] Terence, *Eun.*, II, 2, 33; cf. John of Salisbury, *Policr.*, III, 4: "Tota enim gnathonicorum factio;" and St. Jerome, *Ep.* 50: "ex huius nomine Gnathonici vel Phormionici;" etc.

[2] *Garamantes* must be a corruption of *chiromantes*, the latter form being frequently spelled with an *a* instead of the *i*.

[3] Loewe, *C.G.L.*, II, 586: "domus meretricum vel theatrum."

the twelfth century may be seen when it is recalled that the *mendici*, the beggars, were then and had been for a thousand years, in words at least, the object of love and solicitude, and that one of the commonest of medieval commonplaces is the contrast between the beggar beloved of God and the mime,[1] tool of the devil. The popularity of this Horatian line became so great that it was felt that its power could be maintained by truncated citation, by means of some one catch word or phrase, usually the *hoc genus omne* or the *collegium*. At times the juxtaposition of two or three of its most striking words was resorted to. So Otto of Freising (*Mon. Ger. Scr.*, xx, 244), Chron. vi, 32, speaks of *omne balatronum et histrionum collegium*; the *Summa* of Conrad (Rockinger, *Quellen* etc. ix, 429), presents the *ambubaiarum collegia* by the side of the *balatrones* and *mendici*; Peter of Blois, *Epist.* xiv,[2] has: *mimi, barbatores,[3] balatrones, et hoc genus omne.[4]*

A well known scholar in the field of dramatic history, De Bartholomaeis, seems to be even less aware of the fact that these enumerations are nothing but rhetorical outbursts made up of outdated material having little or no connection with contemporary social conditions. He quotes in his *Storia della poesia drammatica italiana*, page 26, some of the terms used by John of Salisbury in the latter's long string of infamous professional amusements (*Policr.*, i, 8) and thinks that they correspond to as many recognized varieties of more or less histrionic pursuits. As an example he asks us to take (*op. cit.*, p. 26, n. 3) *salii, saliares, aemiliani, gignadii* and adds: "as for the meaning of these terms it is sufficient to refer to Du Cange s.vv." But if we follow his instructions we discover that Du Cange knows these terms only in so

---

[1] Passages in which kings and potentates are praised for feeding the poor and driving the *histriones* from their tables, or rebuked for doing the opposite, are frequent. See: Alcuin (*Mon. Ger. Ep.*, iv, 439; *loc. cit.*, p. 183); Agobard *Epist.* (a. 836); Henry III (a. 1044) is extolled (*Mon. Ger. Scr.*, ii, 243) because at his marriage feast he fed the poor and *infinitam histrionum et ioculatorum multitudinem sine cibo et muneribus abire permisit*. For the disagreement between Alcuin and Angilbert (Homer) on the question of dramatics see: *Mon. Ger. Ep.*, iv, 290, 381.

[2] De Bartholomaeis, *Storia*, etc., p. 33, erroneously attributes this passage to Eude Rigaud.

[3] The most helpful reference for the understanding of this term is not in Du Cange. It is found in the *Lex Romana Raetica Curiensis*, viii, 4 (*Mon. Ger. Leges* v, 361) and reads thus: "quando aliqua publica gaudia nunciantur, hoc est elevatio regit aut nuptiae aut *barbatoria* etc." The reference to Petronius (Fr. Trag., p. 73) is both too fragmentary and uncertain, the reading being the result of an emendation.

[4] For additional instances of the popularity of this quotation see ALT. *Theater und Kirche*, pp. 401-402, and VIELLARD, *Gilles de Corbeil*, p. 380.

far as they appear in the same John of Salisbury, so that all he can do, for three of them, is to refer us back to the passage quoted above and as for the fourth (*salii*) ignore it altogether. As a matter of fact *emiliani* occurs only in this passage and one man's guess as to its meaning is as good as another. *Salii* and *saliares* in the sense of dancers appear in old glossaries but very rarely: the former in *Exc. Cod. Vat.* 1468 (Loewe *C.G.L.*, v, 513), the latter in *Exc. Cod. Cass.* (Loewe *C.G.L.*, v, 578), both defined as *striones* (*histriones*). This meaning probably goes back to Diomedes (Keil, I, 476) or to Servius (in *Aen.*, VIII, 285). *Gignadii*, finally, is obviously connected with *gymnasium* and may be a variant of the common *gignici*; but it too is found nowhere else. All of this shows how well, to use De Bartholomaeis' words (page 26), "the nomenclature adopted by these writers mirrors, naturally enough, the actual state of things."

De Bartholomaeis moreover informs us (page 70) that *balatrones* was the current term for dancers in this period. This information, it may be added, has been accepted and occasionally utilized. In reality, however, there is not a single text that could be adduced to sustain such an interpretation.

Balatro as all know is an old word. Its meaning was wavering and uncertain already in the classical period. It was supposed to be applied now to a jester, now to a rake (*luxuriosus*), occasionally to a spend-thrift, being then spelled *barathro* (*quia bona sua in barathrum mittit*). Porphyrio (3rd century) says (in Hor. *Sat.*, I, 2, 1) *balathrones a balatu et vaniloquentia dicuntur*. The *Scholia in Horatium* explain (*loc. cit.*) *balatrones a balatu intortae vocis dicuntur qui idem et blatterones*, thus giving the word a meaning very close to our *babbler*.

Du Cange favored the derivation from *balare* but apparently thought the word meant not *to bleat* but *to dance*, for he enters *balatro* under that heading. He does not however give any reason for this departure, nor furnish any example. De Bartholomaeis, either originally or through Du Cange, comes to the same strange conclusion and with great assurance informs us that the dancers in this period were regularly called *balatrones*. He too fails to give any reason and offers no example except the well-known quotations in which the meaning of the word is in no manner indicated, being a mere repetition of the text of Horace or of some other classical writer.

One might perhaps say that people in the twelfth century coming across this unusual word istinctively connected it with *ballare* because of similarity in sound. For this, however, we should need a clear statement, something more definite than the usual string of vague learned revilements. Moreover, if we examine the medieval MSS, both those of classical authors and those of contemporary ones, we do indeed find a steady tendency toward a catachresis, but one which completely does away with the meaning of *dancers*. For the word is with extreme frequency spelled *baratrones* or *barathrones*, showing that the scribes were thinking of *barathrum* and not of *ballare*. In fact, the MSS of Pierre de Blois' text above quoted read *barathrones* and the form *balathrones* which appears in the printed editions is the result of an emendation.

The practice of incorporating old texts in one's own discourse for the purpose above described is very old. We find Leidradus (*Mon. Ger. Ep.*, IV, 541) saying: "Velut cum theatrorum moles extruuntur et effodiuntur fundamenta virtutis, cum ex his quae divitibus abundant luxuriantur histriones, et necessaria vix habent pauperes... Si circensibus quispiam delectetur, si athletarum certamine, si mobilitate hystrionum, si formis mulierum... per oculorum fenestras animae est capta libertas. Rursum auditu si vario organorum cantu... et carmine poetarum et comoediarum mimorumque urbanitatibus et strophis etc.," which is a patchwork from two or three old texts but is mainly derived from St. Jerome, *Adversus Jovinianum*, II, 8.[1]

It is interesting in this regard to point out a mistake by Isidore (*Etym.*, XVIII, 42, and in part again in *Etym.*, XV, 2.34), repeated after him by practically all subsequent writers from the 9th to the 13th centuries who have dealt with the matter, viz. that people *stood up* in the theater (*quo stantes* omnes inspiciunt... quod in eo *populus stans* etc.). Isidore is giving us here an antiquated view that had ceased to be true more than half a millennium before his days. He must have read some text like the following from Tacitus (*Annales*, XIV, 20): "Si vetustiora repetas *stantem populum* spectavisse;" or more likely from Livy (48th *Periocha*) "cum locatum a censoribus theatrum extrueretur... ex S.C. destructum est *populusque* aliquamdiu *stans* ludos spectavit."

II. The failure to recognize this antiquarian quality of medieval texts was responsible for Gregorovius's statement that there were

---

[1] This passage is quoted by JOHN OF SALISBURY, *Policr.*, VIII, 6.

theaters in Italy in the tenth century.[1] In his *History of the City of Rome in the Middle Ages* (Book VI, Chapter 7) we read the following:

It is an established fact that in the tenth century theatrical perfomances took place in northern Italy. At that time when so many Greek expressions came into use, actors received the name of *Thymelici*, so that the ancient *Thymele* of the Sophoclean stage in an age which no longer had any notion of tragedians came to give its name to Comedians. Atto of Vercelli protests against ecclesiastics who appear on scenes of theatres; he urges them to leave the table as soon as the *thymelici* appear... The *Graphia* dedicated two paragraphs to theatrical amusements. Poets, Comedians, Tragedians, scenes and orchestras, histrions, dancers and gladiators are mentioned and the expression *thymelici* which was then actually employed shows that at least one feature of what the *Graphia* relates was something more than a mere antiquarian reminiscence. It is not too bold to assert that at the court of Hugo, Marozia and Alberich mythological scenes were performed.

How much truth is there in all this?

The passage of the *Graphia* on which he bases his argument is the following (Schramm, *Rom*, etc., II, 91-92):

De scena et orcistra. In scena que fit infra theatrum in modum domus cum pulpito quod orcistra vocatur cantant comici tragici atque saltant histriones et mimi. In orcistra vero saltator saltat et duo inter se disputant. In ea poete, comedi et tragedi ad certamen conscendunt hisque canentibus alii gestus edunt virorum et feminarum. De Offitiis scene. Offitia scenica tragedi, comedi thymelici histriones et saltatores... In amphitheatro pugnant gladiatores etc.

All this, of course, is taken verbatim from Isidore, *Etym.*, XVIII, 43, 44, 45, 52, and all it shows again is that the author of the *Graphia* had the text of Isidore before his eyes. The affirmation, moreover, that this is the first time Roman spectacles are mentioned since the days of Cassiodorus is wrong, for Isidore comes in between, also Rhabanus Maurus, and a dozen others. The Greek word *thymele* was not, as Gregorovius says, then introduced into Italy, but had been used there and elsewhere continuously for the last ten centuries.

---

[1] This view was shared by DAVIDSOHN, *Storia di Firenze*, p. 1170, n. 2. The recent Italian translation of Gregorovius accepts it without challenge.

This last point is interesting enough and has been perplexing enough to justify here a detailed refutation of Gregorovius' statement in the course of which we pass from literary to juridical antiquarianism.

Gregorovius gives in his notes as evidence for the statement above quoted the following passage from Atto's *Capit.*, 42 (*M.P.L.*, 134-38): "non oportet ministros altaris vel quoslibet clericos spectaculis aliquibus quae in *nuptiis* aut in *scenis* exhibentur interesse sed antequam thymelici ingrediantur surgere eos de convivio et abire debere." These words, however, are an exact quotation from the ancient translation of c. 54 of the Council of Laodicea (fourth century), except that where Atto has *scenis* it reads *caenis*, correctly enough, for the Greek original has: δέίπνοις. This law was in subsequent centuries frequently and correctly quoted either in part or as a whole. When we come however to the Council of Aix-la-Chapelle (a. 816) we see that a significant change has taken place for there we find (chapter 83): "non oportet sacerdotes aut clericos quibuscumque spectaculis in *scenis* aut nuptiis interesse sed antequam thymelici ingrediantur exsurgere." Is the alteration due to the changed meaning of *caena* and the consequent supposition that the word represented a scribe's misspelling of *scena*?

The correct reading was apparently known to Pope Hadrian I (a. 773) who in his *Epitome Canonum* (*Mansi*, XI, 868) says "ne clerici ludicris spectaculis intersint in cenis vel nuptiis sed ante discedant quam thymelici veniant." It is still known to Regino of Prüm, who, in his *De Eccl. Discipl.*, I, 327 (*M.P.L.*, vol. 132), states: "non licet sacerdotibus vel clericis aliqua spectacula in nuptiis vel conviviis spectare sed oportet antequam ingrediantur etc." As we see, Regino Prumensis has kept the sense but has seen fit to change the word from *cenis* to *conviviis* perhaps for the reason above stated.

Gratian gives official and universal validity to this provision which appears in his *Decretum* (III pars. dist. v, 37) with the exact wording of the old translation of the Laodicean council's provision except for the substitution of *scenis* to *cenis*.[1]

So then the word *thymelici* had not, as Gregorovius says, been introduced for the first time in northern Italy in the tenth century. It had been there (and elsewhere) all along and it was being used by people who like Atto were interested in the discipline of the church

---

[1] For more precise determination of all these variations a careful study of the various MSS would be needed.

and who naturally invoked the authority of the old Councils in their endeavors to check disorders of their day, even though the outward form of these disorders had changed from what it had been in the fourth century. The tenth-century *scenae* owe their existence to a scribe's attempt at text emendation.

Another legal fossil found in the text of Atto of Vercelli has more recently been utilized to establish Gregorovius' contention. It is the injunction contained in Atto's *Capit.* chapter 78 (*M.P.L.*, 134.43) which states: "Nec non et illud petendum ut spectacula *theatrorum* caeterorumque ludorum die dominica vel caeteris christianae religionis diebus celeberrimis amoveantur. Maxime quia Sancti Paschae octavarum die, populi *ad circum* magis quam ad ecclesiam conveniunt, deberent trasferri praefiniti ipsorum dies quando evenerint nec debet ullus *christianus cogi ad spectacula.*" The obvious anachronistic elements of this provision are explained by the fact that this is a mere repetition of an order of the *Concilium Africanum* of 424 (see *Conc. Omn. Regia Coll.*, IV, 531).

If we turn from canon to civil law we encounter the same process. Gualcausus tells us (Fitting, *Institutionenglossen des Gualcausus*, page 97), "rerum aliae sunt nullius... quaedam *universitatis* ut *theatra.*" But his words are not called forth by an eleventh-century situation; they are a quotation from Dig. 1, 8, 6, "*universitatis* sunt... *theatra.*"

The process by which these legal residues are deposited is to be seen in the following definition of *scena* which we find in the early thirteenth century jurist Accursius: "scena est obumbratio cortinarum quae posita sunt in publico vel in privato loco et dicitur scena a *scenen* quod est corda, quia ioculatores faciunt ire caballos per chordam et similia" (*Glos. Digest*, III, 2, 3).

Here the term "obumbratio" comes from Servius (*In Aen.*, I, 164): "scena inumbratio et dicta est scena ἀπὸ τῆς σκιᾶσ." The element: "in publico et in privato loco" is quoted from Labeo (*Digest*, III, II, 2, 25): "scena ut Labeo definit quae ludorum faciendorum causa... *in publico privatove...*". Then follows the late pseudo-derivation of *scena* from σχοῖνος (rope), which is found also in Uguccione: "scenofactor i.e. funium factor et ars scenofactoria unde in Actibus Apostolorum (18) legitur de Paulo quod erat scenofactorie artis." With this development we pass from archeology to actuality and are confronted with an early thirteenth century show of the *balestelli* performed in a tent, on a public square, a feature of which was the rope by which the wooden horses were pulled. This game is fully discussed by the jurist Odofredo (first half of thirteenth century), who says: "Exemplificamus in ludis de *balestelli* qui fiunt quando fit aliqua curia (corte bandita). Nam veniunt joculatores et ponunt *cortinas (tende)* in aliquo loco et habent equos ligneos et stant intus cortinas et faciunt ire caballos per cordas" (Tamassia, *Odofredo*, p. 175).[1]

Another example of this stratification of ancient and contemporary layers we find in the following passage from Galveneus Flamma (early fourteenth century) published by Ceruti, *Misc. Stor. Patr.*, VII, 467:

De amphitheatro civitatis mediolanensis: Amphitheatrum fuit hedifitium rotundum altissimo muro circumspectum [*sic*] habens duas portas... Quocienscumque instabat alicuius cause controversia vel criminis impositio non requirebatur iurista aut lex sed illi duo inter quos erat questio *galeis aureis* ornati *equis albis insidentes alter per orientalem alter per occidentalem* (portam) calcaribus perurgentibus destriarios in tantum astis et gladiis *perseveranter dimicabant quousque alter in alterius mortem prosilleret.* Unde in civitate non fuit opus lege ubi gladius insaniens disputabat... et ex hoc Romani principes in arcu triumphali inscribi iusserunt: 'Qui vult modico tempore vivere Mediolanum inhabitet ubi vires pro legibus et iura in ossibus describuntur.'

What we have here is a confusion of actuality, archeology and fiction. The contemporary feature is the unmistakable burgher's dislike for feudal customs, an admiration for Roman law and a general antipathy to the Longobardic tradition. But the story and the picture are unreal. The texts come mainly from Isidore, *Etym.*, 18, 53. (The words exactly taken from Isidore are italicized.)

III. The attempts on the part of medieval authors to explain what actually went on in theaters in pagan days again prove nothing for they offer almost invariably mere repetitions of ancient texts. So the famous passage in Dantis Petrus' commentary to the Divine Comedy (prologue):

Antiquitus in theatro quod erat area semicircularis et in eius medio erat domuncula quae scena dicebatur in qua erat pulpitum et super id ascendebat poeta ut cantor, et sua carmina ut cantiones recitabat. Extra vero erant mimi id est joculatores carminum pronuntiationem gestu corporis effigiantes per

---

[1] For the game of *equi lignei* see: *Just. Cod.*, III, 43.

adaptationem ad quemlibet ex cuius persona ipse poeta loquebatur: unde cum loquebatur, pone, de Junone conquerente de Hercule privigno suo mimi, sicut recitabat ita effigiabant Junonem invocare furias infernales ad infestandum ipsum Herculem: et si tale pulpitum seu domunculam ascendebat poeta qui de more villico caneret talis cantus dicebatur comedia.

In other words, we are told that the theater was semicircular; that in it was a little "domus" which was called *scena*; that in this *scena* there was a "pulpitum" which was also called "orchestra"; and that on this *pulpitum* the poets sang their poems and the mimes enacted it by gestures. All of which is taken bodily out of Isidore's *Etymologiae* ("theatrum semicirculi figuram habens," xv, 2, 35; "scena erat locus infra theatrum in modum domus instructa cum pulpito qui pulpitus orchestra vocabatur ubi cantabant comici tragici," xviii, 43; "ibi enim [on the orchestra] poetae... conscendebant hisque canentibus alii gestus edebant," xviii, 44; "mimi... habebant suum auctorem qui antequam mimum agerent fabulam pronuntiaret," xviii, 49). The only contemporary feature is the example given. It is taken from Seneca's *Hercules Furens* and it schows that Peter had kept up with the progress made in the field of classical scholarship. The closing lines are an abbreviated quotation of a statement that goes back to Diomedes, Donatus and Suetonius.

Boccaccio (and naturally Da Buti) in the prologue to his commentary (*Laterza*, i, 115) agrees mainly with this except that he makes the mimes talk as well as gesticulate. In his commentary to *Inferno* I however (*op. cit.*, p. 144) he seems to fall back upon the accepted position:

Queste cotal commedie poi recitavano [i.e. una spezie di poeti comici] nella scena cioè in una piccola casetta la quale era costituita nel mezzo del teatro, stando dintorno alla detta scena tutto il popolo. E non gli traeva tanto il diletto e il desiderio di udire quanto di vedere i giuochi che dalla recitazione del commedo procedevano; i quali erano in questa forma: che una spezie di buffoni chiamati "mimi" l'uficio dei quali è sapere contraffare gli atti degli uomini, uscivano di quella scena, informati dal commedo in quegli abiti ch'erano convenienti a quelle persone...[1]

Moving backward we find the already quoted passage from the *Graphia* again with the description of Isidore unchanged. The same in

---

[1] The references by BOCCACCIO to ancient theaters are: *Dec.*, x, 6 Fiammetta, 91, 109, 167 etc.

the eleventh century Papias. An eleventh century *Vita Terentii* (Wester-hovius, I, XXX, III) presents this general situation with, however, an interesting addition: "comedia enim," he says, "ita constabat ut non res gestas more historiarum narret, sed ex colluquutione personarum res gesta comprehendatur *quasi inter eos tunc agatur.*" This commentator, in addition to the *recitator* and the *mimi*, has also a *modulator.*

The definition and description of *scena* is accompanied by a considerable stress on the fact that the word has something to do with "umbra" and "adumbratio" and "unabraculum," etc. But this too is antiquarianism. Pio Rajna (*Studi Danteschi*, IV, 13) seems to think that this is a medieval development. As a matter of fact it goes back to classical antiquity. Servius says (*In Aen.*, I, 164): "scena *inumbratio*, et dicta scena ἀπὸ τῆς σκιᾶς. Apud antiquos enim theatralis scena parietem non habuit sed de frondibus *umbracula* quaerebant..." Vitruvius likewise (*De Arch.*, I, 2, 2) says: "scenographia est frontis et laterum abscedentium *adumbratio.*" And Cassiodorus (*Varia.*, IV, 51): "Frons autem theatri scena dicitur ab *umbra* luci densissima ubi a pastoribus inchoante verno diversis sonis carmina cantabantur." This is echoed in the Glossaries. The most interesting restatement is in Placidus, *Libri Glossarum* (Loewe V, 983: "scena est *camera* hinc inde composita que *inumbrat* colum in teatro in quo ludi actitantur; item scena dicitur arborum in se incumbentium quasi concamerata condensatio ut subterpositos tegere possit." The same statement is found in *Codex Parisinus*, *loc. cit.*, p. 148; and with slight variations in the *Libri Romani*, *loc. cit.*, p. 41.

Uguccione likewise tells us s.v. *scenos*: "et a *scenos* quod est umbra dicitur *hec scena, scene*, id est umbra et scena id est umbracu-lum, locus obumbratus in theatro et *cortinis coopertus* similis tabernis mercenariorum que sunt asseris vel cortinis operte. Et secundum hoc scena posset dici a *scenos* quod est *domus* quia in modum domus erat constructa; in illo *umbraculo* latebant persone larvate."

Here the ancient elements reappear with the addition of something drawn from contemporary life. The shade, moreover, is no longer given by the trees but by tents or sheds. And the mimes appear as masks. So again in John of Genoa s.v. *scena*: "in illo *umbraculo* latebant personae larvatae quae ad vocem recitatoris exibant ad gestos faciendos."[1]

---

[1] The word *scena* had early come to mean an *arbor* (*Laube*). EINHART, *Ep.* 57 (*Mon. Ger. Ep.*, V, 138), so treats it and quotes Vitruvius above referred to. In the *Vita S. Anscari* ch. 19 (*Mon. Ger. Scr.*, II, 702), we read "scena in campo ad colloquium

There was however another account of the old theaters which, though completely erroneous, is worth considering. It appears in the *Chronicon Extravagans* of Galvaneus Flamma (thirteenth-fourteenth century) (see Ceruti, *Misc. di Stor. Ital.*, VII, 466): "Teatrum fuit hedificium semicirculare altissimum, fenestratum. Exterius erant scalae per quas ascendebatur ad fenestras et totus populus stabat in fenestris exterius intus aspiciens." (The theater has windows, the spectators stay outside and look through these windows which they reach by means of external stairways.) What follows is somewhat more orthodox: "In medio theatri erat unum puplitum [*sic*] rotundum ex marmore. In puplito *ystoriones* [*sic*] cantabant aliquas pulcras ystorias bellorum. Finito cantu *ystorionum* adveniebant mimi pulsantes lyras et cytharas et decenti motu corporis se circumvolvebant. Et fuit istud hedificium in loco qui dicitur ecclesia Sancti Victoris ad theatrum sive ad Trenum." Here the place of the *comedus*, of the *poeta* as recitator has been taken by the *histriones*. The "lyras et cytharas" go back to Isidore, *Erym.*, XVIII, 47.

The word *ystoriones* (for *ystriones*) should be kept. It is purposely connected with *historia* and this connection goes far back. Isidore has it (*Etym.*, XVIII, 48): "dicti autem histriones quod perplexas hystoriis fabulas exprimerent quasi historiones." This connection has noticeable significance in connection with the meanings the word acquired in Italian.

The theatrical terms which we find in medieval texts can be accounted for frequently on purely rhetorical or stylistic grounds. The theater, its parts, its performances were relied upon to furnish metaphors particularly in connection with the commonplace of the tragedy and comedy of life, of the world's stage, etc., which the Middle Ages inherited from the Romans as they in turn had got it from the Greeks. So Aldhelm in *De Virg.* (*Mon. Ger. Auct. Ant.*, XV, 233) speaks of an "Apium... *theatrali* quodam spectaculo" and page 253, of an "angelicum coelestis *theatri consessum*." Rhabanus Maurus (*De Univ.*,

---

comparata." Papias s.v. *scena* says "Umbraculum ubi poetae recitabantur quasi lobia." This Longobardic word was kept alive by the Lombards and finally passed into the cultural language of Italy. GREGORY OF TOURS (*De Virt. S. Mart.*, ch. 9) also uses it figuratively but in a different sense: "Hi in scena montis aquosi dependent," where the word seems to have the meaning of *facies*, a usage natural enough, *scena* being considered from the point of view of the spectators. So in TERTULLIAN, *Adv. Valentinianos*, ch. 20: "coelorum septemplicem scenam" (see Apuleius, *Met.*, IV, 20).

xx, 36): "Mystice autem theatrum praesentem mundum significare potest..." Lambertus Herzfordensis (*Mon. Ger. Script.*, vi, 236) speaks of
"lugubrem trajediam toto mundi huius theatro decantandam" and page
242 "deferens secum de vita... scenicis figmentis consimilem trajediam."[1]

To this we may add in a somewhat different sense Honorius, *De
Gemma Animae*, i, 83 (*M.P.L.*, 172, 570): "Sciendum quod hi qui in
theatris recitabant, actus pugnantium gestibus populo representabant.
Sic tragicus noster pugnam Christo populo Christiano in *theatro* Ecclesiae gestibus suis repraesentat"; which is but an echo and a development of St. Augustine *In Johan.*, chapter i, tr. 7; also of St. Augustine
De Symbolo (Benedictine edition, vi, 407); of Tertullian *De Spect.*,
chapters 29 and 30, and *Ad Mart.*, chapter 3; finally of Pseudo-Cyprian
De Spect., 9 and 10.

Similar to this is the use of some of these words in connection with
the mannerisms of oratorical delivery. Limiting our attention to *tragedia* we find that in addition to *luctuosum* its standing epithet was some
word meaning: "thundering." So Sedulius (*Carm. Pasch.*, i, 18) who
speaks of "tragico boatu." Cassiodorus *Var.*, iv, 51, informs us that
"tragedia ex vocis vastitate nominatur." This was handed down by the
Glosses of Placidus (Loewe *C.G.L.*, v, 41): "Tragedia est enim genus
carminis quo poetae res... *alto sonitu* describunt" and again page 59:
"trajedi qui in theatro ducturi [*sic*] sunt alta et *intonanti* voce," which
explains expressions such as the following from the Council of Clovesho
(Haddan and Stubbs, iii, 359) "ut presbiteri... in ecclesia non garriant
tragico sono."

The use of the words *theatrum, theatrales* and the rest then proves
nothing as to the existence of the theater. This is brought home to us
when we recall that the adjective *theatralis* was regularly used for performances in churches, and was an official designation. See among many
instances the following from Innocent III (Lateran Council): "interim
ludi fiunt in *ecclesiis theatrales.*" (*Greg. Decr.*, iii, 1, 12). Likewise the
text of the Synod of Trier and Liège (Hartzheim, iv, 17). To conclude
therefore that the word *theatralis*, unless some other place is indicated,
refers to a theater, would be as reasonable as to say that the verb

---

[1] Cf. PASCHASIUS RADBERTUS *Praef.*, lib. iii (*Mon. Ger. Ep.*, vi, 143). For a frequent
use of *trajedia* see *Ekkehardi IV Casus S. Galli* (*Mon. Ger. Scr.* ii, 103, 107, 137). Also
in JOHN OF SALISBURY, iii, 8, the long chapter entitled: "de mundana comedia et
tragedia."

"sails" when nothing to the contrary is stated implies that we are dealing with a sailing vessel.

IV. The same conclusion is reached if we reverse the process and
try to determine from an examination of the medieval texts what places
were mentioned as actually used for purposes of amusements.

Starting with Pirminius (*M.P.L.*, 89, 104) we read: "Nullus christianorum neque ad *ecclesiam*, neque in *domibus*, neque in *trivio* nec
in ullo loco balationes, cantationes, saltationes jocos et lusa diabolica
facere non praesumat." Louis the Pious orders (*Mon. Ger. Leges,* II,
2, 83): "balationes et saltationes, canticaque turpia ac luxoriosa et illa
lusa diabolica non faciat nec in *plateis* nec in *domibus* neque in ullo
loco." Theganus writing this king's life says (*Mon. Ger. Script.*, II,
895): "procedebant thymelici, scurre et mimi cum coraulis et citharistis
ad *mensam* coram eo." Noticeable is Abelard's invective (*Theol. Christ.*,
Cousin, II, 445). He assails the bishops, because, he says, "joculatores, saltatores, incantatores, cantatores turpium acciunt and mensam totum diem ac noctem." Yet, he adds, the devil is not satisfied "nisi
etiam scaenicas turpitudines in *ecclesiam* Dei introducat" where "Ve-
neris celebrantur vigiliae."

King Richard, says Muratori (*Antiq. diss.* 29, V, 150): "Rogerio
Hovedeno teste," called over from France "cantores et ioculatores" who
were to sing his praises "*in plateis.*" About a century later the people
of Bologna decreed "ut cantatores francigenorum in *plateis* communis
ad cantandum omnimo morari non possint." The same in Pierre de
Blois, *M.P.L.*, 207, 49. In the *Historia Eliensis Eccl.* (Gale, *Hist. Brit.
Scr.*, p. 463) we read that "gentilium figmenta et deliramenta" were
"in gymnasiis et scholis publice celebrata." John of Salisbury in the
above quoted passage makes it clear that the performances that were
indulged in his days were not carried on in buildings for the purpose.

The place mentioned at the Synod of Trier (1227) is the *ecclesia*;
at Utrecht (1293) "ecclesiae et coemeteria." In the *Statutes* of John,
Bishop of Liège (Hartzheim, III, 693) we read: "praecipimus ut joculatores, histriones, saltatrices in *ecclesia, coemeterio* vel *porticu* eiusdem
vel in processionibus vel in rogationibus joca vel ludibria non exer-
ceant." And as late as the fifteenth century we find the Council of
Sens (Mansi, IX, 1525) decreeing that "per choreas, ludos theatrales,
ludificationes solent templa domini profanare."

If we turn to some Italian secular performances we reach the same
conclusion. Muratori (*Antiq.*, IV, 1126) refers to a "Ludus in Prato

Vallis cum gigantibus" at Padua in 1224, and to a "magnus ludus de quodam homine salvatico" (page 1130) in the same place (in the year 1209, as we gather from the *Lib. reg. Pad.*). The *Cronica Rolandini* (Mur., *Rer. it. scr.*, new ed., cap. 10) gives a full description of an elaborate pageant and masquerade, enacted likewise in "*Prato* Vallis" at Padua.

Omitting many such performances recorded in medieval writings, we might refer to one which deserves special notice. It took place in 1214 at Treviso in an open square where a temporary mock castle was erected for the occasion. Rolandini in his Chronicle describes the "revue" as follows (chapter 13):

"De ludo quodam facto apud Tarvisium... anno scilicet MCCXIV, ordinata est quedam curia (corte bandita) solacii et leticie... *factum est* enim ludicrum *quoddam castrum* in quo posite domine cum virginibus... que sine alicuius viri auxilio castrum prudentissime defenderunt." This mock castle, defended by ladies and damsels, was fortified with the following materials: "variis et griseis et cendatis, purpuris samitis et ricellis scarlatis et baldachinis et armerinis." The ladies had for helmets golden crowns with precious stones. The attack was made with the following weapons: "pomis, datalis et muscatis, tortellis, piris et coctanis, rosis, liliis et violis," also perfumes and spices of many sorts. Venice sent a goodly troop which, carrying "Sancti Marchi preciosum vexillum, prudenter et delectabiliter pugnaverunt." Unfortunately a real fight developed and the show had to be suspended by the umpire.

A century later (1304) the Florentines staged their famous and disastrous spectacle of the Hereafter on the bridge of the Carraia, with the painter Buffalmacco aiding in the building of the *pulpita*.

V. Conversely every time a theater building is mentioned the reference is clearly to ancient times.

So in Honorius, *M.P.L.*, 172, 1243: "Sciendum quod hi qui in teatro *recitabant*, actus pugnantium gestibus *repraesentabant*." So in Hugo of St. Victor, *Erud. did.*, II, 28 (*M.P.L.*, 176, 762): "Theatrica dicitur scientia ludorum a theatro, quo populus ad ludendum convenire *solebat*." So again, in the same author's *Except. Priores*, I, 21 (*M.L.P.*, 177, 201): "ludorum alii *fiebant* in theatris... in theatris gesta *recitabantur*." So in St. Thomas, *IV Sent. dist.*, 16 qu. 4, art 3: "quidam enim ludi sunt qui in theatris *agebantur*." So Pseudo-Thomas (Fretté 32.438): "Scena locus umbrosus in theatro ubi *abscondebantur* personae pronuntiantes carmina tragica vel comica." When however St. Thomas spoke of contemporary amusements and delivered his memorably liberal views on shows then he used the present tense: "ludus *est* necessarius ad conversationem humanae vitae. Ad omnia autem quae sunt utilia conversationi humanae deputari possunt aliqua officia licita. Et ideo etiam officium istrionum quod ordinatur ad solatium hominibus exhibendum non est secundum se illicitum...." But this applies to the *ludi* in the places we have been considering.

These texts show, it seems to me, that from the use of theatrical words found in Professor Loomis' quotations we may not draw any conclusion as to the existence of the theater. He has another argument however and that is the description of a show in an actual theater drawn from Roger of Wendover's *Flores Historiarum* (Hewlet, ii, 24).

Unfortunately the show therein described is an imaginary one seen in a vision. It represents the devils amusing themselves in the next world torturing the damned in a place which looks like the ruins of an ancient theater.

We have here an example of a very ancient *genre*: Judgment Day described as a theatrical show. Tertullian already has it (*De Spect.*, 29, 30): "quale autem *spectaculum* in proximo est adventus Domini... et tamen per fidem spiritu imaginante *repraesentata*." He then proceeds to place in this imagined fiery hell kings, poets, actors and the like.[1]

The ingenious and original trait of Roger of Wendover's vision is that the imagined diabolical tortures are set in a place which has always been regarded by Christians as a favorite abode of the Devil — the Theater.[2]

The unreal traits of this vision are obvious; the walls are *ferrei*; the blazing seats are also of iron. The only conclusion therefore we can draw from the passage is that the author knew something of the existence of ancient theaters and their use, which of course was to be expected. In order to use it as an argument for the actual existence of theaters we should have to assume that the acts, persons and things of a vision must of necessity belong to the time in which the vision takes place.

---

[1] For Judgment Day Tertullian uses the image of another ancient place of amusement: the gymnasium. He says (*Ad Mart.*, ch. 3): "Bonum agmen subituri estis in quo Agonothetes Deus vivus est; Xystarchus spiritus Sanctus."

[2] For a late and mock reference to this belief, cf. the famous Coliseum scene in Benvenuto Cellini's *Autobiography*.

VI. Professor Cohen's commentary on this vision brings out the elements of actuality which naturally would be introduced in a vision of this sort. There is something, however, in his discussion that, if it means what it seems to say, must be very sharply questioned. He tells us (pages 96-97): "This association of the word *theatricus* with religious plays removes many of our doubts in interpreting *theatrum* in Ailred as a theatre in the *classical sense of the word, that is to say an amphitheatre.*" To make matters worse Professor Cohen after identifying the theater with the amphitheater carries the confusion one step further (page 98) and speaks of a "*circus*-shaped theatre." Thus the so-often mentioned show places of antiquity are reduced from four to one.

Of course there is nothing better established in the architecture and in the social life of antiquity than the distinction between *theatrum, amphitheatrum* and *circus* and it might seem otiose even to discuss the matter. However, since this question has come up before and has given rise to what seem to be misinterpretations and unnecessary emendations of texts it might not be amiss to present certain facts and discuss their meaning.

Tertullian enumerates and describes the four different show places of ancient Rome, viz. 1. circus (hippodromus), 2. theatrum, 3. stadium (agon, xystos, gymnasium), 4. amphitheatrum (arena) in as many chapters of his *De Spectaculis*, viz. 16, 17, 18, 19. He repeats this enumeration in the 20th chapter of the same work and takes them up anew in *Apol.*, 38.4. In *De Spect.*, 30 he transfers the four of them to the next world.

The distinction therefore between the places (1) where races took place, (2) those where dramas were read or performed, (3) those where gladiatorial battles were waged and (4) those where athletic contests were held, was clear to everybody. Isidore saved these distinctions for posterity. He says, correctly (*Etym.*, XVIII, XVI, 3): "Ludus autem aut gymnicus aut circensis aut gladiatorius aut scenicus." In Chapter 59 of the cited book however, he sums up the genus with the four species in describing the moral filth connected in each and gives us five instead of four. Lupus of Ferrières (*Mon. Ger. Ep.*, VI, 115) refers to them correctly: "Ludi aut gymnici aut gladiatorii aut circenses aut scenici nominabantur." Aldelmus mentions them in *De Metris (Mon. Ger. Auct. Ant.*, XV, 166), but confusedly. They are remembered in the intervening centuries and reappear in Helinand (*De Rep. Laps.*); "non scena, non circus, non amphitheatrum, non amphicircus," where the *stadium* has become the *amphicircus*.

When we turn to Hugo of St. Victor we encounter them along with contemporary forms in the usual blend of past lore and actual doings. He says (*Erud. Did.*, II, 28): "Theatrica dicitur scientia ludorum a theatris quo populus ad ludendum convenire solebat. Fiebant autem ludi alii in *theatro*, alii in atriis, alii in *gymnasiis*, alii in *amphicircis*, alii in *arenis*, alii in conviviis, alii in fanis." The circus has here become the amphicircus, with the meaning, however, fairly well maintained. For he says: "In amphicircis cursu certabant vel pedum vel equorum, vel curruum." And again (*Except. Priores*, I, 21) "Ludorum alii in theatris, alii in gabulis, alii in gymnasiis."

The stadium dropped out. In St. Jerome we already have but three: "arena saeviat, circus insaniat, theatra luxurient" (*Epist.* 43, 3). That this threefold division is becoming a real one and is not merely a case of literary exemplification can be seen by referring to the official utterance of Justinian (*Novella* 105, 1), which in the Latin version (the Authenticum) reads as follows: "haec autem a nobis determinentur in circensibus, et bestiarum spectaculis, et thymeles delectatione." Du Cange (s.v. *balisteum*) believes he finds these three places in a French text as translations, he says, of leg. 9 cap. *De feriis*: "aut scena theatralis, aut circense spectaculum, aut ferarum lachrymosa spectacula."

Each of these places had its patron devil: Mars for the arena, Mercury for the stadium; for the circus Neptune, for the theater Liber and Venus (Isidore, Tertullian, Salvianus, *et al.*). Each one of them got its standing epithets and its attributes of opprobrium: *insania* or *mania* belongs to the circus; to the "saeva arena" was assigned "immisericordia" (Tertullian *et al.*). The "theatrum" is more generously endowed. Some of the commonest names connected with it are: "impudicitia, spurcitia, impuritas, turpitudo, licentia, luxuria, foeditas, obscenitas." Naturally the gymnasium was let off easily with such phrases as "vanitas xysti."

The difference in shape between Theatrum and Amphitheatrum is given approximately enough by Isidore, XVIII, II, 2: "Amphitheatrum rotundum est, theatrum vero ex medio amphitheatro est semicirculi figuram habens." These words are frequently quoted, as we saw above. They are again met with when the term "arena" replaces "amphitheatrum," and "harengum" in turn displaces "arena." Galvaneus Flamma (*Chronicum Majus*, 43) says "Inter ecclesiam majorem et ecclesiam

Sancte Thecle fuit quoddam aedificium dictum arena, nunc dicitur Arengum et erat rotundum et magnum," and Bentius of Alessandria (was in Holy Land 1284) in the opusculum *De Civitate Mediol.* (from his *Chronicon*) published by Ferrai in *Bull. Istituto Stor. Ital.*, IX (1890), p. 15, says: "Arena quae est arengum erat... rotunda in cuius circuito erant camerae quot in anno sunt dies per occultos meatus inclusae." Of course the forms were not quite as described by these authors: the amphitheater was elliptical; the theater normally consisted of semicircular rows of seats (the *cavea*) concentric with the semicircle of the orchestra and facing the stage. The circus was a space enclosed within two parallel *straight* lines, one slightly longer than the other, connected at one end by a semicircle and at the other by a curve whose cord was not perpendicular to the rectilinear sides.

These distinctions were perpetuated in the toponymy of the medieval cities and it has been possible to locate buried structures by the names surviving in the localities where they once stood. So for instance in Milan we have the "Ecclesia Sancti Victoris ad Theatrum," built close to the site where the Roman theater stood until 1162. The amphitheater of Milan was early lost sight of. When excavations began a few years ago the men in charge proceeded to make minor assays in the locality called Via *Arena*. What they unearthed was enough to convince them that they had found part of an elliptical wall. They then proceeded to calculate the dimensions of the ellipse, determine its curvature and thus reduce the work of excavating to a minimum: viz. to the spots pre-established by calculations. All of which turned out successfully.[1]

The same situation obtained in connection with the circus. Excavations were again guided by the existence of the old church, "Ecclesia Sanctae Mariae ad *Circulum*" (Santa Maria al *Cerchio*), that pointed to the existence of the *Circus* in the proximity. Excavations again led to the unearthing of parts of the rectilinear walls, of the connecting semicircle, and finally of the oblique *carceres*.[2]

The names of the *theatrum* and *amphitheatrum* were often confused in common parlance. New terms arose, some of them limited to certain buildings. "Arena" remained the commonest term for the amphitheater; regularly so at Verona, Capua, Nîmes, etc. The term Laby-

---

[1] See A. CALDERINI, *L'Anfiteatro*, etc. (1940).
[2] See ALBERTO DE CAPITANI D'ARZAGO, *Il Circo Romano* (1939).

rinthus was occasionally used as substitute; see the eighth century *Descriptio Veronae* in Muratori, *Rer. Ital. Scr.*, II, 2, 1095, which says: "Habet autem Labyrinthum magnum per circuitum" (cf. Maffei *Istoria dei diplomi*).

More frequent was the term Colosseum, Colyseum, Colossum and the like. So naturally at Rome, so at Verona, so at Capua. In the last place we have very interesting developments. Erchempert in his late ninth century *Historia Lang. Benev.* gives us ample information on the subject. In chapter 41 he calls it *Berelais* ("Adveniens Berelais hoc est amphitheatrum"). So again in chapter 40 ("Berelais et Suessam"). In chapter 44 he calls it *Colossum*: "super *Colossum* quo filii Landonis degebant insedit illos... qui residebant in thermis iuxta aerenam... filiis Landonis in Amphitheatro circumseptis." Again in chapter 73: "Hinc inchoavit omnia sata eorum qui in *Colossum* morabantur diripere." Owing to this name the leader of the troops defending the amphitheater bore the title of *Colossensis* and his soldiers were called *theatrales*: "ille vero sugerente hoc vel maxime Guaiferio *Colossense* ex abditis Grecos Neapolites una cum *theatralibus* viris..." (chapter 56).

The term *Berelais* was changed to *Vorolasu* (A. Di Meo, *Annali del Regno di Napoli*, IV, 253) and finally became *Verlasci*, in which form it still lives today. The word itself *Berelais* is well established. It became the name of an Episcopal See (*Epist.* 273 of Pope John VIII: *Mon. Ger. Epist.*, V, 242, 246). The catalogue of the Counts of Capua (*Scr. Rerum Lang.*, p. 449) says: "inditione 6, post dies 11 capitur *Berelais* a domno Atenolfo."

This seems to be the same word as *Parlascium*[1] (parlascio, pirolascio, perilasium, etc.) so frequently referred to in Tuscany: Lucca, Florence, Pisa and elsewhere.[2] For Lucca see *Mem. e Doc. Lucch.*, IV, I, p. 199: "Iuxta theatrum quod Parlascium vocant" (a. 808). This place came to be called: "Le prigioni vecchie." For Florence see Davidsohn, *Storia di Firenze*, II, 1023. This place came to be used as a prison and was called *Burelle*. (Is the word connected with *Berelais*?). Dante was reminded of these dark, *man-made* caverns when he was groping through *natural* dungeons, back from the center to the

---

[1] The usual derivation is from: *Palatium*.
[2] The word is not in Du Cauge.

surface of the earth. A Tuscan village that grew around an Arena came to be called *Parlascio* (see Repetti s.v.).

The term *Theatrum* likewise had interesting vicissitudes. It was changed to:

1. *Zatrum*;* cf. Mirabilia (*Codex Pragensis*), Urlichs *Codex*, etc., p. 135: "theatrum Pompei, juxta palatium eius, ubi dicitur *Zatro.*"

2. to *Zadrum* * (*Cod. dipl. Padovano*, I, 259 [a. 1079], 304).

3. to *Jadrum*:* *Maffei degli Anf.*, lib. II, cap. 16: "habet ibi [Pola] duo antiqua palatia scilicet Iadrum et Harenam."

4. Azadrum (see below).

5. Zairum. This word was used throughout the Middle Ages and in modern times to indicate a place in Padua which had long ceased to be connected with the ancient theater. Muratori quotes documents in which it appears but does not try to define it. Du Cange incorporates one of Muratori's texts but he too fails to define or derive the term. Yet the text is very clear in that it describes the main use which Roman theaters in the Middle Ages were put to, viz. that of a marble quarry: "ut concedas mihi fodere de Zairo aliquas petras" (Placit ann. 1077 apud Murat. *Antiq.*, I, 457).

The failure to identify these forms has caused scholars to read texts erroneously and introduce new words in the vocabulary.

Ughelli (*Italia Sacra*, II, 187), publishing a false *charta* of Charles le Gros which exists in a twelfth-century "copy," prints the word: "Azidium." Again on page 203 he has it but in the form of: "Azadium." Du Cange takes both of these over without change or definition. The text however was correctly read by Affò (*St. Parm. I App.*, XXII, 298) as follows: "*arenam*, carnarium, *azadrum*, publica pascua etc."

Muratori (*Ant. diss.* 19, II, 73) quotes a "confirmatio *privilegiorum... episcopo Patavino... ab Henrico IV*" as follows: "nominatim quoque *Ladrum* cum pratis et pontem cum arcubus." Where, again, the correct reading is: *Zadrum*. Migne, *P.L.*, 151, 1149, reproduces the document with the erroneous reading.

A diploma of the year 1090 reads in the copy of Gloria (*Cod. Dipl. Pad.*, 328-329) as follows: "Arenam quoque sum satyro etc." And scholars have tried to discover some ancient theatrical structure called *satyrum*. This form may be due to a scribe who not understanding *Zatrum* replaced it by a reading that seemed to suit the context.

---

* See note 2, page 177.

VII. When these buildings ceased to be used as places of spectacles, which is a question raised by Professor Cohen, it is hard to say. St. Augustine tells us, *De Cons. Evang.*, I, 33: "Per omnes civitates cadunt theatra"; but things did not move, as all know, very fast. Usually the last example of some sort of a show in an ancient theater is supposed to have been at Barcelona in the reign of Sisebut and with the authorization of Bishop Eusebius. Du Merit (*Orig.*, page 13) refers to this event and quotes the following passage which he attributes to Mariana: "Quod in theatro quaedam agi concessisset [*i.e.* episcopus] quae ex vana deorum superstitione traducta aures christianae abhorrere videantur." E. K. Chambers (*The Medieval Stage*, I, 21, n. 4) tells us that he cannot find "in Sisebut or in Mariana who writes Spanish the words quoted by Du Meril," which is doubly remarkable. For in the first place Mariana did publish his history in Latin: in 20 books (1592); in 25 books (1595); in 30 books in 1606. Also the passage quoted by Du Meril is to be found in the Latin version (De Hondt, I, 203) as well as in the Spanish, in the spot where one would naturally look for it, viz. in the three pages devoted to Sisebut.

Most of the arenas were turned into fortresses, then used as quarries; their underground parts became prisons and finally disappeared. A few of them remained standing. That of Verona was for a while turned into a tournament camp. At the Colosseum of Rome bull fights held in the early fourteenth century were brought to an end by the tragic events of 1332. (See *Annali di Ludovico Monaldeschi*, in Muratori, *Rer. it. scr.*, x, 2, 535.) Later it came to be used for the passion plays of the Compagnia del Gonfalone.

Much has been written on these sacred performances in the Colosseum and some misinformation has found its way into standard works. The *Compagnia del Gonfalone* started to produce its passion plays in the Flavian Amphitheatre in the closing years of the fifteenth century. These performances came to an end in 1522. They were taken up again in 1525; suspended by the Sack of Rome and forbidden in 1539 by Paul III. An attempt in 1561 to resume them was followed by an order in the same year that put an end to them permanently. (See documents in Mons. Vattasso, *Per la storia*, etc., and Ruggeri, *L'Arciconfraternita del Gonfalone*.)[1]

---

[1] The information given on the subject by J. H. PARKER in "The Roman Amphitheatre" p. 29 is mostly inaccurate.

VIII. It is not sufficient, however, to dispose of the above mentioned arguments for there are certain texts, which I will now produce, which might point to the existence of theaters in the twelfth and thirteenth centuries. Some of these texts we can explain by recalling that *theatrum* meant *market*, or *market square*, for which see Du Cange s.v., also Bartal *Glossarium*, etc., s.v. and Fumagalli *Antichità Longobardico-Mediolanensia*, I, 165.

There are others, however, that cannot be explained away on this ground.

The references, for instance, to the *theatrum* of Milan anterior to 1162 become meaningless if we follow Fumagalli's explanation (endorsed by Pertile) and say that its meaning is that of an open market. The theater was still standing when Barbarossa ordered the destruction of the city. It was either demolished by his forces, or immediately afterwards by the Milanese themselves in the endeavor to get materials with which to rebuild their city and its defenses. We gather this from Gunther's *Ligurinus*, a book which we can confidently accept as genuine, and from the *argumentum* to Book VII which though slightly inaccurate in its topography is none the less authentic. He says: "speculatur providus Urbem Caesar et antiqui *theatri* procul aspicit arces." A document of the year 1130 dated "civitate Mediolani in *theatro* publico ipsius civitatis" (*Arch. Catt. Bergamo*, I, IX, A) shows that the building was indeed standing though used for administrative purposes. Calchi, moreover, in his *Historia Patria*, VII (a. 1119: Graevius, II, 209) confirms this when he says of an event of 1119: "qui populum in *theatro* sedentem (durabat enim adhuc antiquissimi operis usus), etc."

In view of all this what does Landulphus Senior (eleventh century) mean when he says: "Harembaldus... quasi solus dux, *theatrum*, suos confortando ac cohortando ad bellum, regens, praelii necessaria ordinabat... His itaque compositis praecepit militibus ut armati in *theatro* dato signo convenirent" (*Mediol. Hist.*, III, 29; Murat., *Rer. it. scr.*, IV, 117)? It seems as though the *theatrum* had been turned into a fortress, which of course regularly happened in the case of the amphitheaters.

Landulphus Junior (1137) furnishes new difficulties and also an important clue. He says (*Hist. Mediol.*, chapter 31, in *Mon. Ger. Scr.*, XX) "in prato Sancto quod dicitur Brolium ubi archiepiscopus et consules duo *theatra* constituunt; in uno archiepiscopus... in altero consules." *Theatrum* here is equivalent to "platform," a meaning which is borne out by another passage of the same author when, referring to the synod of Rome of 1116, he says: "Jordanus vero coram ipsa Synodo *theatrum* ascendit et ibi ad pedes apostolici stratus... gratiam et virgam pontificalem in ipso *theatro* suscepit."

These texts may help us to interpret the following from Caesarius of Heisterbach (*De Miraculis Dist.*, x, cap. 28): "De theatro in Saxonia fulminato. Sacerdos quidam de Saxonia nuper mihi retulit miraculum stupendum.... Hoc, inquit, anno [a. 1222] in terra nostra, in quodam *theatro* fulminati sunt viginti homines solo sacerdote evadente." And the following (Hilka, *Die Wundergeschichten des Caesarius von Heisterbach*, iii, 38): "in Hertene villa dyoccsis Coloniensis dives quidam arietem sericis vestitum malo imposuit atque juxta *theatrum* erexit." Follows the description of an idolatrous rite of buck worship, for which cf. the Longobardic practice referred to by Gregory the Great (*Dial.*, iii, 28). A description by Caesarius of the same Germanic rite (Hilka, *op. cit.*, p. 39) may help to further clarify the situation: "Oliverus [died 1227] scholasticus Coloniensis cum ante aliquot annos per villam quandam transiret arietem vidit erectum et circa illum, choream cum canticis et musicis instrumentis, etc."

Theatrum then seems to be equivalent in the eleventh, twelfth and early thirteenth centuries to "scaffolding," "platform." This sense is borne out a century later by the following passage from Mussato's *De Gestis Italic. IX intr.*, where he tells us the reasons that made him change from prose to verse: "et solere etiam inquitis [*i.e.* you notaries] amplissima regum documque gesta, quo se vulgi intelligentiis conferant pedum syllabarumque mensuris variis linguis in vulgares traduci sermones et in *theatris* et *pulpitis* cantilenarum modulatione proferri." The identity of *theatris* and *pulpitis* above established is here maintained. We find it in an author of the eighteenth century, Concina (*Maffei dei Teatri*, page 70) who says "at nostri circulatores qui... in plateis publicis tabulata seu *pulpita* seu *theatra* vocare vis, erigunt et populo spectacula praebent"; and in the last century the people of the Tuscan countryside still called the half dozen planks on which the *maggi* were played: the "teatro."

Another passage must also be considered because it has recently again been utilized. It is from Muratori (*Antiq. Ital. diss.* 29) and states: "In Chronico Msto Mediolanensi quod anonymus quidam ex aliis chronicis consarcinavit *antiquum* Mediolanensium *theatrum* describitur super quo Histriones cantabant sicut modo cantantur [*sic*] de Rolando et Oliverio."

Pio Rajna in his article: *Il Teatro di Milano etc.* (*Arch. Stor. Lomb.*, xiv) was able to clear the matter. He discovered what the chronicles were from which this anonymous proceeded. He gave us the ancient texts which did away entirely with the notion of an ancient theater used for dramatic purposes.

These texts were primarily from the early fourteenth-century historian Galvaneus Flamma. It is sufficient to quote one of them from the *Cronica Major* (*op. cit.*, p. 17): "In loco ubi nunc est ecclesia Sancti Victoris ad Trenum sive ad *theatrum* fuit quoddam hedifitium semicirculare dictum theatrum.... In medio theatri erat unum puplitum [*sic*] altum super quod historiones cantabant aliquas pulcras et virtuosas ystorias sicut nunc in *foro* cantatur de Rolando et Oliverio."

The theater of Muratori's anonymous has disappeared and the *forum* has taken its place. De Bartholomaeis (*op. cit.*, p. 27, note 2), who does not seem to know about the article of Rajna and the original texts published by him, still refers us to the passage in Muratori above quoted as though it had not completely lost its value.

Less easy to explain is the following from *Vita Sancti Brunonis Querfordensis* (1009 — Kauffmann): "adhuc puer... more solito pedibus superius calciatis plantis vero desubtus penitus denudatis in secretiori loco *theatri* stabat. Oculis ac manibus in celum fideliter intendebat, circumstrepentes et ignicis [lege: gimnicis] ludisque *theatricis* occupatos proximos ac sodales minime reputans nec attendens." We obviously have here a private gymnasium and sports building. The passage may receive some light by the following from Lambert of Ardres (1203) in his *Hist. Com. Ghisn.* (*Mon. Ger. Scr.*, xxiv, 597): "muros autem infra quorum ambitum pugiles et athletas sepius conflictantes aspeximus" speaking of structures that were then being built.

IX. It seems therefore as though the utilization of a text from a medieval author becomes valid for historical purposes only after the history of the passage and the value of its terms are known. We can see what hasty conclusions could be reached by the uncritical use of the following text from the Appendix to Hugo of St. Victor, *De Bestiis*, ii, chapter 32 (*M.P.L.*, 177, 78): "sic et illi qui deliciis huius *saeculi* et pompis et theatralibus voluptatibus delectantur tragediis et comediis dissoluti velut gravi somno sopiti adversariorum praeda efficiuntur...." We might be presented with tragedies in the twelfth century.

So when we read in the medieval documents of Verona the phrase "ire ad theatrum" we might decide that there was here some sort of an amusement. But in reality the people there considered were going to kill or to be killed, as we gather when we come across the fuller statement which is the following (see *Maffei degli Anfiteatri*, 149): "ire ad theatrum pro custodiendo battaiam cum hominibus armatis."

NOTE

This volume owes its existence to the initiative of Professor Giuseppe Prezzolini. Mindful of the long-standing concern of learned colleagues that such a collection of Professor Bigongiari's studies be made generally available, he arranged for prompt publication of the writings in Italy and asked me to select and introduce them. Professor Peter Riccio graciously offered to facilitate distribution of the volume in the United States through the Casa Italiana of Columbia University. Special thanks are, of course, due to the original publishers of these Bigongiari writings. The following list specifies the source of each of the pieces reprinted here:

The Liberal Arts Press: "The Political Doctrine of Dante," Introduction, *On World Government or De Monarchia*, H. W. SCHNEIDER, tr., New York, 1949, pp. xi-xiv.

Speculum: "The Text of Dante's *Monarchia*," Vol. II, No. 4, Oct. 1927, pp. 457-462; "Notes on the Text of the *Defensor Pacis* of Marsilius of Padua," Vol. VII, No. 1, Jan. 1932, pp. 36-49; "B. Nardi's *Saggi di filosofia dantesca*," Vol. VII, No. 1, Jan. 1932, pp. 146-153; "J. E. Shaw's *Essays on the Vita Nuova*," Vol. VII, No. 2, April 1932, pp. 296-302.

The Romanic Review: "Girolamo Fracastoro," Vol. XVII, No. 3, July 1926, pp. 264-268; "A. H. Gilbert's *Dante's Conception of Justice*," Vol. XVII, No. 3, July 1926, pp. 359-362; "Were There Theaters in the Twelfth and Thirteenth Centuries?," Vol. XXXVII, No. 3, Oct. 1946, pp. 201-224; "C. S. Singleton's *An Essay on the Vita Nuova*," Vol. XL, No. 4, Dec. 1949, pp. 285-288; "Notes on the Text of Dante," Vol. XLI, No. 1, Feb. 1950, pp. 3-13 and No. 2, April 1950, pp. 81-95.

Henry Regnery Co.: "The Political Ideas of St. Augustine," *The Political Writings of St. Augustine*, H. Paolucci, ed., Chicago, 1962, pp. 343-358.

Hafner Publishing Co.: "Introduction," *The Political Ideas of St. Thomas Aquinas*, Dino Bigongiari, ed., New York, 1953, pp. vii-xxxvii.

H. P.

HENRY PAOLUCCI

At the time of his death, on January 1, 1999, Henry Paolucci had been retired for eight years from St. John's University and held the title of Professor Emeritus of Government and Politics. He had also continued to serve, until his death, as Vice-Chairman of the Conservative Party of New York State.

He graduated from The City College of New York in 1942 with a BS degree and promptly joined the United States Air Force as a navigator. He flew many missions over Africa and Italy and, toward the end of the war in Europe, was placed in charge of 10,000 German prisoners of war. In that capacity, he remained in Italy for over a year. Immediately after his discharge, he resumed his education and received a Master's Degree and a Ph.D. from Columbia University. In 1948 he was Chosen Eleanora Duse Traveling Fellow in Columbia University and spent a year studying in Florence, Italy. In 1951, he returned to Italy as a Fulbright Scholar at the University of Rome.

His wide range of intellectual interests was reflected in the variety of subjects he taught, including Greek and Roman history at Iona College, Brooklyn College, and The City College; a graduate course in Dante and Medieval Culture at Columbia; and, since 1968, graduate and undergraduate courses in U.S. foreign policy, political theory, St. Augustine, Aristotle, Machiavelli, Hegel, astronomy and modern science.

A frequent contributor to the Op Ed pages of the *New York Times* and magazines like *National Review* and *Il Borghese* (Rome), Professor Paolucci wrote numerous articles for the Columbus quincentenary and helped prepare three volumes of *Review of National Literatures* from materials drawn from the massive eight-volume work of Justin Winsor, the great historian of early America. He translated Cesare Beccaria's *On*

Crimes and Punishments, Machiavelli's Mandragola (in 34th printing), portions of Hegel's massive work on the Philosophy of Fine Arts, *Hegel and the Arts,* and edited Maitland's *Justice and Police,* as well as a notable collection of *The Political Writings of St. Augustine* and, first of its kind, selections drawn from Hegel's entire opus into a single volume, *Hegel on Tragedy.* His books on political affairs and foreign policy analysis include the classic *War, Peace and the Presidency* (1968), *A Brief History of Political Thought and Statecraft* (1979), *Kissinger's War* (1980), *Zionism, the Superpowers, and the P.L.O.* (1964) *and Iran, Israel, and the United States* (1991).

In 1964, he was asked by William F. Buckley to accept the New York State Conservative Party nomination for the U.S. Senate, running against Kenneth Keating and Robert F. Kennedy. His stimulating campaign drew considerable interest, and he was written up in the *New York Times* as the "Scholarly Candidate." In 1995, the Party honored him with its prestigious Kieran O'Doherty Award.

Founder and President of The Walter Bagehot Research Council on National Sovereignty (a non-profit educational foundation), Professor Paolucci was for many years the chief editor of its newsletter, *State of the Nation,* (a collection containing the 1969-1980 issues will soon be published) and organizer of the Council's annual meetings at the American Political Science Association. He contributed also to the international series *Review of National Literatures* and its companion series, *CNL/World Report.*